MESSAGE OF THE FATHERS OF THE CHURCH
General Editor: Thomas Halton

Volume 5

MESSAGE OF THE FATHERS OF THE CHURCH

Early Christian Baptism and the Catechumenate

West and East Syria

Thomas M. Finn

A Michael Glazier Book
THE LITURGICAL PRESS
Collegeville, Minnesota

A Michael Glazier Book published by The Liturgical Press

Cover design by Lillian Brulc

1	2	3	4	5	6	7	8	9

Library of Congress Cataloging-in-Publication Data

Finn, Thomas M. (Thomas Macy), 1927–
    Early Christian baptism and the catechumenate : west and east
Syria / Thomas M. Finn.
        p.   cm. — (Message of the fathers of the church; v. 5)
    "A Michael Glazier book."
    Includes bibliographical references and index.
    ISBN 0-8146-5345-6. — ISBN 0-8146-5317-0 (pbk.)
    1. Baptism—History—Early church, ca. 30-600. 2. Conversion-
-History of doctrines—Early church, ca. 30-600. 3. Syria—Church
history. 4. Christian literature, Early—History and criticism.
I. Title. II. Series.
BV803.F55 1992
265'.13'09394—dc20

92-1215
CIP

For Marielena—
And she loved with salvation,
and guarded with kindness,
and declared with grandeur.
Hallelujah.
Odes of Solomon, 19:11

Contents

Editor's Introduction ix

Acknowledgments xi

Abbreviations xiv

General Introduction 1
    Conversion: A Ritual Journey 2
    Catechumens and Catechumenate 3
    Baptism... 7
    Postbaptismal Rites 15
    Anointing and the Holy Spirit 18
    The Bible and the Baptismal Liturgy 22

Chapter 1: West Syria 29
    The *Didache*................................... 32
    Melito of Sardis 36
    The *Didascalia Apostolorum* 38
    Jerusalem: Cyril and Egeria 41
    The *Apostolic Constitutions* 55
    Gregory of Nyssa 60
    John Chrysostom 70
    Theodore of Mopsuestia 81
    The *Ordo of Constantinople* 97
    Dionysius the Pseudo-Areopagite 101

Chapter 2: East Syria................................111
 The *Odes of Solomon* 115
 The *Gospel According to Philip* 120
 The *Acts of Judas Thomas*.........................127
 Aphrahat 134
 Ephrem 150
 Narsai 169
 Jacob of Serugh 188
 The Teaching of St. Gregory 197

Suggestions for Further Reading 207

Synoptic Chart 210

Index...212

Editor's Introduction

The *Message of the Fathers of the Church* is a companion series to The *Old Testament* and The *New Testament Message*. It was conceived and planned in the belief that Scripture and Tradition worked hand in hand in the formation of the thought, life and worship of the primitive Church. Such a series, it was felt, would be a most effective way of opening up what has become virtually a closed book to present-day readers, and might serve to stimulate a revival in interest in patristic studies in step with the recent, gratifying resurgence in scriptural studies.

The term "Fathers" is usually reserved for Christian writers marked by orthodoxy of doctrine, holiness of life, ecclesiastical approval, and antiquity. "Antiquity" is generally understood to include writers down to Gregory the Great (+604) or Isidore of Seville (+636) in the West, and John Damascene (+749) in the East. In the present series, however, greater elasticity has been encouraged, and quotations from writers not noted for orthodoxy will sometimes be included in order to illustrate the evolution of the Message on particular doctrinal matters. Likewise, writers later than the mid-eighth century will sometimes be used to illustrate the continuity of tradition on matters like sacramental theology or liturgical practice.

An earnest attempt was made to select collaborators on a broad interdisciplinary and interconfessional basis, the chief consideration being to match scholars who could handle the Fathers in their original languages with subjects in which they had already demonstrated a special interest and competence. About the only editorial directive given to the selected contributors was that the

Fathers, for the most part, should be allowed to speak for themselves and that they should speak in readable, reliable modern English. Volumes on individual themes were considered more suitable than volumes devoted to individual Fathers, each theme, hopefully, contributing an important segment to the total mosaic of the early Church, one, holy, catholic and apostolic. Each volume has an introductory essay outlining the historical and theological development of the theme, with the body of the work mainly occupied with liberal citations from the Fathers in modern English translation and a minimum of linking commentary. Short lists of Suggested Further Readings are included; but dense, scholarly footnotes were actively discouraged on the pragmatic grounds that such scholarly shorthand has other outlets and tends to lose all but the most relentlessly esoteric reader in a semi-popular series.

At the outset of his *Against Heresies* Irenaeus of Lyons warns his readers "not to expect from me any display of rhetoric, which I have never learned, or any excellence of composition, which I have never practiced, or any beauty or persuasiveness of style, to which I make no pretensions." Similarly, modest disclaimers can be found in many of the Greek and Latin Fathers, and all too often, unfortunately, they have been taken at their word by an uninterested world. In fact, however, they were often highly educated products of the best rhetorical schools of their day in the Roman Empire, and what they have to say is often as much a lesson in literary and cultural, as well as in spiritual, edification.

St. Augustine, in *The City of God* (19.7), has interesting reflections on the need for a common language in an expanding world community; without a common language a man is more at home with his dog than with a foreigner as far as intercommunication goes, even in the Roman Empire, which imposes on the nations it conquers the yoke of both law and language with a resultant abundance of interpreters. It is hoped that in the present world of continuing language barriers the contributors to this series will prove opportune interpreters of the perennial Christian message.

Thomas Halton

Acknowledgments

I owe a debt of gratitude to many and wish first to acknowledge with gratitude permissions from the following authors, journals, publishers, and serials to publish from their copyrighted texts:

Rev. Thomas L. Campbell, *Dionysius: The Pseudo-Areopagite: The Ecclesiastical Hierarchy* 2:1–3, Studies in Sacred Theology, 2nd series, 83 (originally published, Washington: The Catholic University of America Press, 1955).

The Catholic University of America Press, the Fathers of the Church Series (1946–), ed. Thomas Halton, the following volumes:

FC 1 (J. Merique, trans.): *The Shepherd of Hermas:* The Third Vision, 3; The Ninth Parable, 14.

FC 6 (T. Falls, trans.): *Justin Martyr: The First Apology,* chs. 61, 65, 67.

FC 23 (S. Wood, trans.): *Clement of Alexandria: Christ the Tutor:* Book 1, 6:5–28; Book 3, 12:101.

FC 34 (E. Hunt, trans.): *Pope Leo the Great: Epistle* 16, 68–77.

FC 38 (M. Muldowney, trans.): *Augustine: Sermon* 227.

FC 44 (R. Deferrari, trans.): *Ambrose: On the Sacraments, Homilies* 1–4.

FC 51 (R. Donna, trans.): *Cyprian, Letters* 60, 70.

FC 64 (A. Stephenson, trans.): *Cyril of Jerusalem: Catecheses* 1–3.

FC 67 (R. DeSimone, trans.): *Novatian: On the Trinity* 29.

FC 81 (R. Heine, trans.): *Origen: Homily 5, On Exodus,* 1–2.

Doubleday, a division of Bantam Doubleday Dell Publishing Group, Inc., *The Gospel According to Philip,* fragments 22, 37,

41, 47, 51, 58, 59, 60, 67, 68, 72, 78, 79, 80, 83, 84, 86, 90, 92, 94, 106, 107, from Bentley Layton, ed., *The Gnostic Scriptures: A New Translation with Annotations and Introductions* (Garden City, 1987); also *The Odes of Solomon,* 11, 19, 42, from James Charlesworth, ed., *The Old Testament Pseudepigrapha,* vol. 2 (Garden City, 1985).

Eastern Churches Review/Sobornost 3 (1970) S. Hackel, ed., R. Murray, "Hymns on Faith, X: A Hymn of St. Ephrem to Christ on the Incarnation, the Holy Spirit, and the Sacraments," 142-150; also, ECR/S 4 (1975), S. Brock, "Hymni de Ecclesia 36" in "St. Ephrem on Christ as the Light in Mary and in the Jordan," 133-144.

Thomas Halton, "Zeno of Verona: Invitations to the Baptismal Font," from *Baptism: Ancient Liturgies and Patristic Texts,* ed. A. Hamman, trans. T. Halton (Staten Island: Alba House, 1967) 64-66.

Harvard University Press, *The Teaching of St. Gregory* 409-415, 418, 420, 429-438, 441, 442, 446, 447, from R. W. Thompson, ed., *The Teaching of St. Gregory: An Early Armenian Catechism,* Harvard Armenian Texts and Studies 3 (Cambridge, 1970).

Patrologia Orientalis, ed. F. Graffin, "A Homily on the Epiphany of Our Lord," from F. McLeod, ed., *Narsai's Metrical Homilies on the Nativity, Epiphany, Passion, and Resurrection,* PO 182 (1979).

Paulist Press, *Didache* 1-7, from J. Kleist, trans., Ancient Christian Writers 6 (New York: Paulist Press 1948); also, *Egeria: Diary of a Pilgrimage* 45-47, from ACW 38 (1970), trans. G. Gingras.

St. Paul Publications, E. Yarnold, ed., *The Awe-Inspiring Rites of Initiation* (Slough, UK, 1972), the following: John Chrysostom, *Baptismal Homily* 11; Theodore of Mopsuestia, *Baptismal Homily* 3.

Theological Studies, ed. R. J. Daly, Innocent I, *Epistle 25, to Decentius,* from G. Ellard, "How Fifth Century Rome Administered the Sacraments," TS 9 (1948) 5-11.

Without the Woodstock Theological Center Library at Georgetown University and its wealth of patristic holdings this study of early Christian baptism and the catechumenate might never have seen the light of published day. Special thanks are due to its excellent professional staff for their unfailing generosity and always timely help: Rev. Eugene M. Rooney, S.J., and Mr. Paul Osmanski.

The chapter on the Syriac-speaking baptismal tradition would have been thin fare without the suggestions of Professor Susan A. Harvey of Brown University; the scholarly advice, studies, and translations of Professors Sebastian Brock of the Oriental Institute, Oxford University, and Robert Murray, S.J., of Heythrop College, University of London; and the holdings of the Institute for Christian Oriental Research at the Catholic University of America, together with the help of Professor Sydney H. Griffith, director, and of Ms. Monica Blanshard, librarian.

I am also deeply grateful to the general editor, Thomas Halton, professor of Greek and Latin at the Catholic University of America, for the opportunity to do the fifth and sixth volumes in the Message of the Fathers of the Church series, for his deft editorial hand, and for his invaluable bibliographical help.

In addition, I wish to acknowledge that several grants from the National Endowment for the Humanities and from the College of William and Mary, and a Joseph H. Malone Fellowship from the National Council on U.S.-Arab Relations enabled me to do preliminary studies, the fruits of which nourish the General Introduction and the chapters on Italy, North Africa, and Egypt.

Finally, I am once again pleased to acknowledge my lifelong indebtedness to the late Rev. Johannes Quasten, professor of ancient Church history and Christian archaeology at the Catholic University of America, who initiated me into the world of the Fathers of the Church and ancient Christian liturgy.

Abbreviations

ACW	*Ancient Christian Writers*
ANF	*Ante-Nicene Fathers*
BAP	*Baptism: Ancient Liturgies and Patristic Texts,* ed. A. Hamman, trans. Thomas Halton. Staten Island: Alba House, 1967
CCL	*Corpus Christianorum Series Latina*
CSCO	*Corpus Scriptorum Christianorum Orientalium*
CSEL	*Corpus Scriptorum Ecclesiasticorum Latinorum*
DBL	*Documents of the Baptismal Liturgy,* ed. E. C. Whitaker. 2nd ed., London: SPCK, 1970.
FC	*Fathers of the Church*
FP	*Florilegium Patristicum*
LCC	*Library of Christian Classics*
Mansi	Johannes D. Mansi, ed., *Sacrorum Conciliorum nova et amplissima collectio.* Paris, 1901
NCE	*New Catholic Encyclopedia*
NPNF	*Nicene and Post-Nicene Fathers*
PG	*Patrologia Graeca*
PL	*Patrologia Latina*
PO	*Patrologia Orientalis*
PS	*Patrologia Syriaca*
Quasten	Johannes Quasten, *Patrology.* 3. vols. Utrecht-Antwerp/Westminster, Md.: Spectrum/Newman, 1950 ff.; vol. 4, ed. Angelo Di Berardino, trans. Placid Solari. Westminster, Md.: Christian Classics, 1986
SC	*Sources Chrétiennes*
SCA	*Studies in Christian Antiquity*
SL	*Studia Liturgica*
SeT	*Studi e Testi*
TS	*Theological Studies*
TU	*Texte und Untersuchungen*

General Introduction

Baptism, whether ancient or modern, is the hinge upon which Christian identity turns. To understand what the rite discloses about Christian identity today, however, one must understand what it disclosed in antiquity. This book is about baptism "then," specifically, baptism in the first five Christian centuries.

Practically from the beginning Christians insisted, and the creeds taught, that there was one baptism for the forgiveness of sins, just as there was one Lord and one faith. The rite, however, presented many faces, adopted many shapes, and yielded many shades of meaning. As a result, a narrative history of baptism is neither practicable nor desirable. Not practicable, because the evidence is fragmentary, leaving large gaps. Not desirable, because when it comes to the deep matters of the human heart, in this case salvation, it is preferable to let people speak for themselves.

Yet to do so poses a special problem, because the early Christians spoke in ancient tongues (Armenian, Coptic, Greek, Latin, Syriac), lived in a remote world that encompassed many complex histories and cultures, and expressed their deepest experiences largely in the language of myth, symbol, and drama. In short, what they have to say is not easily accessible. As a result, one needs help to hear and understand them. These volumes are designed to help. What the early Christians have to say about baptism and the preparations for it is organized into Volumes 5 and 6 of this series, which represent the five major cultural areas: Volume 5: West Syria (ch. 1), East Syria (ch. 2); Volume 6: Italy (ch. 1), North Africa (ch. 2), and Egypt (ch. 3). In addition to a General Introduction, each chapter has an introductory section that depicts the establishment of Christianity in the area together with its distinctive baptismal characteristics, themes, preparations, and practices. The readings, arranged chronologically, are representative rather than comprehensive and have their own introduc-

1

tions. Preference has been given to those forms of baptismal teaching and practice that the ordinary Christian heard and followed. Prominent are the homily, hymn, and Church-order book (a pastoral book of rituals and rules). Correspondence, however, is in evidence (Italy and North Africa), as are the baptismal treatise (North Africa) and sayings-collections (East Syria and Egypt). The setting is normally a congregation assembled in church, whether small and rural or large and urban. The occasion is generally instruction, more accurately, that distinctive form of religious instruction called "catechesis," about which more later. The audience is both the faithful and those seeking baptism. Specific form, setting, and occasion are described in connection with each reading.

Accessible translations, where possible, have been used and, where necessary, adapted for the contemporary reader. Some readings have been especially translated for this book. For the reader who wishes to consult the original language, an accessible up-to-date text has been cited for each reading.

Conversion: A Ritual Journey

A striking event in ancient history is the geographical spread of early Christianity from rural Palestine eastward to the Indus Valley and westward all the way to Roman Britain in less than two centuries. Even more striking is its social survival and spread from the religion of an obscure Jewish sect to the established religion of the Roman Empire in a matter of four centuries. The details of survival and spread are discussed in the chapter introductions. In general, however, the new religion moved outward and upward in the backpacks of immigrants. It was a traveling faith, largely urban, which in four centuries moved from synagogue to marketplace to house and, finally, to imperial palace.

The key was conversion, itself a journey, or as the ancients put it, a change ("turning," *epistrephein/conversio*) from one "way of walking" to another. The destination was frequently called "salvation," and many embarked. Jews might journey from one Jewish sect to another in search of a greater righteousness; pagans, from civic religion to mystery cults in search of divinity and immortality; intellectuals from an aimless life to philosophy in search of truth. The readings contain two examples of such philosophical quests (see vol. 6, ch. 1, Justin; and ch. 3, Clement). Indeed, the search for salvation however conceived was a hallmark of the period, often called the "Age of Anxiety." Its anxious roots lay in the shattering changes that saw old ways in flight before the onrush of new ways, especially those represented by the rise of the Roman Empire (27 B.C.E.)—a rise followed by the incursions of the barbarians (ca. 250 C.E.).

Some conversions seemed sudden (like that of Paul of Tarsus) and had a strong emotional overlay (like that of Augustine). Most, however, were gradual, the result of time and testing. For those ancients who sought the Christian "Way," the journey had clearly marked stages: (1) a period of preparation that emphasized instruction and testing and involved personal struggle; (2) penultimate preparations for baptism also characterized by instruction, testing, and ritual struggle; (3) baptismal immersion; and (4) post-baptismal "homecoming" celebrations, which included the Eucharist. In second-century Rome the stages could occupy three years; in fifth-century North Africa they might take the better part of a lifetime or only the weeks of Lent; in first-century East and West Syria and Palestine it might be a matter of days.

Central, however, is the fact that conversion, whether Christian, Jewish, or pagan, was a complex ritual process through which the subjects passed from an old way of life to a new way. They were considered reborn, emerging from the process with a new network of relations and responsibilities, new values, and a new status in society, or as the ancients put it, a "new home and family." Anthropologists are accustomed to call the process "rites of passage" (sometimes, "rites of initiation"), which typically exhibit three phases: (1) rites signaling separation from the "old way"; (2) rites effecting transition from old to new, emphasizing a state of "liminality," or of being on the boundaries *(limina)* between old and new; and (3) rites yielding initiation into the new way of life (or reintegration into the old with a new and different status).

Catechumens and Catechumenate

The rites distinctive of the journey to Christianity developed quickly into a rich, extended, and dramatic liturgical journey. Perhaps more than any other possession of the Church, they account for early Christian survival and spread—such is the power of ritual. In addition, they reveal the fundamental meaning of the Church to early Christians as the place of salvation, more accurately, that community where one finds access to Christ the Savior. For prospective converts, incorporation into the "saving" community (Church), therefore, was the destination of the journey.

Enrollment

The rite that signaled the candidates' separation from their old way of life and launched the journey proper was called "enrollment" or "enlistment." The heart of it was a searching inquiry into their personal life, status, and occupation. From that point on, candidates admitted to the process and enrolled in the Church's "book" journeyed on the boundaries between society and Church—of both but in neither—the subjects of intense and extended catechetical instruction and exorcism.

Instruction

The importance of instruction is suggested by two ancient technical terms. As already noted, "catechesis" was the term for the kind of instruction involved. Its Greek root, *echo,* gives the early Christian sense of the term: Instructions were to be so internalized that they "echoed" not only in one's mind but in one's conduct. As a result, the candidates bore the name "catechumens," designating those under instruction for baptism. Indeed, the whole process of conversion, from enrollment to the threshold of immersion, came to be called the "catechumenate."

The syllabus of instruction was twofold. For the ordinary catechumen it was the Bible as read and commented on in church, often daily. In Origen's Caesarea (vol. 6, ch. 3), for instance, a catechumen in the mid-third century would have heard both the Old and New Testaments, to some extent selectively, over the course of the several years prior to baptism.

For those approved for baptism (called the "competents," the "elect," the "baptizands," or the "photizands"), the syllabus was the creed, which almost invariably was the Nicene Creed, at least from the fourth century on. Orally and article by article the catechist (usually the bishop) delivered the creed to the competents shortly before baptism (the rite came to be called *traditio symboli,* "handing over the creed"). He then commented on the articles, sometimes briefly, sometimes at length. Close to baptism, sometimes as part of the rite, the competents, having committed the creed to memory, were required to make a public profession of faith (*redditio symboli,* "returning the creed"). As evidence of the occasion's drama, Augustine of Hippo has left a record of the public profession made by Marius Victorinus, the celebrated Neoplatonic philosopher (see vol. 6, ch. 2, *Confessions*).

From very early times, however, instruction continued after baptism as well; the focus was the religious significance of the baptismal rites and the Eucharist. Indeed, it is largely from these postbaptismal instructions (often called "mystagogical catecheses") that we discover the early Christian meaning of baptism. As the reader will quickly learn, the theology of the early Christians was the result of symbols deeply lived. The primacy of experience is further underscored by the fact that instruction on the baptismal rites was delayed until after baptism, given usually during the Easter season. Conditioned by ancient mystery-cult practice, the Church felt that the intimate meaning of the ritual drama should be spread before and understood only by the initiated.

Exorcism

Catechesis was only half the battle, and "battle" is the correct word: The purpose of the catechumenate was literally to "re-form" the candidate. Formation rather than information was its thrust ("resocialization," as the social scientist might call it). For the early Christian was persuaded that conduct mirrored conviction. Thus, as the catechumens' convictions changed from old values to new, their conduct had also to change from old ways to new. This formative task was assigned to exorcism, because the obstacle to conversion was a literally terrifying field of forces—physical, psychological, and spiritual—which the catechists identified with graphic specificity: the gods, their cultic processions, the races, the theater, the gladiatorial extravaganzas, every conceivable vice, even the instruments of the Muse of music. Invariably the forces were the institutions of pagan, usually Greco-Roman, culture, and sometimes, especially before Constantine (311/313), when it was a capital crime to be a Christian, the naked power of Rome itself.

The unseen enemy, however, was Satan and his legions—the real obstacle to conversion. The pagan institutions were only their servants. As a result, catechesis was linked to exorcism. For the Holy Spirit to enter, as the catechists put it, the evil spirit had to be driven out. Thus, exorcist was counterpart of catechist. Indeed, by the mid-third century, the exorcist corps at Rome numbered forty-two.

Although the rites differed, the dynamics of exorcism remained fairly constant. They were at their most striking in the solemn exorcism that marked the end of the catechumenate, an ordeal called the "scrutiny." It first appears (ca. 200) in the *Apostolic Tradition* of Hippolytus (vol. 6, ch. 1) as a searching inquiry into the life of the catechumens in order to gauge the quality and progress of their conversion, specifically, to determine whether anything of the "evil spirit" remained. By the late fourth century in North Africa, the rite had become an intense psychological ordeal (see vol. 6, ch. 2, Augustine). It was public, involved a physical examination, an exsufflation (a hissing and spitting) that would lead to the charge of demeaning the emperor were it done to an imperial statue, the imposition of hands, and ringing curses. Held at the end of the vigil on the Saturday night before what is now Palm Sunday, it was presided over by the bishop, who delivered the commands, expelling Satan in the name and power of Christ and the Trinity. Not everyone passed scrutiny, but those who did were anointed on the ears and nose against the possible return of Satan and his legions. These, as already noted, were the competents, or elect, that is, chosen for baptism.

But exorcism, whether daily or in the form of a scrutiny, was an awesome experience calculated to excite lively fear in the candidates and an abhorrence of the very thought of evil. Written into the rite was the early Christian theology of sin, specifically, the fall of Adam and its consequences for his descendants: They were Satan's slaves, enlisted in his ranks and yoked to his service. Perhaps a bizarre practice by modern standards, the early Church nonetheless dramatized in rite and symbol its realistic sense of the sway that culture, habit, and life's addictions held over the individual. But written into the rite as well was the conviction that God, Christ, and the Church could collectively bring to bear on the candidates the power needed to put Satan and the demons to flight, enabling them to break out of his ranks and shed his yoke. The script for exorcism, although beyond detailed reconstruction, was biblical, largely based on the encounters between Jesus and the demons.

Renunciation and Allegiance

Thus "scrutinized," the candidates could now stand on their own two feet and in their own voices formally renounce Satan and his works. Renunciation, which signaled the end of the preliminary rites, took place on the threshold of baptism itself, sometimes, as in the case of North Africa, right after the solemn scrutiny and a week before baptism, or, as was more often the case, just outside the baptistery immediately before baptism. The rite was often coupled with a pledge of allegiance to Christ that spoke of entering his ranks and accepting his yoke. Occasionally, however, the baptismal profession of faith constituted the pledge. In either case, the rite concluded with an anointing of the entire body, apparently for protection against the further assaults of the devil, now formally denounced, and, as was the custom among athletes, in preparation for the decisive Olympic struggle with Satan in the baptismal font. Whatever the precise order, the rites of renunciation and allegiance dramatized the early Christian conviction that conversion to Christ was a long, collaborative ritual process through which catechumens gradually acquired the freedom to break the powerful hold of an old way of life and to embrace the new. That there was nothing routine or automatic about the process is underscored by the fact that some, perhaps many, did not pass scrutiny or survive the renunciation.

Baptism

The journey was almost over. As we have seen, for some it lasted a lifetime, for others, several years, for still others, especially after the Church instituted Lent in the fourth century (see ch. 1, Cyril and Egeria), six weeks. Whatever the duration, the goal was the baptismal font, in its earliest form a stream or river. By mid-third century the font was often a converted domestic bathing facility. Elaborate cruciform and octagonal (occasionally round) baptisteries were the norm in the fourth century and thereafter. The earliest extant baptismal document, the *Didache* (ch. 1) speaks of baptism in "living waters," that is, flowing water. There is some indication that streams were diverted to flow through the font. However, the earliest archaeological evidence of a baptistery comes from a Roman garrison town on the Euphrates, Dura Europos, in modern Iraq. It was in a private house converted to a house-church a decade or two before 256, when the building was partially destroyed in a Parthian invasion. The earliest description of a specially built baptistery comes from Jerusalem in the mid-fourth century (see ch. 1, Cyril and Egeria).

Whether stream or richly ornamented building, however, the baptistery was the place of the final act of the sacred drama. Here was what the Latin-speaking Christians called *sacramentum* (sacrament), and the Greek-speaking, *mysterion* (mystery). Although borrowed from Greco-Roman culture, the terms designated those rites that gave the catechumens direct access to Christ as Savior, the heart of which was immersion in water usually consecrated for the purpose. Although liturgical customs differed strikingly, the candidates invariably were naked and immersed in the baptismal water three times in the name of the Father and of the Son and of the Holy Spirit—the medievals would term the water and the words "matter" and "form."

Time and again the question came up: Why such ordinary things as water, oil, gestures, and words for such a sacred event as salvation? Underneath differences of custom lay a widely shared conviction about what happened in the font. Enunciated by Tertullian (vol. 6, ch. 2), who gave the West so much of its theological vocabulary, the answer is fundamental to all early Christian sacramental thinking: "The flesh is the hinge of salvation" *(caro salutis est cardo).* He explains: "The flesh is washed that the soul may be made spotless; the flesh is anointed that the soul may be consecrated; the flesh is signed [with the cross] that the soul too may be protected; the flesh is overshadowed by the imposition of the hand that the soul may also be illumined by the Spirit; the flesh feeds on the body and blood of Christ so that the soul may be replete with God" *(On the Resurrection of the Flesh* 8).

Symbolic Participation

Tertullian's younger contemporary Origen, however, is the first of the Fathers to address the question of how candidates gained direct access to salvation. The answer lies in the dynamics of symbol, for he says about the three days Christ spent in the tomb that "those who have been taken up into Christ by baptism have been taken up into his death and been buried with him, and will rise with him" (vol. 6, ch. 3, *Homilies on Exodus* 5:2). As a result, he calls baptism the "mystery of the third day." By "mystery" he means immersion in the baptismal water, through which one participates not only in Christ's death and burial but also in his resurrection. Indeed, Origen, who appears to have retrieved it from the Gnostics, is the first Church Father to bring Paul's doctrine of symbolic participation in the death and resurrection of Christ (see Rom 6:1-11) to bear on baptism. As a result, the baptismal font came to be seen as at once a tomb and a womb. Gregory of Nyssa, Origen's disciple, in his *Homily on the Baptism of Christ,* explains that the water which receives the baptismal candidate, like the earth which received Christ's body, is a tomb from which, like a womb, Christ and the newly baptized arise new-born (see ch. 1).

But it is another disciple of Origen, Cyril of Jerusalem, who takes the decisive step. In his baptismal instructions he explains that the recipient of baptism, through the enactment of Christ's death, burial, and resurrection in baptismal rite and symbol, participates in the redemption that these events have accomplished. In short, the rites of baptism give the baptismal candidate living access to redemption through participation in the baptismal drama, especially immersion. Although the Church Fathers distinguish between the historical events of Christ's crucifixion, death, and resurrection as once-for-all and the baptismal ritual, which reenacts them, they insist that "by sharing his sufferings in a symbolic enactment we may really and truly gain salvation" (ch. 1, Cyril of Jerusalem, *Baptismal Catechesis* 2:5). The key is the participatory character of the liturgical symbolism that undergirds baptismal instruction in both East and West.

Culture, however, conditioned perception. Theodore of Mopsuestia (ch. 1), for instance, has a different perspective. Imbued with Neoplatonism, he sees the sacraments as the link between what he calls the "two ages." The first age is the visible and ever-changing world of time, space, and human life and choice; the second, the invisible and immutable future—Paradise regained. The ages are linked invisibly by the risen Christ and visibly by the sacrament, which makes present the second age through sign and symbol enacted in the first. As Theodore sees it, the sacraments make present the second age, or future, because they participate in its reality, the core of which is resurrection. Already achieved by Christ, resurrection, even though inchoative, is Paradise regained for the Christian.

Further east, in Syriac-speaking Christianity (ch. 2) with its deeply Semitic culture, past and present and heaven and earth all intersect in Christ, to whom the sacrament is linked by the Holy Spirit. Everything converges: Creation, the Exodus from Egypt, crossing the Jordan, Christ's baptism, and the Christian's baptism. The Holy Spirit, who hovered over the primal deep, over the Red Sea, over the Jordan, and as the dove over Christ, is the very Spirit who hovers over the baptismal waters, sanctifying the recipient (see ch. 2, Ephrem). Thus, what happened to Christ in the Jordan happens also to the Christian in the baptismal font.

In the West, the emphasis is on representation (anamnesis). First used in the *Apostolic Tradition* of Hippolytus (vol. 6, ch. 1), this biblical term (see 1 Cor 11:23-25; Luke 20:19) is often taken to mean "in memory of" or "commemoration." The underlying sense, however, is that the liturgy of baptism (and the Eucharist) renders present the events signified, especially the hinge event upon which the entire early liturgy turns: the death and resurrection of Christ. Thus, a more adequate translation is "re-presentation." Christ's redeeming death and resurrection are "re-presented" at a later time and in a different place (without being repeated).

Whether East or West, however, the underlying conviction was about the resurrection of Christ, which, as early Christians saw it, shattered the normal boundaries of space and time. For them Christ's resurrection made him and the saving events of his life accessible in their own present through the sacramental liturgy, in this case, baptism.

The Efficacy of Baptism

As for the power of baptism, early Christians were convinced that the sacrament receives its saving power from the Christ who is risen and in glory but who died on the cross. The passion of Christ was literally the crucial event. Meditating on the spear the soldier thrust into Christ's side (see John 19:34-35), the Church Fathers both Eastern and Western see the sacraments of baptism and the Eucharist embodied in the blood and water that gush forth. John Chrysostom (ch. 1), for instance, insists that the water came out first and then blood, since, in the order of things, baptism comes first and then the Eucharist; he then adds, "It was the soldier, then, who opened Christ's side and dug through the rampart of the holy temple, but I am the one who has found the treasure and gotten the wealth" (*Baptismal Homily* 3:16).

The catechist is not breaking new ground but only handing on a tradition at least as old as the second century (see vol. 6, ch. 2, Tertullian, *On Baptism* 9) and as far reaching as Jacob of Serugh (ch. 2, *Memra* 7, *On the Baptism of the Law,* ll. 185–191). Indeed, the Council of Florence reflects this ancient tradition when, a thousand years later, its *Decree for the Armenians* explains that the passion of Christ is the "efficient" cause of the sacramental efficacy, including the sacrament of baptism (Mansi 31:1054).

The Pattern of Baptism

Directly related to efficacy is the widespread patristic view of the pattern according to which sacraments accomplish their effects. (Subsequent ages would call it the "institution" of the sacraments.) In the Eucharist, for instance, the pattern is the Last Supper; for baptism it is Christ's own baptism. For both, the power of the sacrament issues from Christ's institution. Tertullian sets the tone for the West when he writes that Christ was fashioning baptism throughout his life, but particularly when he was baptized, walked on water, changed water into wine at Cana, washed the feet of his disciples, and finally (as we have just seen), "when he receives a wound [and] water bursts forth from his side, as the soldier's spear can tell" (vol. 6, ch. 2, *On Baptism* 9). Years later, Ambrose of Milan (vol. 6, ch. 1, *On the Sacraments* 3:4) attempts more precision when he proposes (not persuasively, as it turned out) that Jesus instituted the sacrament when he washed the feet of the disciples at the Last Supper (see John 13:12-18).

For Origen and the Eastern tradition generally, however, the focus is squarely on Christ's own baptism: What happened at the Jordan happens also in the baptismal font. Indeed, the baptismal font is often called "Jordan." Narsai, the East Syrian disciple of Theodore of Mopsuestia, sums up much patristic tradition on the subject when he writes that Christ descended into the water, bathed in it, sanctified it, and conferred on it the power of the Holy Spirit to give life and make it a "womb which begets people spiritually" (ch. 2, *Homily on the Epiphany*, 1. 294). Indeed, Christ entering the Jordan is the pattern to which Egyptian consecratory prayers over the baptismal font appeal (see vol. 6, ch. 3, Serapion; Coptic Rite).

Sacrament as Sign

Thanks largely to Augustine, sacraments came to be regarded as signs composed of "words" and "things," which cause what they signify. He holds that the spoken word is the quintessential human sign because it actualizes what it signifies, that is, it renders its referent present to the mind. As the incarnate Word of God, Christ, therefore, he argues, is the perfect sign because he embodies God. The sacraments, for Augustine, are of the same order—perfect Word—because they are signs that embody Christ to such an extent that even "if Judas baptizes, it is Christ who baptizes" (*Commentary on John*, 5:18, 6:7). His contemporary, Leo the Great (vol. 6, ch. 1), puts the matter even more strikingly: "What was visible in Christ has passed over into the sacraments of the church" (*Sermon* 74).

Reminiscent of Tertullian, for whom, as we have seen, the flesh is the hinge of salvation, the point Augustine and Leo seek to maintain is that precisely as signs composed of words, gestures, and material elements, baptism renders accessible the saving action of Christ. As a result, there is an enduring quality established by the words joined to the material elements and celebrated by the minister. Indeed, Augustine and his predecessor Optatus (vol. 6, ch. 2) argue that the recipient of a sacrament receives "something" from the sacrament irrespective of the minister's moral character (i.e., whether he is a known or public sinner) or of his ecclesiastical status (heretic or schismatic). As a result and contrary to North African tradition (see Cyprian, vol. 6, ch. 2), they hold that even when a schismatic (one separated from the Church) or a heretic (i.e., one of erroneous belief) baptizes, the sacrament is valid.

Augustine goes even further, arguing that baptism imprints a "mark" ("seal" and "character" are his other terms) on the recipients quite irrespective of their "worthiness" or dispositions, in virtue of which the "benefit" or "grace" of the sacrament revives (see vol. 6, ch. 2, *On Baptism* 10-13). Quite apart, then, from the minister's situation or the recipient's dispositions, Christ offers salvation, or, as the two North Africans also put it, the sacrament is valid. In arguing thus, Optatus and Augustine establish for their medieval successors the distinction between the validity of a properly celebrated sacrament and its fruitfulness: Validity depends on the act of Christ embodied in the sign rather than on the moral character or ecclesiastical situation of the minister; fruitfulness depends on the dispositions of the recipient. Coupled with the patristic doctrine of symbolic participation discussed above, their approach sets the foundation for the medieval teaching that in their very celebration sacraments effect what they signify *(ex opere operato)*.

The Minister

In his incisive way (as we have just seen) Augustine asserts that even if Judas baptizes, it is really Christ who baptizes. Nonetheless, the usual ecclesiastical minister of the sacrament is the bishop. As Chrysostom puts the matter, he is the "visible high priest," whereas the "unseen great High Priest is Christ" (ch. 1, *Baptismal Homily* 11:12). But we learn from Tertullian that presbyters, deacons, and laymen can baptize (see vol. 6, ch. 2, *On Baptism* 17). Ultimately, however, the minister is the Trinity. In commenting on the passive and impersonal baptismal formula used in Syrian Christianity ("N. is baptized in the name . . ."), for instance, both Chrysostom and his friend Theodore of Mopsuestia insist that the sacrament summons Father, Son, and Spirit in their consubstantiality to baptize. Both are convinced (as are the North Africans, Optatus and Augustine) that the visible minister is only instrumental in the hands of the Trinity. As much as the two friends might excoriate a bishop or other minister of baptism for immoral character, moral condition, they hold, cannot impede God's action. Nonetheless, they require orthodox faith in the Trinity for validity. Chrysostom, for instance, argues against the validity of Arian baptism by asserting that unless the minister professes true (Nicene) Trinitarian faith neither remission of sin nor filial adoption is granted (see ch. 1, *Baptismal Homily* 2:26). His conviction was widespread in the fourth-century East, though not in the West, where the issue was settled by the Council of Arles (314), namely, that neither schism nor heresy could render an otherwise properly celebrated baptism invalid. Medieval theology would clarify the ministerial issue by insisting that the minister need only intend to do what the Church intends done (Council of Florence, *Decree for the Armenians,* Mansi 31:1054).

Faith and Baptism

From the outset faith entered into the very constitution of baptism, not precisely the divine gift by which one believed—that was presupposed, because the norm was adult baptism. Rather, the faith in question was the creed. In one form or another it was elicited from the candidates as they stood in the baptismal pool. In fact, in second-century Rome the creed constituted the form according to which baptism was administered and required the candidates' explicit assent of faith (see vol. 6, ch. 1, *Apostolic Tradition* 20).

At different times different customs obtained. In fourth-century Syria, as we have already seen, the creed was given to the candidates approved for baptism orally, article by article, at the beginning of Lent; they returned it by public profession just before baptism. In North Africa the custom was for the candidate to profess the creed in the presence of the assembled congregation the Sunday before (Easter) baptism and to repeat profession at baptism. Whatever the custom, an explicit act of creedal faith was an integral part of baptism; indeed, many, including Augustine (*Letter to Bonanus* 98:9), call baptism the "sacrament of faith." The Council of Orange (529), looking back over the long journey to the baptismal font, calls the first stirrings, which prompted one to start out on the journey, the "beginnings of faith" (cann. 5, 7, 8, and conclusion; Mansi 8:718).

The inner disposition of the recipient, however, was not thereby downplayed. We have already seen in detail (see above, on catechesis, exorcism) the intense screening process characteristic of the catechumenate. Yet not everyone who passed scrutiny was truly converted. About the unconverted, Gregory of Nyssa (ch. 1) warns, "Though it may be a bold thing to say, yet I will say it and will not shrink; in these cases the water is but water, for the gift of the Holy Spirit in no way appears in him who is thus baptismally born" (*Great Catechetical Oration* 40).

A note of caution. Early Christian baptism had clearly in view adults; yet infants and children (and the incapacitated) were not thereby excluded. In the *Apostolic Tradition* of Hippolytus, for instance, an important rubric enjoins the baptism of children, including infants, ahead of everyone else (see vol. 6, ch. 1). Although the North African Tertullian rejects infant baptism (vol. 6, ch. 2, *On Baptism* 18), Cyprian, bishop of Carthage, who considers Tertullian his "master," urges his people not even to wait the customary eight days after birth to baptize their children (vol. 6, ch. 2, *Letter* 74). Origen (vol. 6, ch. 3) gives the reason. "The church has received from the apostles the custom of administering baptism even to infants," he writes, "for those who have been entrusted with the secrets of the divine mysteries [the apostles] knew very well that all are tainted with the stain of original sin, which must be washed off by water and the spirit" (*Commentary on Romans* 5:9).

Although early Christian baptismal liturgies had primarily in view the adult, they reached out also to embrace infant and incapacitated alike. For that faith that entered into the very constitution of baptism was the faith of the Church. Where circumstance dictated, the Church's faith could supply for the faith of the individual, and, in any case, early Christians did not think that God was hemmed in by the sacraments.

Postbaptismal Rites

What prevents a narrative history of the sacrament of baptism is the sometimes striking variation of rite and custom in time and cultural area. Nowhere is this more apparent than in the rites that followed baptism. For instance, the earliest Church order, the *Didache* (ch. 1), leaves the postbaptismal record blank, whereas the late second-century Roman liturgy paints the portrait of the naked newly baptized coming up out of the font to be greeted by a presbyter and a rich variety of rites.

According to the *Apostolic Tradition* of Hippolytus (vol. 6, ch. 1), first they were anointed with oil in the name of Christ. When dried and dressed, they entered the church, there to be met by the bishop, who imposed his hands and prayed about baptismal remission of sins, rebirth, and grace. He embraced each and then poured blessed oil on their heads, signed them on the forehead, and embraced them with a kiss. The newly baptized then prayed together with the congregation, were welcomed with the kiss of peace, and celebrated their first Eucharist, at which they received a cup of milk mixed with honey and a cup of water (in addition to the bread and wine). This "first Communion" included a homily in which the bishop explained to the newly baptized the meaning of the rites they had just celebrated.

In a comparatively short space of time but in different places with differing customs, the postbaptismal liturgy became a drama in its own right. Although the following picture is a composite, it is nonetheless fairly representative by the late fourth century. As the newly baptized came up out of the baptismal pool, they prayed the Lord's Prayer, sent prayers of intercession heavenward, vested in white garments, received lighted candles, and sometimes were crowned with garlands. They processed to the Eucharist, often chanting Psalm 22 (23) interpreted to extol baptism and the Eucharist (see below, on baptismal typology): "The Lord is my shepherd, I shall not want; he makes me lie down in green pastures. He leads me beside still waters; he restores my soul. . . ."

An entire week of daily Eucharistic celebrations followed in which the newly baptized occupied center stage. A striking feature was instruction in the meaning of the baptismal rites, several sets of which are included in the readings.

The rites reveal the depth and timbre of early Christian thinking about the effects of baptism. The nakedness of the newly baptized as they emerged from the font emphasized rebirth, an image of baptism at least as old as the letters of Paul and John's Gospel. They could pray the Lord's Prayer (Our Father) because they were now new-born and sinless children in that family of which God was Father. Their intercessory prayers were especially valued because they could now speak boldly to their Father, an intimacy claimed particularly by the children of the family. The white garment, the counterpart of the "tunics of shame" they had stripped off (Paul's "old" or "sinful man") before entering the font, dramatized the conviction that they "had put on Christ," that is, possessed the grace of resurrection and immortality. The baptismal candle stressed the sacrament as enlightenment—a theme that first appears in the Letter to the Hebrews (see 6:4) and develops many associations in the early centuries, prominent among them the baptismal gift of faith and the interior renovation accomplished by the grace of baptism. Among others, the *Ordo of*

Constantinople (ch. 1) recapitulates the themes by then (ca. 420) deeply traditional:

> As one in need, you lift your hands to heaven. In this you may know how poor you are whom the Master receives, how he enriches your nakedness with his grace, how with the chrism he puts on you the odor of good deeds [a reference to the full anointing before baptism], how with the oil, he makes you shine brilliantly, how you lay aside your corruption in the grave of the bath, how the Spirit raises you up to a new life, how he clothes your body with shining garments, how the lamps you hold in your hands symbolize the illumination of the soul.

Where the work of baptism was crowned by coronation—doubtless drawn from marriage customs—the rite emphasized an ancient theme: baptism as marriage between Christ and the newly baptized. Reflecting an ancient tradition, for instance, John Chrysostom says to the newly enrolled before him: "Come let me talk to you as I would to a bride about to be led to the holy nuptial chamber. . . . But let no one who hears these words of mine fall into a crass or carnal interpretation. I am talking of the soul and its salvation" (ch. 1, *Baptismal Homily* 1:3-4; see also ch. 2, Jacob of Serugh, *Memra* 7, ll. 29-36).

Generally, the members of the congregation tendered the newly baptized a familial embrace. In so doing they signified that baptism initiated the newly baptized into the family, which had not only God as Father but Christ as elder brother, the Holy Spirit as its bond, and the baptized as brothers and sisters—in short, the Church. Although beyond the scope of this book, the Eucharist (see vol. 7 of the series), as the meal of their new family (the Church), awaited.

An early and widespread Eucharistic custom was to give the newly baptized (in addition to the bread and wine) a cup of baptismal water and one of milk and honey mixed. The water symbolized the penetration of baptism to their inmost being, and the milk and honey, their entry into the Promised Land of gifts and grace, together, as we shall see, with their return to Paradise.

About the bread and wine, the newly baptized could now be nourished by that "other" sacrament that gushed from the pierced side of Christ, the Eucharist—for the two sacraments combined to bring the Church into being. Again, Chrysostom: "I said that there was a symbol of baptism and the mysteries [the Eucharist] in that blood and water. It is from both of these that the church is sprung. . . . It is from his side, therefore, that Christ formed his church, just as he formed Eve from the side of Adam" (ch. 1, *Baptismal Homily* 3:17).

Anointing and the Holy Spirit

The crucial act in the baptismal rites was "the washing." Yet anointing was almost as important; its significance was closely allied to immersion. The reason reflects the bedrock Christian conviction that Jesus was the "Messiah" or "Anointed One" and that the Christian, as incorporated into Christ, is similarly an anointed one—a "christ." It was a conviction rich in history and custom.

Background

From bathing to cult, almost every aspect of life in the Greco-Roman world involved the use of oil, especially anointing, or smearing with scented oil (chrism). The Bible reflects Greco-Roman practice, terminology, and world-view, but with this difference: Biblical literature shows a marked tendency to emphasize sacred anointing. The biblical terminology provides a rich background for early Christian thought and practice. The root word "to anoint" (Hebrew, *masah,* Greek, *chriein*) gave the name "messianic" to an ancient tradition in Israel.

Although Israel itself was God's anointed, kings, priests, and prophets were typically the anointed ones and, as such, the bearers of God's spirit. After the Babylonian Exile (587–533 B.C.E.), the history of God's people, though it had its bright spots, was largely the history of subjugation to foreigners: Persians, Greeks, and Romans. Understandably, a certain preoccupation with the future came to the fore (ca. 200 B.C.E.). Grounded in the ancient traditions, people began to look for God to intervene as he had in the past to save his people. This expectation often centered around an "anointed one"—a David, a Moses, an Elijah, an Enoch—as God's agent to usher in a better future. In short, an "anointed one," a *messiah/christos.* Messianism was especially characteristic of the Jewish sectarian groups that abounded in the first century of our common era.

Early Christianity

Against this background and the expectations to which it gave rise, early Christians saw Jesus as the Anointed One—at once king, priest, and prophet—sent to fulfill the hope for a new age and redemption. Jesus' baptism at the hands of John came quickly to the fore as the privileged moment when he was revealed as the Anointed One, that is, anointed with the Holy Spirit and attested by the Father as his well-loved Son (see Mark 1:11; Matt 3:16-17; Luke 3:21-23).

When Christ's baptism emerged as the pattern for Christian baptism, the details of the Jordan scene called for ritual attention. In time, anointing became part of the baptismal rite to signify the "christening" of the candidates—they had become "christs," according to Tertullian (see vol. 6, ch. 2, *On Baptism* 7). Like their Master, the newly baptized emerged from the font as God's royal, priestly, and prophetic sons and daughters (see 1 Pet 2:9) and the bearers of the Spirit.

Anointing also yielded one of the earliest terms for baptism, the "seal." Although the term denoted a mark of ownership and protection (sheep of the flock, etc.), it pointed beyond itself to another mark, circumcision, which was also called the "seal," that is, the mark of God's covenant with Abraham. As the mark of the new covenant, baptism was the new or "second" circumcision (see vol. 6, ch. 3, Origen, *Homily on St. Luke* 14; see also ch. 2, Aphrahat, in this vol.). There is reason to believe that "seal" was transferred from baptism itself to anointing, because widespread custom called for the baptismal candidates to have the sign of the cross traced on their foreheads, very often with oil. The cross was the distinctively Christian mark of ownership—sign of the new covenant in Christ's blood, as circumcision was the sign of the old covenant. The washing and the anointing were linked well before the end of the second century, possibly as early as the end of the first.

Two Traditions

Although anointing in the baptismal rites differed from place to place, two dominant patterns developed early, the Western and the Syrian. At Rome, for instance, there were two separate anointings: One took place just before baptism and the other, just after. The first sought to exorcize, heal, and strengthen the candidate for combat with Satan; the second, performed with consecrated and scented oil (chrism), was associated with the gift of the Holy Spirit (see vol. 6, ch. 1, *Apostolic Tradition;* Ambrose). Both anointings covered the whole body, but the latter was done in two stages: (1) When the newly baptized emerged from the water, a presbyter anointed their bodies with chrism; (2) after they had dried, dressed, and entered the church, the bishop imposed hands on them, poured chrism on their heads, and signed their foreheads with the sign of the cross. Eventually the full anointing after baptism would disappear, and only the anointing and signing of the forehead would survive. Cyril of Jerusalem provides the earliest explanation of its meaning: "Christ was anointed with a mystical oil of gladness; that is, with the Holy Spirit, called the 'oil of gladness' because he is the cause of spiritual gladness; so you, being anointed with ointment, have become partakers and fellows of Christ" (ch. 1, *Baptismal Catechesis* 3:2).

The second pattern is Syrian (both Greek- and Syriac-speaking) and knew only an anointing before baptism. Also given in two stages, the first consisted of anointing the forehead in the sign of the cross; the second was a full anointing from head to foot. Both anointings sought to put the candidate under Christ's protection and to exorcise, heal, and strengthen. In Greek-speaking Syria this prebaptismal anointing had no connection with the Holy Spirit. In Syriac-speaking Syria, however, there was a more kaleidoscopic view. Ephrem (ch. 2), for instance, sees many splendors in the prebaptismal anointing, especially the radiance of the Holy Spirit: "The oil is the dear friend of the Holy Spirit, it serves him, following him like a disciple. With it the Spirit signed priests and anointed kings; for with the oil the Holy Spirit imprints his mark on his sheep. Like a signet ring whose impression is left on wax, so the hidden seal of the Spirit is imprinted by oil on the bodies of those who are anointed in baptism; thus they are marked in the baptismal mystery" (*Hymns on Virginity* 6).

The importance of the disparate Syrian and Western patterns of anointing is twofold: The Syrian emphasized the fact that baptism itself is the privileged moment of transformation through the descent of the Holy Spirit, while the Western focused attention on the continuing work of the Holy Spirit in baptismal rebirth and life after baptism. Ambrose of Milan, for instance, associates postbaptismal anointing with the outpouring of the seven gifts of the Spirit, which perfect baptism and empower the newly baptized to live a Christian life (see vol. 6, ch. 1, *On the Sacraments* 3:8–10). At almost the same time, John Chrysostom in Syrian Antioch exhorts his candidates to recognize that the Holy Spirit in his fullness descends at the moment of immersion (see ch. 1, *Baptismal Homily* 2:25).

A Shift in the West: Confirmation

No one disputed that the Holy Spirit was the treasured gift of baptism. Gradually in the West, however, changing custom drove a wedge between baptism and the postbaptismal anointing (coming to be called "consignation"). By the fifth century, for instance, the rite was regularly separated from baptism and reserved to the bishop (see vol. 6, ch. 1, Innocent, John the Deacon). Given the pressure from the conversion of the Western barbarian tribes and coupled with the rise of infant baptism as normal practice, it proved to be only a matter of time before the separable rite became a separate sacrament.

The development was largely set by mid-ninth century when the Benedictine abbot Rabanus Maurus (d. 856), doubtless shaped by the tradition handed on by Ambrose and, to some extent, by the "strengthening" significance inherent in anointing, proposed its theology, namely, that the rite confers that distinctive gift by which the Holy Spirit (already received in baptism) strengthens the gifts of baptism (*On the Institution of Clerics* 1:28–30). In short, as the West came to see it, the work of baptism was "confirmed" by the special outpouring of the Spirit signified by the anointing, which strengthens one to overcome the difficulties of living in Christ—a sacrament of confirmation. In his celebrated theological textbook, *On the Sentences,* Peter Lombard (ca. 1150), for instance, numbers confirmation among the seven sacraments, concluding that its distinctive grace is the "gift of the Holy Spirit for strength, whereas in baptism the Spirit is given for the remission of sin" (book 4, distinction 7:3).

A Shift in the East: Chrismation

The first mention of a postbaptismal anointing in the unalloyed Syrian tradition, albeit West Syrian, is in the baptismal homilies of Theodore of Mopsuestia (ca. 420). He writes that when the bishop sealed the newly baptized on the forehead in the name of the Father and of the Son and of the Holy Spirit, "this sign shows you that, when the Father, the Son and the Holy Spirit were named, the Holy Spirit came upon you" (*Baptismal Homily* 3:27).

In East Syria (ch. 2) a postbaptismal anointing first clearly appears during the early sixth century in two contemporaries of Jacob of Serugh, Philoxenus of Mabbug (d. 523) and Severus of Antioch (d. 538). When outlining the baptismal liturgy, the former simply mentions a postbaptismal "imprinting," which the latter identifies as a symbol of the Holy Spirit.

Whether the shift to a postbaptismal anointing in the Syrian traditions, sometimes called "chrismation," signifies a gift distinct from the baptismal gift of the Holy Spirit is not clear. Looking at the ancient Syrian tradition as a whole, however, it is not a question of either/or: The Holy Spirit in his fullness is given through the water *and* the oil. Beyond the scope of this work is a discussion of the complex history of the postbaptismal anointing and its significance for the Churches that stand in continuity with the Syrian tradition.

The Bible and the Baptismal Liturgy

As we have already seen, a single principle binds together like a golden thread all the disparate traditions about baptism: The flesh is the hinge of salvation. The thread that binds together the disparate baptismal theologies is biblical. The genius of the early Christian catechists lies in their unique ability to unite Bible and liturgy by drawing the theology of the rites from key events narrated in the Bible.

The biblical events important for the meaning of baptism have water as their focus. Those in the Hebrew Bible that stand out are Creation (Gen 1–3), the Flood (Gen 7–8), crossing the Red Sea (Exod 14), crossing the Jordan (Josh 3), and Elisha, Naaman, and the Jordan (2 Kgs 5). Two events in the New Testament that have special importance, as we have seen in detail, are Christ's baptism in the Jordan (Mark 1:9-11; Matt 3; Luke 3:1-21) and his pierced side from which water and blood flowed (John 19:34).

Some catechists, like those of the Antioch school (see ch. 1), were restrictive in their use of the applicable biblical events. Others, like the Alexandrians (see vol. 6, ch. 3, especially Origen), were expansive and explored the events with the lenses of allegory. Still others, especially the Syriac-speaking commentators, were allusive and worked as if by the free association of biblical ideas.

Yet undergirding their several attempts to link biblical event and liturgical rite was the deep conviction that God intervenes in the movements, achievements, and crises in human affairs to save humankind. More pertinent, they were convinced that the history of salvation narrated in the Bible is one long and continuous sweep of saving events from creation to Christ, such that the earlier event signals and anticipates the later event, which fulfills it. To adapt Tertullian's sacramental principle: Key biblical events are the hinge (like the flesh) upon which the history of salvation turns.

Called "typological thinking," the dynamics of this early Christian approach to the Bible are complex. For instance, the primeval waters of the Book of Genesis over which the spirit of God moves and from which light and life spring; the flood waters bearing Noah's ark; the waters of the Red Sea through which the Israelites pass to a new way of life; the waters of the Jordan through which Joshua leads the Israelites to a second circumcision and the better life of the Promised Land—in typological Christian thinking each of these points beyond itself to the waters of the Jordan, in which John the Baptist immerses Jesus, who summons all to a new and better life in the kingdom of God. In turn, Jesus' baptism points ahead to his death and resurrection. The God who intervenes to create, to save Noah and his precious cargo, to bring the fugitive Hebrews dry-shod through the Red Sea, to lead the people of Israel across the Jordan, is the very God who intervenes at the Jordan through John the Baptist to bring to fruition in Jesus the salvation prepared from the beginning of time.

Thus linked to the key events of the past, the baptism of Jesus in the Jordan fulfills and redefines the historic significance of each of the earlier events. Conversely, each of the earlier events, a saving event in its own right, prepares for, anticipates, and reveals something of the historic significance of Jesus' baptism, which in turn illuminates the death that he himself calls a baptism (see Mark 10:38-39). To early Christians the key biblical events, like a rich Oriental tapestry, are woven into the fabric of biblical history as patterns that lead to a central figure and then lead away to the sacramental events that lie beyond the biblical border.

Although the catechists vary the term with "figure," "shadow," and "image," they call the earlier (Old Testament) event, which points to the New Testament event as its fulfillment, a "type." The New Testament fulfillment is the "antitype," "reality," "substance," or "truth." Thus, for instance, the Exodus from Egypt is the type and the baptism of Jesus, the antitype. Cyril of Jerusalem (ch. 1), whose baptismal catecheses have been classics for a millennium and a half, sees the significance of the rite of the renunciation of Satan through the lenses of the Exodus account (12–14). After recounting its highlights, he writes:

> Pass, pray, from the old to the new, from the figure [lit. "type"] to the reality. There Moses sent by God to Egypt; here Christ sent from the Father into the world. Moses' mission was to lead out from Egypt a persecuted people; Christ's to rescue all the people of the world who were under the tyranny of sin. There the blood of a lamb was the charm against the destroyer; here, the blood of the unspotted Lamb, Jesus Christ, is appointed your inviolable sanctuary against demons. Pharaoh pursued that people of old right into the sea; this outrageous spirit, the impudent author of all evil, followed you, each one, up to the very verge of the saving streams [of the baptistery]. That other tyrant is engulfed and drowned in the Red Sea; this one is destroyed in the saving water (*Baptismal Catechesis* 1:3).

Typology such as this, however, was not an early Christian invention, for the catechists found biblical warrant. Paul, for instance, developed a powerful typological lesson for his turbulent Corinthian Christians from the experience of the Israelites in the Sinai Desert (see 1 Cor 10:1-6). Origen (vol. 6, ch. 3) comments: "Writing to the Corinthians he says in a certain passage, 'For we know that our fathers were all under the cloud, and were all baptized in Moses in the cloud and in the sea. . . .' Do you see how much Paul's teaching differs from the literal meaning? What the Jews supposed to be a crossing of the sea, Paul calls a baptism; what they supposed to be a cloud, Paul asserts is the Holy Spirit" (*Homilies on Exodus* 5:2). Although Origen here considers the Jewish interpreters of his time "literalists," typological thinking had its origin among Jewish scholars, as Paul is witness. Indeed, for them the bath that formed part of the rite of proselyte conversion was an extension of the waters of the Red Sea, and they had long understood the Passover Seder, which both Paul and Origen saw as a type of the Eucharist, as a new Exodus.

Against this background, the early Christian catechists saw the liturgy, in this case the baptismal liturgy, as the ongoing biblical history of salvation narrated—more accurately, enacted—in myth, symbol, and ritual drama. Although the events of the old dispensation were linked indissolubly to those of the new, both were linked to the sacraments, which rendered accessible the God who saves. In his incisive way, Augustine, for instance, counsels that the counterpart of the biblical miracles is to be found in the sacraments of baptism and Eucharist (see vol. 6, ch. 2, *On Baptism* 3:21). In the allusive way of the East Syrians, Jacob of Serugh (ch. 2) links the Exodus through the Red Sea, John the Baptist at the Jordan, and Christ's gift of baptism:

> Thus you should understand that there are three different categories of baptism for those who have been baptized as we have described:
> One is of the Law, another is of John, while this third one was
> opened up by the Son of God.
> The baptisms in the Law are a shadow,
> while the baptism of John is of repentance,
> whereas the baptism of the Son of God gives birth to the "first
> born,"
> providing sons to be brothers to the Only-Begotten.
> Moses in the wilderness depicted the image of baptism,
> John opened it up, so that it might be for repentance,
> then Christ came and kindled it with the Holy Spirit and Fire,
> so that it might be giving birth to new and immortal children.
> The great Moses with his baptism marked out
> the baptism wherein the whole world is to receive forgiveness;
> John cleansed off the filth of his own people in baptism
> in order to sanctify them and so they might then see the Son
> of God.
> Christ came and opened up baptism on his cross
> so that it might be, in the place of Eve, a "mother of living
> beings" for the world;
> water and blood, for the fashioning of spiritual children,
> flowed forth and so baptism became the mother of life (*Memra,*
> 7:159-190).

Nowhere in early Christian literature, however, is early Christian theology of baptism better recapitulated than in the typol-

ogy of Paradise. The first Adam, whose disobedience drove him
from the "garden of delights," gave place to the Second Adam,
Christ, whose death, as the Good Thief was to discover (see Luke
23:43), opened Paradise anew. The gates once opened, baptism
was the way of return. The Jordan, which, as some thought flowed
from Paradise, in fact flows back into Paradise whence it came;
so also its surrogate, the font. In one of the earliest and most
remarkable of the Syriac baptismal poems, the *Odes of Solomon*
(ch. 2), the odist limns:

> And [the Most High, my God] took me to his Paradise,
> wherein is the wealth of the Lord's pleasure.
>
> (I contemplated blooming and fruit-bearing trees,
> and self-grown was their crown.
>
> Their branches were flourishing
> and their fruits were shining;
> their roots [were] from an immortal land.
>
> And a river of gladness was irrigating them,
> and the region round about them in the land of eternal life.)
>
> Then I adored the Lord because of his magnificence.
>
> And I said, blessed, O Lord, are they
> who are planted in your land,
> and who have a place in your Paradise,
>
> And who grow in the growth of your trees,
> and have passed from darkness into light (*Ode* 11).

An ancient theme, it also endured. As if instructed by the odist,
Gregory of Nyssa (ch. 1), the architect of the Eastern Christian
mystical tradition, could lead his congregation two centuries later
in the following prayer from the conclusion of his *Homily on the
Baptism of Christ* (Epiphany):

> For you truly, O Lord, are the pure and eternal fount of good-
> ness, who did justly turn away from us, and in loving kindness
> did have mercy upon us. You did hate, and were reconciled;
> you did curse, and did bless; you did banish us from Paradise,
> and did recall us; you did strip off the fig-tree leaves, an un-
> seemly covering, and put upon us a costly garment; you did
> open the prison, and release the condemned; you did sprinkle
> us with clean water, and cleanse us from our filthiness. No
> longer shall Adam be confounded when called by you, nor hide

himself, convicted by his conscience, cowering in the thicket of Paradise. Nor shall the flaming sword encircle Paradise around, and make the entrance inaccessible to those that draw near; but all is turned to joy for us that were the heirs of sin: Paradise, yes, heaven itself may be trodden by man: and the creation, in the world and above the world, that once was at variance with itself, is knit together in friendship.

For early Christians the religious meaning of baptism embedded in the rites and symbols of the liturgy was disclosed by the types and antitypes, which, tutored by an ancient tradition, they drew from the Bible.

Chapter 1

West Syria

The Syrians

The earliest, most extensive, and richest baptismal tradition is Syrian. But the term "Syrian" is ambiguous; in antiquity it referred at once to territory, culture and language, and political centers. As a geographical term "Syrian" included Asia Minor (Turkey), Syria, Palestine, and the lands to the east as far as Mesopotamia (Jordan, Iraq, and to some extent Iran). In language and culture the term embraced both Hellenized largely Greek-speaking Syria (West Syria) and Semitic largely Syriac-speaking Syria (East Syria). When it comes to spheres of influence, at least among Christians, the term points to the great urban centers of Antioch and Edessa, and eventually to Constantinople and Nisibis.

Although there is a discernible unity to Syrian baptismal tradition and a good deal of bilingualism, the Hellenized Greek-speaking Syrian Christians and the Semitic Syriac-speakers differed not only in language but in patterns of thought, literary genius, and historical circumstances. The former, for instance, lived within the shifting eastern borders of the Roman Empire, were oriented to the Mediterranean world, and spoke its language, primarily Greek. The latter lived beyond Rome's borders in the land of ancient Sumer, were oriented toward Persia, and spoke Syriac, a dialect of the Aramaic that Jesus used. West Syrian baptismal instruction tends to be analytic and expository; the Eastern tradition tends to the symbolic and poetic. These differing patterns of thought and modes of expression will be immediately apparent to the reader.

For our purposes "West Syrian" denotes the predominantly Hellenized Greek-speaking Christianity of Asia Minor, Syria, and Palestine, whose principal center of influence was Antioch and then Constantinople (Istanbul, Turkey). "East Syrian," the subject of the next chapter, refers to the predominantly Semitic, Syriac-speaking Christianity east of Palestine as far as Mesopotamia, whose principal centers were Edessa and Nisibis.

Antioch and the Christians

Antioch is now Antakya, a small city in the southwestern tip of modern Turkey. But in its golden days the city ranked with Rome, Carthage, and Alexandria as the empire's leading cities. Founded in 300 B.C.E. by Seleucus, one of Alexander the Great's generals, Antioch was the seat of Seleucus' dynasty for the better part of three hundred years. Then it continued as the seat of Roman government for the Near East until it was eclipsed by Constantinople in the fourth century; Antioch largely disappeared from sight during the Arab conquests of the seventh.

A city of half a million in the first century, Antioch had a large and influential Jewish population from its founding to the Arab conquest. Because of strong Antiochene links with Palestine, Palestinian Christians, primarily Greek speaking (see Acts 6), arrived in the city early, gravitating to its synagogues. Given their convictions about Jesus as Messiah, the immigrants eventually caused friction in the synagogues. Many among them, especially among the Greek speaking, turned to the Gentiles, which led to the bitter controversy between Jew and Gentile in the Church (see Acts 15, and Gal) and in turn led to the birth of "Gentile" Christianity and the inauguration of the mission to the Gentiles. In fact, Antioch is where people first learned to distinguish the messianic immigrants from Jews, calling them *Christianoi* (Christ's people, or Christians; see Acts 11:26), and it is an Antiochene Christian (Ignatius, ca. 110) who first used the term "Christianity."

Although the break between Christians and Jews happened early in the city, the two communities encountered one another day in and day out. As a result, the impact of Judaism on Antiochene Christianity was lasting, especially on its baptismal tradition (see below, Melito). Further, the ancestral religion remained a permanent attraction to the city's Christians, so much so that Antiochene homilists (see below, Chrysostom) regularly inveighed against Jewish belief and practice, sometimes with great bitterness. What they feared was Christians flocking to the synagogue, a much more likely possibility than the sight of Jews flocking to the church.

Antioch long remained a dynamic mission center whose influence reached as far as Armenia, and where Antiochenes went, its liturgy went. But the city was also a center for biblical study and theological reflection. Among its leading lights were Lucian (d. 312), founder of the Antioch school; Diodore, later bishop of Tarsus (378–394); John Chrysostom (below); Diodore's most celebrated pupil, Theodore of Mopsuestia (below); Theodore's pupil Nestorius; and Theodore's disciple Narsai (ch. 2).

The Antioch School

Antiochene biblical interpretation runs toward history rather than allegory, which the Alexandrians preferred (see vol. 6, ch. 3). Their commentaries on baptism use typology with restraint, centering on creation, Paradise, and the Exodus from Egypt as the classical types that disclose the religious significance of baptism. And their understanding of Christian life strongly emphasizes earnest moral effort (Chrysostom), an emphasis quite consistent with their theological concentration on the humanity of Christ. Repeatedly, for instance, Theodore and his followers speak of the "man" Jesus and the "one assumed." Unlike the Alexandrians, the Antiochenes seemed determined to give full play to the human in the quest for salvation, whether it is to Jesus' humanity or to the effort of the catechumen.

By the end of the fourth century, Constantinople, which Constantine had founded as the new capital of the Roman Empire in 330, eclipsed Antioch as the cynosure of West Syrian Christianity. The city's decline was further hastened over the next two centuries by earthquakes and by the controversies about the divine and human in Christ, followed finally by the rise of Islam. Nonetheless, the rich Antiochene baptismal heritage continued to shape the Christian experience of Syrian Christianity both West and East, as will be evident to the reader from the texts that follow in this and the next chapter.

The Readings

The selections range from the first century to the fifth and reflect a variety of literary forms: ritual books or Church-order books *(Didache, Apostolic Constitutions, Ordo of Constantinople),* pastoral manuals *(Didascalia),* homilies (Melito of Sardis, Gregory of Nyssa), catechetical instructions (Cyril, Chrysostom, Theodore of Mopsuestia), and mystical theology (Dionysius the Pseudo-Areopagite).

Important studies of Antiochene Christianity are Glanville Downey, *Ancient Antioch* (Princeton: The University Press, 1963); and Robert L. Wilken, *John Chrysostom and the Jews* (Berkeley: University of California Press, 1983). For Antiochene theology and biblical interpretation see W. J. Burghardt, "On Early Christian Exegesis," TS 11 (1950) 78–116, and his "Free Like God: Recapturing Ancient Anthropology," *Theology Digest* 26 (1978) 343–364. See also R. V. Sellers, *Two Ancient Christologies: A Study in the Christological Thought of the Schools of Alexandria and Antioch* (London: SPCK, 1940).

The Didache

Unknown until 1883, the *Didache* is the earliest of the Church-order books, works that concern themselves with the organization, liturgy, and customs in Christian communities. Sacramentaries (vol. 6, ch. 1), Missals, Books of Hours, and the like are among their medieval successors. Appropriating the mantle of apostolic authority (the full title is *The Teaching of the Twelve Apostles*), the *Didache* is a compilation from Syria, dating from the turn of the first century through the mid-second century, possibly a manual for missionaries. The relevant chapters are the first seven, containing a baptismal instruction and the rubrics for baptism. The remaining chapters (8–16, not included) deal with fasting, the Lord's Prayer, the Eucharist, missionaries, community leaders, the Lord's Day, and apocalyptic prayer.

To become a Christian (the candidates were largely pagan) in *Didache* communities required an indeterminate period of instruction that included the "Two Ways," a method of oral instruction familiar to Greeks, to the synagogues of the Greek-speaking Jewish Diaspora, and to early Christian communities. The reading opens with the "Two Ways" instruction characteristic of early outreach to Gentiles. When the candidate was deemed ready for baptism, several days of communal fasting preceded the rite. Preference was for immersion in running (literally, "living") waters—streams or rivers—largely because John the Baptist baptized Christ in the running waters of the Jordan. The formula was Matthew's Trinitarian form (see Matt 28:19), which would also become the norm. Unquestionably, the rite was followed by the Eucharist celebrated according to the rubrics in chapters 8–10 (not included). The tenor of the document suggests that these "disciples of the Way of the Teaching" eagerly anticipated Jesus' return as "the Lord of the sky" (6). Baptism and the Eucharist appear to have been an anticipation of the return, and the "Lord's Day" (Sunday) a weekly preparation and reminder of its imminence.

There is good reason to believe that this early structure of baptism—instruction, fasting, immersion, and the Eucharist—was to some extent inspired by the ritual for the initiation of proselytes in Judaism. The rite included instruction in, and acceptance of, the Law; inquiry into motives; circumcision; baptismal immersion (normally seven days later); and the offering of sacrifice (that is, prior to the destruction of the Temple in 70). Indeed, possibly as early as Paul of Tarsus (ca. 50), baptism was called "circumcision," recalling the "second circumcision" the Israelites underwent after crossing the Jordan into the Promised Land (Josh 5:2-7).

Originally composed in Greek, the text of the *Didache* is that of W. Rordorf and Andre Tuillier, SC 248 (1978); the translation is adapted from James A. Kleist, ACW 6 (1948) 15-19.

The *Didache*
An Instruction of the Lord Given to the Heathen by the Twelve Apostles

1:1. Two ways there are, one of life and one of death, and there is a great difference between the two ways. 2. Now the way of life is this: "first love the God who made you; secondly, your neighbor as yourself": do not do to another "what you do not wish" to be done to yourself [Matt 22:37-39; Deut 6:5; Lev 19:18; see Matt 7:12]. 3. The lesson of these words is as follows: "bless those that curse you, and pray for your enemies"; besides, fast "for those that persecute you." For "what thanks do you deserve when you love those that love you? Do not the heathens do as much?'' For your part, "love those that hate you" [Matt 5:44, 46; Luke 6:27, 32]; in fact, have no enemy. 4. "Abstain from gratifying the carnal [and bodily] impulses" [1 Pet 2:11]. "When anyone gives you a blow on the right cheek, turn to him the other as well, and be perfect" [Matt 5:39, 48]. When "anyone forces you to go one mile with him, go two with him"; when anyone takes "your cloak away, give him your coat also" [Matt 5:40]; when anyone robs you of your property, demand no return. You really cannot do it. 5. "Give to anyone that asks you, and demand no return" [Luke 6:30]; the Father wants his own bounties to be shared with all. Happy the giver who complies with the commandment, for he goes unpunished. Trouble is in store for the receiver: if someone who is in need receives, he will go unpunished; but he who is not in need will have to stand trial as to why and for what purpose he received; and, if he is thrown into prison, he will be questioned about his conduct, and "will not be released from that place until he has paid the last penny" [Matt 5:25]. 6. However, in this regard, there is also a word of Scripture: "Let your alms sweat in your hands until you find out to whom to give" [not in Scripture].

2:1. A further commandment of the teaching: 2. Do not murder; do not commit adultery; do not practice pederasty; do not fornicate; do not steal; do not deal in magic; do not practice sorcery; do not kill a fetus by abortion or commit infanticide. Do not covet your neighbor's goods. 3. Do not perjure yourself; do not bear false witness; do not calumniate; do not bear malice. 4. Do not be double-minded or double-tongued, for a double tongue is a deadly snare. 5. Your speech must not be false or meaningless, but made good by action. 6. Do not be covetous, or rapacious, or hypocritical, or malicious, or arrogant. Do not have designs upon your neighbor. 7. Hate no man; but correct some, pray for others, for still others sacrifice your life as a proof of your love.

3:1. My child, shun evil of any kind and everything resembling it. 2. Do not be prone to anger, for anger leads to murder. Do not be fanatical, not quarrelsome, not hot-tempered; for all these things beget murder. 3. My child, do not be lustful, for lust leads to fornication. Do not be foul-mouthed or give free rein to your eyes; for all these things beget adultery. 4. My child, do not be an augur, because it leads to idolatry. Do not be an enchanter, not an astrologer, not an expiator, and do not wish to see [and hear] these things; for they all beget idolatry. 5. My child, do not be a liar, for lying leads to theft. Do not be a lover of money, or a vain pretender. All these things beget thievery. 6. My child, do not be a grumbler, because it leads to blasphemy; or self-willed, or evil-minded. All these things beget blasphemy. 7. On the contrary, be gentle, for the gentle will inherit the land. 8. Be long-suffering, and merciful, and guileless, and quiet, and good, and with trembling treasure forever the instructions you have received. 9. Do not carry your head high, or open your heart to presumption. Do not be on intimate terms with the mighty, but associate with holy and lowly folk. 10. Accept as blessings the casualties that befall you, assured that nothing happens without God.

4:1. My child, day and night remember him who preaches God's word to you, and honor him as the Lord, for where his lordship is spoken of, there is the Lord. 2. Seek daily contact with the saints to be refreshed by their discourses. 3. Do not start a schism, but pacify contending parties. Be just in your judgment: make no distinction between man and man concerning transgressions. 4. Do not waver in your decision. 5. Do not be one that opens his hands to receive, but shuts them when it comes to giving. 6. If you have means at your disposal, pay a ransom for your sins. 7. Do not hesitate to give, and do not give in a grumbling mood. You will find out who is the good Rewarder. 8. Do not turn away from the needy; rather, share everything with your brother, and do not say: "It is private property." If you are sharers in what is imperishable, how much more so in the things that perish! [9–14: There follows a domestic code that regulates behavior toward children and slaves, counsels against concern with status, rank, and sham, and enjoins holding fast to the traditions, confessing sins in church, and praying without a guilty conscience.] Such is the way of life.

5:1. The way of death is this. First of all, it is wicked and altogether accursed: murders, adulteries, lustful desires, fornications, thefts, idolatries, magical arts, sorceries, robberies, false testimonies, hypocrisy, duplicity, fraud, pride, malice, surliness, covetousness, foul talk, jealousy, rashness, haughtiness, false pretensions. 2. It is the way of persecutors of the good, haters of the truth, lovers of falsehoods; of men ignorant of the reward of right living, not devoted to what is good but what is evil; of strangers to gentleness and patient endurance, of men who love vanities, and fee hunters; of men that have no heart for the poor, and are not concerned about the oppressed, do not know their Maker; of murderers of children, destroyers of

God's image; of men that turn away from the needy, oppress the afflicted, act as counsels to the rich, are unjust judges of the poor—in a word, of men steeped in sin. Children, may you be preserved from all this!

6:1. See that no man leads you astray from this way of the teaching, since any other teaching takes you away from God. 2. Surely, if you are able to bear the Lord's yoke in its entirety, you will be perfect; if you are not able, then do what you can. 3. And in the matter of food, do what you can stand; but be scrupulously on your guard against meat offered to idols; for that is a worship of dead gods.

7:1. Regarding baptism. Baptize as follows: after first explaining all these points [above], "Baptize in the name of the Father and of the Son and of the Holy Spirit" [Matt 28:19], in running water. 2. But if you have no running water, baptize in other water; and if you cannot in cold, then in warm. 3. But if you have neither, pour water on the head three times "in the name of the Father and of the Son and of the Holy Spirit." 4. Before the baptism, let the baptizer and the candidate for baptism fast, as well as any as are able. Require the candidate to fast one or two days previously.

Melito of Sardis

From the time of Paul of Tarsus, Asia Minor (Turkey) was the site of an extremely dynamic Christianity. Centered around Ephesus (now an archaeological site), it spread north to the Black Sea, west to the Mediterranean, and east across the highlands of Cappadocia as far as Armenia. By the end of the first century, John, the celebrated "Seer of Patmos," had addressed letters to seven "Asian" Churches (see Rev 2:2–3:22), and two decades later the Antiochene Ignatius had also written to some of the same Churches. One Church to whom both wrote was the Church at Sardis in Western Asia Minor, an important city that boasted a large and influential Jewish community. Indeed, the synagogue at Sardis, the subject of recent excavation (1962 +), reveals a building history that dates very likely from the second century. Integrated into the public center of the city *(agora)*, the remains of its last building phase (fourth to sixth century) reveal a building longer than a football field, perhaps capable of holding twenty thousand people.

By comparison the Christian community was small and very much a distant and poor relative. Beleaguered by the municipal authorities, Sardis' Christians were not even well thought of by John, the Seer of Patmos. Nonetheless, the community numbered among its members a leader, Melito, well known for his eloquence. Undoubtedly a native of Sardis, Melito was a celibate, possessed an excellent Greek rhetorical education, flourished between 160 and 170, and very likely was the bishop.

Except for his *Homily on the Passion of Christ,* discovered and identified in 1932, his sixteen works only survive in fragments. The homily is the earliest example of preaching at a Christian Passover celebration. Although many Christians celebrated Christ's death and resurrection on the Sunday following the Jewish Passover (held on the night of the fourteenth of Nisan), many others, especially in the East (see ch. 2, Aphrahat), observed *Pascha* (Easter) on the Jewish Passover. The custom came to be called "Quartodeciman" (*dies quartodecima,* the fourteenth day) and included fasting, gathering for a vigil at sunset, biblical readings, and prayer coupled with instruction, followed by the Eucharist celebrated at cockcrow (dawn). Melito very likely preached the homily during the vigil. Although a case can be made that baptism was part of Quartodeciman custom, the question remains too clouded to warrant including the homily itself.

Nonetheless, the following fragments breathe Melito's spirit, and the second (B) has a strong claim not only to authenticity but also to being a fragment of his lost work *On Baptism.* The text and translation are those of Stuart G. Hall, *Melito of Sardis: On Pascha and Fragments,* Oxford Early Christian Texts (Oxford: Clarendon, 1979) 70–73. A valuable study of ancient synagogues is A. T. Kraabel, "The Diaspora Synagogue: Archaeological and Epigraphic Evidence since Sukenik," *Aufstieg und Niedergang der Römischen Welt* II (1979) Principat, 477–510.

On Baptism

Fragment A

What sort of gold or silver or bronze or iron is not made red hot and dipped in water, in one case to be brightened by the color, in another to be tempered by the dipping? The whole earth, too, bathes in rains and rivers, and after bathing yields well. So also the land of Egypt after bathing in a swollen river increases its corn, fills out its ear, and yields a hundredfold through the goodly bathing. Yes, and even the air itself is bathed by the descents of the rain-drops. The many-colored rainbow, the mother of rains, also bathes, when she swells rivers down channels, summoning them with water-laden breath.

Fragment B

If you wish to observe the heavenly bodies being baptized, make haste now to the Ocean, and there I will show you a strange sight: outspread sea, and boundless main, and infinite deep, and immeasurable Ocean, and pure water; the sun's swimming-pool, and the stars' brightening-place, and the moon's bath. And how they symbolically bathe, learn faithfully from me.

When the sun has with fiery chariotry fulfilled the day's course, having in the whirling of his course become like fire and flared up like a torch, and where he has blazed through his course's meridian, (then) as though reluctant, if he should appear close by, to burn up the land with ten radiant lightning-shafts, he sinks into the Ocean. Just as a ball of bronze, full of fire within, flashing with much light, is bathed in cold water, making a loud noise, and in the polishing process stops glowing; yet the fire within is not quenched, but flares up again when roused: just so also the sun, inflamed like lightning, wholly undying bathes in cold water, but keeps his fire unsleeping; and when he has bathed in symbolic baptism, he exults greatly, taking the water as food. Though one and the same, he rises for men as a new sun, tempered from the deep, purified from the bath; he has driven off the nocturnal darkness, and has begotten bright day. Along his course, both the movement of the stars and the appearance of the moon operate. For they bathe in the sun's swimming-pool like good disciples; for the stars with the moon pursue the sun's track, soaking up pure brilliance.

Now if the sun, with stars and moon, bathes in Ocean, why may not Christ also bathe in Jordan? King of heavens and creation's Captain, Sun of uprising who appeared both to the dead in Hades and to mortals in the world, he also alone arose a Sun out of heaven.

The Didascalia Apostolorum

The *Didascalia Apostolorum,* which stands in the tradition of the *Didache* and which the author knew, also adopts the apostolic mantle (the title is the *Teaching of the Apostles).* Composed in Greek early in the 200s, the work gained wide dispersion in both East and West. The complete text, although with revisions of the original, exists in a fourth- or fifth-century Syriac version; only a remnant of the Greek survives.

The author was a Syrian bishop of a community somewhere in Hellenized Syria to the north and east of Antioch, which had assumed some jurisdiction over neighboring communities. The work is a pastoral manual comprising twenty-seven chapters. It paints a detailed picture of daily provincial Syrian Christian life. The community was centered around the bishop, who appointed the rest of the leaders: a council of presbyters, deacons, deaconesses, widows, subdeacons, and lectors.

Baptism is mentioned only in passing. The first reading indicates briefly some of the rite's effects; elsewhere and in fragmentary fashion we learn that those who seek baptism (1) are largely pagans, (2) have sponsors, (3) gradually become integrated into the community, (4) bear the name "hearer," (5) receive oral instruction from a deacon, though the bishop handles creedal instruction, (6) undergo a twofold prebaptismal anointing, (7) are baptized in the name of the Trinity by immersion, and (8) celebrate the Eucharist. There is no indication about how long the process took, save that it lasted until the community was sure about the solidity of the candidate. Although an entire chapter (21) is devoted to the Christian Passover (Easter), and despite the fact that we learn about a fast lasting the entire week before Easter and that Passover night was spent in vigil, we are not told of an explicit connection between baptism and Easter.

The second reading is the longest baptismal discussion in the *Didascalia* and focuses on the role of the deaconess in the baptism of women. Here the rite is called the "seal" *(sphragis),* a term in Syrian tradition that signified ownership. The term grew out of the original prebaptismal practice of anointing only the candidate's forehead with oil (in the form of a cross). The anointing marked the baptized out as a member of God's new "peoples," just as circumcision had once marked out the member of the "people" (of Israel). Indeed, Paul's letter to the Colossians calls baptism "a circumcision made without hands" (2:11). By the time of the *Didascalia,* however, and probably as a result of customs at the baths, the prebaptismal anointing is extended to the whole body. The significance of the anointing, however, lies in an ancient rite of great importance in Syrian tradition: the anointing of Israel's kings and priests. Like their Master, who was anointed by the Spirit at his baptism, the newly anointed are regal and priestly. Unlike the practice in the West, there is no post-baptismal anointing. In the course of time the rite will emphasize, as in Christ's baptism, sonship.

The text is that of Arthur Vööbus, CSCO 401 (1979) 109-110, 407 (1979) 173-174; the translation is that Sebastian P. Brock, *The Liturgical Portions of the Didascalia* (Bramcote Notts: Grove Books, 1982) 22-23. The Vööbus volumes (CSCO 402, 408) have valuable introductions.

Chapter 9
Concerning the Bishop and Baptism

Hold the bishops in honor, for it is they who have loosed you from sins, who by the baptismal water have given you new birth, who filled you with the Holy Spirit, who reared you with the word as with milk, who established you with doctrine, who confirmed you with admonition, and allowed you to partake of the holy eucharist of God, and made you partakers and joint heirs of the promise of God.

Chapter 16
Concerning Deacons and Deaconesses

For this reason, O bishop, appoint for yourself workers of righteousness as helpers who can co-operate with you, for salvation. Of those who are pleasing to you out of all the people, you should choose and appoint as deacons: a man for the performance of most things that are necessary, but a woman for the ministry of women. For there are houses where you cannot send a deacon to the women, on account of the heathen; but you can send a deaconess. Also, because in many other matters too the office of a woman, a deaconess, is required. In the first place, when women go down into the baptismal water: those who go down into the water ought to be anointed by a deaconess with the oil of anointing; and where there is no woman at hand, and especially no deaconess, he who baptizes must of necessity anoint the woman who is being baptized. But where there is a woman, and especially a deaconess, present, it is not fitting that women should be seen by men, but with the imposition of hand you should anoint the head only. As of old priests and kings were anointed in Israel, so do you likewise, with the imposition of hand, anoint the head of those who receive baptism, whether it be of men or of women; and afterwards, whether you yourself baptize, or you tell the deacons or presbyters to baptize, let a woman, a deaconess, anoint the women, as we have already said. But let a man pronounce over them the invocation of the divine names in the water.

And when the woman who is being baptized has come up from the water, let the deaconess receive her, and teach and instruct her how the seal of baptism ought to be kept unbroken in purity and holiness. For this reason we say that the ministry of a woman, a deaconess, is particularly needed and important. For our Lord and Savior was also ministered to by women ministers, "Mary Magdalene, and Mary the daughter of James and mother of Jose, and the mother of the sons of Zebedee," with other women as well. And you too need the ministry of deaconess for many things; for a deaconess is needed to go into the houses of the heathen where there are believing women, and to visit those who are sick, ministering to them in whatever way they require, and to bathe those who have begun to recover from sickness.

Jerusalem: Cyril and Egeria

Before the Peace of Constantine (311/313), evidence about baptism is comparatively sparse. Although there is other extant literature like the Clementine *Homilies* and *Recognitions* and baptismal fragments in the letter of Ignatius of Antioch (ca. 115), the *Didache* and the *Didascalia* are representative of the period. The fullest description, however, is Roman, about 200 (see vol. 6, ch. 1, *Apostolic Tradition*), and the first and only treatise is Tertullian's (vol. 6, ch. 2), also about 200. With the Constantinian Peace, the Church of the Greco-Roman world acquired what it never had before: legal standing. By the end of the fourth century (390) it was the empire's established religion. One result was that the number of people seeking entry increased dramatically, which had great impact on baptismal preparation and liturgy.

Nowhere is this "new" baptism earlier or more clearly documented than in Jerusalem (see Egeria). Precisely how it developed is shrouded in the obscurity that hovers over the development of Christianity in Palestine. The primary reasons for the obscurity are the Jewish revolts against Roman rule from 66 to 73 and again from 132 to 135. In the former, the Jerusalem Christians, predominantly Jewish, fled east to the Euphrates, south to Egypt, west to Italy and North Africa, and north to Syria and beyond. In the latter revolt, Roman retribution was so severe that Jerusalem was refounded as a Roman colony, renamed "Aelia Capitolina"—a city prohibited to Jews.

From that point on, the Church in and around Jerusalem was Gentile and primarily Greek-speaking, though Syriac was the language of the less cosmopolitan. Further, the Jerusalem Church was subject to the ecclesiastical oversight of Caesarea on the coast, long the seat of Roman government in Palestine (see vol. 6, ch. 1).

Although the Jerusalem Church received some attention in the history of the period, the earliest firsthand evidence of Christian life in the city lies in two remarkable documents, the *Baptismal Catecheses* of Cyril, bishop of Jerusalem (349–389), and the *Diary of Egeria,* composed by a Latin-speaking nun from Galicia in Spain. In the early fifth century she made a pilgrimage to the Holy Land, during which she composed a journal for the members of her religious community at home. Part of Egeria's legacy is an eyewitness account of Easter baptism in Jerusalem. In effect, it provides the visual setting of Cyril's *Catecheses*.

Cyril: Baptismal Catecheses

Although geographically Cyril's baptismal instructions belong to Hellenized Syria, liturgically they look west to Caesarea and ultimately south to Alexandria in Egypt. Theologically they stand in the tradition of Origen (vol. 6, ch. 3), who lived out the last two decades of his life in Caesarea.

The distinctiveness of Cyril's catechetics stems from his typology and approach to symbolic participation, both of which are discussed in the General Introduction (see "Bible and Baptismal Liturgy" and "Baptism: Symbolic Participation"). In the spirit of Origen, Cyril contrasts "figure" (also "likeness" or "type") and "reality" (also "truth" or "antitype"). In the first reading, for instance, the figure is the Exodus from Egypt, in which God led the Israelites out of slavery in Egypt into the Promised Land. The reality is the rite of renunciation and profession, which fulfills the promise of the Exodus, delivering the baptismal candidate from allegiance to Satan and the land of darkness to allegiance to Christ and return to Paradise. The promise of the figure, as Cyril sees it, is achieved in the reality, the baptismal rite.

The second instruction alters the relationship of the referents. The reality is Christ, specifically, the historical events of his "passover": the crucifixion, death, and burial. The figure (or likeness) is baptism, specifically, the ritual stripping and triple immersion. Christian baptism participates in Christ's passion in such a way that the salvation he accomplished by dying is effectively conveyed to the participant through the symbolic drama of the immersion (see his celebrated statement of the case in *Catechesis*, 2:4-5) and its attendant rites.

"Antitype" replaces "figure" in the third reading and designates the postbaptismal anointing, which conveys the descent of the Holy Spirit; the "type" (which replaces "reality") is Christ in the Jordan as he is anointed by the Holy Spirit.

Although Cyril's terminology is fluid, his "participatory" exposition of the sacraments says with eloquence what lay unsaid in much early Christian sacramental thought and, as noted, deeply influenced succeeding generations in East and West. Although there is consensus that Cyril authored the creedal catecheses that preceded baptism, some scholars attribute the mystagogical catecheses (three of which follow) to his successor, Bishop John (386-417). What is more likely the case is that the *Catecheses* became a manual of instruction for his successors (see below, Theodore).

The text is that of Auguste Piédagnel, SC 126 (1966) 82-133; the translation is that of Leo P. McCauley and Anthony A. Stephenson, FC 64 (1970) 153-173. For an important study of Cyril's *Catecheses* see William Telfer, ed., *Cyril of Jerusalem and Nemesius of Emesa* (Philadelphia: Westminster Press, 1955) 19-63; see also T. M. Finn, "Baptismal Death and Resurrection: A Study in Fourth Century Eastern Baptismal Theology," *Worship* 43 (1969) 175-189.

Baptismal Catechesis 1: Renunciation and Profession

[The reading is 1 Peter 5:8ff.: "Be sober, be watchful. . . ."]

1. It has long been my wish, true-born and long-desired children of the Church, to discourse to you upon these spiritual, heavenly mysteries. On the principle, however, that seeing is believing, I delayed until the present occasion, calculating that

after what you saw on that night I should find you a readier audience now when I am to be your guide to the brighter and more fragrant meadows of this second Eden. In particular, you are now capable of understanding the diviner mysteries of divine, life-giving baptism. The time being now come to spread for you the board of more perfect instruction, let me explain the significance of what was done for you on that evening of your baptism.

2. First you entered the antechamber of the baptistery and faced towards the west. On the command to stretch out your hand, you renounced Satan as though he were there in person. This moment, you should know, is prefigured in ancient history. When that tyrannous and cruel despot, Pharaoh, was oppressing the noble, free-spirited Hebrew nation, God sent Moses to deliver them from the hard slavery imposed upon them by the Egyptians. The doorposts were anointed with the blood of a lamb that the destroyer might pass over the houses signed with the blood; so the Jews were miraculously liberated. After their liberation the enemy gave chase, and, on seeing the sea part miraculously before them, still continued in hot pursuit, only to be instantaneously overwhelmed and engulfed in the Red Sea.

3. Pass, pray, from the old to the new, from the figure to the reality. There Moses sent by God to Egypt; here Christ sent from the Father into the world. Moses' mission was to lead out from Egypt a persecuted people; Christ's, to rescue all the people of the world who were under the tyranny of sin. There the blood of a lamb was the charm against the destroyer; here, the blood of the unspotted Lamb, Jesus Christ, is appointed your inviolable sanctuary against demons. Pharaoh pursued that people of old right into the sea; this outrageous spirit, the impudent author of all evil, followed you, each one, up to the very verge of the saving streams. That other tyrant is engulfed and drowned in the Red Sea; this one is destroyed in the saving water.

4. You are told, however, to address him as personally present, and with arm outstretched to say: "I renounce you, Satan." Allow me to explain the reason of your facing west, for you should know it. Because the west is the region of visible darkness, Satan, who is himself darkness, has his empire in darkness—that is the significance of your looking steadily towards the west while you renounce that gloomy Prince of night.

What was it that each of you said, standing there? "I renounce you, Satan, you wicked and cruel tyrant; I no longer" (you said in effect) "fear your power. For Christ broke that power by sharing flesh and blood with me, planning through their assumption to break, by his death, the power of death, to save me from subjection to perpetual bondage. I renounce you, crafty scoundrel of a serpent; I renounce you, traitor, perpetrator of every crime, who inspired our first parents to revolt. I renounce you, Satan, agent and abettor of all wickedness.''

5. Then in a second phrase you are taught to say, "and all your works." All sin is "the works of Satan"; and sin, too, you must renounce, since he who has escaped from a tyrant has also cast off the tyrant's livery. Sin in all its forms, then, is included in the works of the Devil. Only let me tell you this: all your words, particularly those spoken at that awful hour, are recorded in the book of God. Whenever, therefore, you are caught in conduct contrary to your profession, you will be tried as a renegade. Renounce, then, the works of Satan, that is, every . . . deed and thought [contrary to your baptismal promise].

6. Next you say, "and all his pomp." The pomp of the Devil is the craze for the theater, the horse races in the circus, the wild-beast hunts, and all such vanity, from which the saint prays to God to be delivered in the words, "Turn away mine eyes that they may not behold vanity." Avoid an addiction to the theater, with its spectacle of the licentiousness, the lewd and unseemly antics of actors and the frantic dancing of degenerates. Not for you, either, the folly of those who, to gratify their miserable appetite, expose themselves to wild beasts in the combats in the amphitheater. They pamper their belly at the cost of becoming themselves, in the event, food for the maw of savage beasts; of these gladiators it is fair to say that in the service of the belly which is their God they court death in the arena. Shun also the bedlam of the races, a spectacle in which souls as well as riders come to grief. All these follies are the pomp of the Devil.

7. The food, also, which is sometimes hung up in pagan temples and at festivals—meat, bread, and so forth—since it is defiled by the invocation of abominable demons, may be included in "the pomp of the Devil." For as the bread and wine of the Eucharist before the holy invocation of the adorable Trinity were ordinary bread and wine, while after the invocation the bread becomes the Body of Christ, and the wine his Blood, so these foods of the pomp of Satan, though of their own nature ordinary food, become profane through the invocation of evil spirits.

8. After this you say, "and all your service." The service of the Devil is prayer in the temples of idols, the honoring of lifeless images, the lighting of lamps or the burning of incense by springs or streams; there have been cases of persons who, deceived by dreams or by evil spirits, have gone to this length in the hope of being rewarded by the cure of even bodily ailments. Have nothing to do with these practices. The observation of birds, divination, omens, charms and amulets, magic and similar chicanery—all such practices are the cult of the Devil. Shun them. For if you should succumb to such practices after renouncing Satan and transferring your allegiance to Christ, you will find the usurper more cruel than ever. For if formerly, treating you as a familiar, he abated the rigors of your slavery, now he will be furiously exasperated against you. So you will lose Christ and taste Satan's tyranny.

Have you not heard the old story which recounts the fate of Lot and his daughters? Was not Lot himself saved together with his daughters after gaining the mountain, while his wife was turned into a pillar of salt, a monumental warning and a memorial of her wicked choice [her looking back]? So be on your guard: do not turn back to "what is behind" [Phil 3:13], first "putting your hand to the plow" [Luke 9:62] and then "turning back" to the bitter savor of the things of this world. No; flee to the mountain, to Jesus Christ, the "stone hewn without hands" [Dan 2:45] that has filled the world.

9. When you renounce Satan, trampling underfoot every covenant with him, then you annul that ancient "league with Hell" [Isa 28:15], and God's paradise opens before you, that Eden, planted in the east, from which for his transgression our first father was banished. Symbolic of this is your facing about from the west to the east, the place of light. It was at this point that you were told to say: "I believe in the Father, and in the Son, and in the Holy Spirit, and in one baptism of repentance." But these subjects have been treated at large, as God's grace allowed, in the previous discourse [1.6, the creedal instructions before baptism].

10. In the security, then, of this formula of faith, "be sober." For "our adversary, the Devil," in the words just read, "as a roaring lion, goes about seeking whom he may devour" [the reading]. Yet if in former times Death was mighty and devoured, now, in the time of the holy laver of regeneration, "the Lord God hath wiped away all tears from every face" [Isa 25:8]. No more shall you mourn, now that you have "put off the old man"

[Eph 4:22], but you shall ever keep high festival, clad in Jesus Christ as in a garment of salvation.

11. That was what was done in the outer chamber. When we enter, God willing, in the succeeding discourses on the mysteries, into the Holy of Holies, we shall receive the key to the rites performed there. Now to God, with the Son and the Holy Spirit, be glory, power and majesty forever and ever. Amen.

Baptismal Catechesis 2: Baptism

[The reading is Romans 6:3-14: "Do you not know that all who have been baptized into Christ Jesus have been baptized into his death?"]

1. The daily initiatory expositions, with their new teaching telling of new realities, are profitable to you, especially to those of you who have just been renewed from oldness to newness. I shall, therefore, resuming from yesterday, expound the bare essentials of our next topic, explaining the symbolical meaning of what you did in the inner chamber.

2. Immediately, then, upon entering, you removed your tunics. This was a figure of the "stripping off of the old man with his deeds" [Col 3:9]. Having stripped, you were naked, in this also imitating Christ, who was naked on the cross, by his nakedness "throwing off the cosmic powers and authorities like a garment and publicly upon the cross leading them in his triumphal procession" [Col 2:15]. For as the forces of the enemy made their lair in our members, you may no longer wear the old garment. I do not, of course, refer to this visible garment, but to "the old man which, deluded by its lusts, is sinking towards death" [Eph 4:22]. May the soul that has once put off that old self never again put it on, but say with the Bride of Christ in the Canticle of Canticles: "I have put off my garment: how shall I put it on?" [Cant 5:13]. Marvelous! You were naked in the sight of all and were not ashamed! Truly you bore the image of the first-formed Adam, who was naked in the garden and "was not ashamed" [Gen 2:25].

3. Then, when stripped, you were anointed with exorcised olive oil from the topmost hairs of your head to the soles of your feet, and became partakers of the good olive tree, Jesus Christ. Cuttings from the wild olive tree, you were grafted into the good olive tree and became partakers of the fatness of the true olive tree [cf. Rom 11:17-24]. The exorcised olive oil, therefore, symbolized the partaking of the richness of Christ; its ef-

fect is to disperse every concentration of the cosmic forces arrayed against us. For as the breath of the saints upon you [i.e., the exorcists], with the invocation of the name of God, burns the devils like fierce fire and expels them, so this exorcised olive oil receives, through prayer and the invocation of God, power so great as not only to burn and purge away the traces of sin but also to put to rout all the invisible forces of the Evil One.

4. After this you were conducted to the sacred pool of divine baptism, as Christ passed from the cross to the sepulcher you see before you [see Egeria for the church buildings]. You were asked, one by one, whether you believed in the name of the Father and of the Son and of the Holy Spirit; you made that saving confession, and then you dipped thrice under the water and thrice rose up again, therein mystically signifying Christ's three days' burial. For as our Savior passed three days and three nights in the bowels of the earth, so you by your first rising out of the water represented Christ's first day in the earth, and by your descent the night. For as in the night one no longer sees, while by day one is in the light, so you during your immersion, as in a night, saw nothing, but on coming up found yourselves in the day. In the same moment you were dying and being born, and that saving water was at once your grave and your mother. What Solomon said in another context is applicable to you: "A time for giving birth, a time for dying" [Ecclus 3:2]; although for you, contrariwise, it is a case of "a time for dying and a time for being born." One time brought both, and your death coincided with your birth.

5. The strange, the extraordinary, thing is that we did not really die, nor were really buried or really crucified; nor did we really rise again: this was figurative and symbolic; yet our salvation was real. Christ's crucifixion was real, his burial was real, and his resurrection was real; and all these he has freely made ours, that by sharing his sufferings in a symbolic enactment we may really and truly gain salvation. Oh, too generous love! Christ received the nails in his immaculate hands and feet; Christ felt the pain: and on me without pain or labor, through the fellowship of his pain, he freely bestows salvation.

6. Let no one imagine, then, that baptism wins only the grace of remission of sins plus adoption, as John's baptism conferred only the remission of sins. No; we know full well that baptism not only washes away our sins and procures for us the gift of the Holy Spirit, but is also the antitype of the passion of Christ.

That is why Paul just now proclaimed: "Do you not know that all we who have been baptized into Christ Jesus have been baptized into his death? For through baptism we were buried along with him" [the reading]. Perhaps this was directed against those who supposed that baptism procures only the remission of sins and the adoption of sons and does not, beyond this, really make us imitatively partakers of the sufferings of Christ.

7. To teach us, then, that all that Christ endured "for us and for our salvation," he suffered in actual fact and not in mere seeming, and that we have fellowship in his passion, Paul cries aloud in unequivocal language: "For if we have become one planting with him by the likeness of his death, we shall be one with him by the likeness of his resurrection also." "One planting" is apt, for since the true Vine was planted here, we, by partaking in the baptism of his death, have become "one planting" with him. Mark closely the words of the apostle: he did not say: "for if we have become one planting by his death," but "by the likeness of his death" [as in par. 6, above, these citations are from the reading]. For in the case of Christ death was real, his soul being really separated from his body. His burial, too, was real, for his sacred body was wrapped in clean linen. In his case it all really happened. But in your case there was only a likeness of death and suffering, whereas of salvation there was no likeness, but the reality.

8. That should be sufficient instruction on these points. I urge you to keep it in your memory that I too, though unworthy, may be able to say of you: "I love you because at all times you keep me in mind and maintain the tradition I handed on to you" [1 Cor 11:2]. God, "who has presented you as those who have come alive from the dead," is able to grant to you to "walk in newness of life," because his is the glory and the power, now and forever. Amen.

Baptismal Catechesis 3: Chrismation

[The reading is 1 John 2:20-28: "But you have an anointing from God and you know all things."]

1. "Baptized into Christ" and "clothed with Christ" [Gal 3:27], you have been shaped to the likeness of the Son of God. For God, in "predestining us to be adopted as his sons" [Eph 1:5] has "conformed us to the body of the glory" [Phil 3:21] of Christ. As "partakers of Christ" [Heb 3:14], therefore, you are rightly called "Christs," i.e., "anointed ones": it was of you that God said: "Touch not my Christs" [Ps 104:15 LXX].

Now, you became Christs by receiving the antitype of the Holy Spirit; everything has been wrought in you "likewise" because you are likenesses of Christ.

He bathed in the river Jordan and, after imparting the fragrance of his Godhead to the waters, came up from them. Him the Holy Spirit visited in essential presence, like resting upon like. Similarly for you, after you had ascended from the sacred streams, there was an anointing with chrism, the antitype of that with which Christ was anointed, that is, of the Holy Spirit. Concerning this Spirit the blessed Isaiah, in the prophetical book which bears his name, said, speaking in the person of the Lord: "The Spirit of the Lord is upon me because he has anointed me. He has sent me to preach glad tidings to the poor" [Isa 61:1].

2. For Christ was not anointed by men with material oil or balsam; his Father, appointing him Savior of the whole world, anointed him with the Holy Spirit as Peter says: "Jesus of Nazareth, whom God anointed with the Holy Spirit" [Acts 10:38]. The prophet David also made proclamation: "Your throne, O God, is forever and ever: the scepter of your kingdom is a scepter of uprightness. You have loved justice, and hated iniquity: therefore God, your God, has anointed you with the oil of gladness above your fellows" [Ps 44 (45):7-8].

As Christ was really crucified and buried and rose again, and you at baptism are privileged to be crucified, buried, and raised along with him in a likeness, so also with the chrism. Christ was anointed with a mystical oil of gladness; that is, with the Holy Spirit, called "oil of gladness" because he is the cause of spiritual gladness; so you, being anointed with ointment, have become partakers and fellows of Christ.

3. Beware of supposing that this ointment is mere ointment. Just as after the invocation of the Holy Spirit the Eucharistic bread is no longer ordinary bread, but the Body of Christ, so this holy oil, in conjunction with the invocation, is no longer simple or common oil, but becomes the gracious gift of Christ and the Holy Spirit, producing the advent [presence?] of his deity. With this ointment your forehead and sense organs are sacramentally anointed, in such wise that while your body is anointed with the visible oil, your soul is sanctified by the holy, quickening Spirit.

4. You are anointed first upon the forehead to rid you of the shame which the first human transgressor bore about with him everywhere; so you may "reflect as in a glass the splendor

of the Lord" [2 Cor 3:18]. Then upon the ears, to receive ears quick to hear the divine mysteries, the ears of which Isaiah said: "The Lord gave me also an ear to hear" [Isa 50:4], and the Lord Jesus in the Gospels: "He who has ears to hear, let him hear" [Matt 11:15]. Then upon the nostrils, that, scenting the divine oil, you may say: "We are the incense offered by Christ to God, in the case of those who are on the way to salvation" [2 Cor 2:15]. Then on the breast, that "putting on the breast-plate of justice you may be able to withstand the wiles of the Devil" [Eph 6:14, 11]. For as Christ after his baptism and the visitation of the Holy Spirit went forth and overthrew the adversary, so must you after holy baptism and the mystical chrism, clad in the armor of the Holy Spirit, stand firm against the forces of the Enemy and overthrow them, saying: "I can do all things in the Christ who strengthens me" [Phil 4:13].

5. Once privileged to receive the holy chrism, you are called Christians and have a name that bespeaks your new birth. Before admission to baptism and the grace of the Holy Spirit you were not strictly entitled to this name but were like people on the way towards being Christians.

6. You must know that this chrism is prefigured in the Old Testament. When Moses, conferring on his brother the divine appointment, was ordering him high priest, he anointed him after he had bathed in water, and thenceforward he was called "christ" ["anointed"] [Lev 8:5, 12; 4:5], clearly after the figurative chrism. Again, the high priest, when installing Solomon as king, anointed him after he had bathed in Gihon [3 Kgs 1:38-39]. But what was done to them in figure was done to you, not in figure but in truth, because your salvation began from him who was anointed by the Holy Spirit in truth. Christ is the beginning of your salvation, since he is truly the "first hand-ful" of dough and you "the whole lump" [Rom 6:11]: and if the first handful be holy, plainly its holiness will permeate the lump.

7. Keep this chrism unsullied; for it shall teach you all things if it abide in you, as you heard the blessed John declaring just now as he expatiated upon the chrism [i.e., in the reading]. For this holy thing is both a heavenly protection of the body and salvation for the soul. It was of this anointing that in ancient times the blessed Isaiah prophesied, saying: "And the Lord shall make unto all people in this mountain" (elsewhere also he calls the Church a mountain, as when he says: "And in the last days the mountain of the Lord shall be manifest") [Isa 2:2]. ". . .

and they shall drink wine, they shall drink gladness, they shall
anoint themselves with ointment" [Isa 5:6, LXX]. To alert you
to the mystical meaning of "ointment" here, he says: "All this
deliver to the nations: for the counsel of the Lord is upon all
the nations" [Isa 25:7, LXX].

Anointed, then, with this holy oil, keep it in you unsullied,
without blame, making progress through good works and becoming well-pleasing to "the trail-blazer of our salvation" [Heb
2:10], Christ Jesus, to whom be glory forever and ever. Amen.

Egeria's Diary

Although Easter had long been the preferred day for solemn
baptism, the fourth century created Lent as the privileged time
for baptismal preparation. An attempt to cope with both the numbers of candidates and the Church's new legal status, the "Forty
Days" (as Lent is called here and elsewhere, reminiscent of
Christ's forty days in the desert) was a time of concentrated instructional and ritual preparations, which culminated in "Great"
(Holy) Week with baptism during the Easter Vigil.

In Jerusalem the preparations took place in the complex of Constantinian church buildings erected on Golgotha (the place of the
crucifixion, see Mark 15:22). The buildings were aggressively new
in the time of Cyril and Egeria. The major edifice, where the prebaptismal preparation took place, was the basilical church known
as the Martyrium, built on what was thought to be Golgotha. The
Anastasis, where the *Catecheses on the Mysteries* were delivered,
was round and built over what was believed to be Christ's tomb.
It was joined to the Martyrium by a garden court, where the baptistery stood, as well as by a cruciform monument marking the
reputed site of the crucifixion. This complex of buildings, the place
of the *Catecheses,* is the site of Egeria's eye-witness account.

The text is that of E. Franceschini and R. Weber, eds., CCL
175 (1965); the translation, that of George E. Gingras, ACW 38
(1970) 122–126; see also his valuable introduction.

Chapter 45

I must also describe how those who are baptized at Easter are
instructed. Whoever gives his name does so the day before Lent,
and the priest notes down all their names; and this is before
those eight weeks during which, as I have said, Lent is observed
here. When the priest has noted down everyone's name, then

on the following day, the first day of Lent, on which the eight weeks begin, a throne is set up for the bishop in the center of the major church, the Martyrium. The priests sit on stools on both sides, and all the clergy stand around. One by one the candidates are led forward, in such a way that the men come with their godfathers and the women with their godmothers.

Then the bishop questions individually the neighbors of the one who has come up, inquiring: "Does he lead a good life? Does he obey his parents? Is he a drunkard or a liar?" And he seeks out in the man other vices which are more serious. If the person proves to be guiltless in all these matters concerning which the bishop has questioned the witnesses who are present, he notes down the man's name with his own hand. If, however, he is accused of anything, the bishop orders him to go out and says: "Let him amend his life, and when he has done so, let him then approach the baptismal font." He makes the same inquiry of both men and women. If, however, someone is a stranger, he cannot easily receive baptism, unless he has witnesses who know him.

Chapter 46

Ladies, my sisters, I must describe this, lest you think that it is done without explanation. It is the custom here, throughout the forty days on which there is fasting, for those who are preparing for baptism to be exorcised by the clergy early in the morning, as soon as the dismissal from the morning service has been given at the Anastasis. Immediately a throne is placed for the bishop in the major church, the Martyrium. All those who are to be baptized, both men and women, sit closely around the bishop, while the godmothers and godfathers stand there; and indeed all of the people who wish to listen may enter and sit down, provided they are of the faithful. A catechumen, however, may not enter at the time when the bishop is teaching them the law. He does so in this way: beginning with Genesis he goes through the whole of Scripture during these forty days, expounding first its literal meaning and then explaining the spiritual meaning. In the course of these days everything is taught not only about the resurrection but concerning the body of faith. This is called catechetics.

When five weeks of instruction have been completed, they then receive the creed. He explains the meaning of each of the phrases of the creed in the same way he explained Holy Scripture, expounding first the literal and then the spiritual sense. In this fashion the creed is taught.

And thus it is that in these places all the faithful are able to follow the Scriptures when they are read in the churches, because all are taught through those forty days, that is, from the first to the third hours, for during the three hours instruction is given. God knows, ladies, my sisters, that the voices of the faithful who have come to catechetics to hear instruction on those things being said or explained by the bishop are louder than when the bishop sits down in church to preach about each of those matters which are explained in this fashion. The dismissal from catechetics is given at the third hour [9:00 A.M.], and immediately, singing hymns, they lead the bishop to the Anastasis, and the office of the third hour takes place. And thus they are taught for three hours a day for seven weeks. During the eighth week, the one which is called the Great Week, there remains no more time for them to be taught, because what has been mentioned above must be carried out.

Now when seven weeks have gone by and there remains only Holy Week, which is here called the Great Week, then the bishop comes in the morning to the major church, the Martyrium. To the rear, at the apse behind the altar, a throne is placed for the bishop, and one by one they come forth, the men with their godfathers, the women with their godmothers. And each one recites the creed back to the bishop. After the creed has been recited back to the bishop, he delivers a homily to them all, and says: "During these seven weeks you have been instructed in the whole law of the Scriptures, and you have heard about the faith. You have also heard of the resurrection of the flesh. But as for the whole explanation of the creed, you have heard only that which you are able to know while you are still catechumens. Because you are still catechumens, you are not able to know those things which belong to a still higher mystery, that of baptism. But that you may not think that anything would be done without explanation, once you have been baptized in the name of God, you will hear of them during the eight days of Easter in the Anastasis following the dismissal from church. Because you are still catechumens, the most secret of the divine mysteries cannot be told to you."

Chapter 47

When it is Easter week, during the eight days from Easter Sunday to its octave, as soon as the dismissal has been given from the church, everyone, singing hymns, goes to the Anastasis. Soon a prayer is said, the faithful are blessed, and the bishop stands up [see Cyril's *Catecheses*]. Leaning on the inner railing, which is in the grotto of the Anastasis, he explains everything which is accomplished in baptism. At this hour no catechumen goes into the Anastasis; only the neophytes and the faithful who wish to hear the mysteries enter the Anastasis. Indeed, the doors are closed, lest any catechumen come that way. While the bishop is discussing and explaining each point, so loud are the voices of praise that they can be heard outside the church. And he explains all these mysteries in such a manner that there is no one who would not be drawn to them, when he heard them thus explained.

A portion of the population in this province knows both Greek and Syriac; another segment knows only Greek; and still another, only Syriac. Even though the bishop may know Syriac, he always speaks Greek and never Syriac; and, therefore, there is always present a priest who, while the bishop speaks in Greek, translates into Syriac so that all may understand what is being explained. Since whatever scriptural texts are read must be read in Greek, there is always someone present who can translate the readings into Syriac for the people, so that they will always understand. So that those here who are Latins, those consequently knowing neither Greek nor Syriac, will not be bored, everything is explained to them, for there are other brothers and sisters who are bilingual in Greek and Latin and who explain everything to them in Latin. But this above all is very pleasing and very admirable here, that whatever hymns and antiphons are sung, whatever readings and prayers are recited by the bishop, they are said in such a manner as to be proper and fitting to the feast which is being observed and to the place where the service is being held.

The Apostolic Constitutions

Compiled in Greek between 360 and 380 in eight books with an appendix *(epitome)* of eighty-five canons, the *Apostolic Constitutions* stands in the Church-order tradition of the *Didache* and the *Didascalia*. Indeed, the compiler incorporated both works, albeit revised. Much other material is incorporated, including the important *Apostolic Tradition* of Hippolytus (bk. 8; see vol. 6, ch. 1).

As for authorship and provenance, the compilation was done somewhere in or around Antioch in the ancient equivalent of a publishing house. Late fourth-century religious turmoil in Hellenized Syria seems to have occasioned the publication; An-

tiochene Christianity at that time numbered some twelve different groups of Christians—from Arians of several stripes through
Gnostics to the Orthodox, or Catholics, among whom were at
least two opposing bishops. The *Apostolic Constitutions* is the
work of one of those groups (most think Arian), which sought
to bring some unity of discipline and liturgical practice to a torn
Church or at least to an important group within it.

Although the work records an evolving Greek-speaking Syrian
baptismal tradition, it has a number of correspondences with Cyril
of Jerusalem and knows a postbaptismal anointing that grants
"participation" in the Holy Spirit (7:22). In addition, we learn
of a slightly different syllabus for prebaptismal instruction (7:39)
and that the creed constitutes the profession of allegiance that
follows the renunciation of Satan (7:40–41). The work also records a long prayer for the consecration of the baptismal water
that recapitulates the history of salvation (7:43) and discloses that
the newly baptized pray the Lord's Prayer facing east (7:45).

The baptismal section of Book 3 is brief and reflects Cyril (see
3:17–18). The reading, therefore, is drawn from Book 7, which
represents some distinctive Antiochene customs. The text is that
of F. X. Funk, ed., *Didascalia et constitutiones apostolorum,* 2
vols. (Paderborn: F. Schoeningh, 1905); the translation is based
on that of James Donaldson ANF 7 (1886), conformed by E. C.
Whitaker (DBL 30–35) to Funk's text. There is a helpful introductory study in Marcel Metzger, ed., SC 320 (1985).

The *Apostolic Constitutions:* Book 7

Chapter 22

Now concerning baptism, O bishop, or presbyter, we have already given direction, and we now say, that you shall so baptize
as the Lord commanded us, saying: "Go and teach all nations,
baptizing them in the name of the Father, and of the Son, and
of the Holy Spirit, teaching them to observe all things what-
soever I have commanded you" [Matt 28:19]: of the Father who
sent, of Christ who came, of the Comforter who testified.

2. But you shall first anoint the person with holy oil, and
afterward baptize him with water, and finally shall seal him with
the chrism; that the anointing with oil may be a participation
of the Holy Spirit, and the water a symbol of the death, and
the chrism a seal of the covenants.

3. But if there be neither oil nor chrism, the water is sufficient both for the anointing, and for the seal, and for the confession of him that is dead, or indeed is dying together with [Christ (baptism in emergency)].

4. But before baptism, let him that is to be baptized fast.

Chapter 39

2. Let him, therefore, who is to be taught the knowledge of piety be instructed before his baptism in the knowledge of the unbegotten God, the understanding of his only begotten Son, the certainty of the Holy Spirit. Let him learn the order of the several parts of the creation. . . .

4. Let him that offers himself to baptism learn these and the like things during his instruction; and let him who lays his hands upon him adore God, the Lord of the whole world, and thank him for his creation, for his sending Christ his only-begotten Son, that he might save man by blotting out his transgressions. . . .

5. And after this thanksgiving, let him instruct him in the doctrines concerning our Lord's incarnation, and in those concerning his passion, and resurrection from the dead, and assumption.

Chapter 40

1. And when it remains that the catechumen is to be baptized, let him learn what concerns the renunciation of the Devil, and the joining himself with Christ; for it is fitting that he should first abstain from things contrary, and then be admitted to the mysteries.

Chapter 41

1. Let, therefore, the candidate for baptism declare thus in his renunciation:

2. "I renounce Satan, and his works, and his pomps, and his service, and his angels, and his inventions, and all things that are under him."

3. And after his renunciation let him in his act of adherence say: "And I adhere to Christ,

4. "And believe and am baptized into one unbegotten Being, the only true God Almighty, the Father of Christ, the creator and maker of all things, 'of whom are all things' [1 Cor 8:6];

5. "And into the Lord Jesus Christ, his only-begotten Son, 'the firstborn of the whole creation' [1 Cor 1:15], who before the ages was begotten by the good pleasure of the Father, not created, 'by whom all things' [1 Cor 8:6] were made, both those in heaven and those on earth, visible and invisible;

6. "Who in the last days descended from heaven, and took flesh, and was born of the holy Virgin Mary, and did converse holily according to the laws of his God and Father, and was crucified under Pontius Pilate, and died for us, and rose again from the dead after his passion the third day, and ascended into the heavens, and sits at the right hand of the Father, and is to come again at the end of the world with glory 'to judge the quick and the dead' [2 Tim 4:1] 'of whose kingdom there shall be no end' [Luke 1:33].

7. "And I am baptized into the Holy Spirit, that is, the Comforter, who wrought in all the saints from the beginning of the world, but was afterwards sent to the apostles by the Father, according to the promise of our Savior and Lord Jesus Christ; and after the apostles to all those that believe in the holy catholic Church;

8. "Into the resurrection of the flesh, and into the remission of sins, and into the kingdom of heaven, and into the life of the world to come."

Chapter 42

1. And after this vow, he comes in order to the anointing with oil.

2. Now this is blessed by the priest for the remission of sins, and the first preparation for baptism.

3. For he calls upon the unbegotten God, the Father of Christ, the King of all sensible and intelligible natures, that he would sanctify the oil "in the name of the Lord Jesus" [Acts 8:16], and impart to it spiritual grace and efficacious strength, the remission of sins, and the first preparation for the confession of baptism, that so the candidate, when he is anointed, may be freed from all ungodliness, and may become worthy of initiation, according to the command of the Only-Begotten.

Chapter 43

1. After this he comes to the water.

2. He blesses and glorifies the Lord God Almighty, the Father of the only-begotten God; and the priest returns thanks

that he has sent his Son to become man on our account, that he might save us; that he has permitted that he should in all things become obedient to the laws of that incarnation, to preach the kingdom of heaven, the remission of sins, and the resurrection of the dead.

3. Moreover, he adores the only-begotten God himself, after his Father, and for him, giving thanks that he undertook to die for all men by the cross, the type of which he has appointed to be the baptism of regeneration.

4. He glorifies him also, for that God who is Lord of the whole world, in the name of Christ, and by his Holy Spirit, has not cast off mankind, but has suited his providence to the difference of seasons: at first giving to Adam himself Paradise for an habitation of pleasure, and afterwards giving a command on account of providence, and casting out the offender justly, but through his goodness not utterly casting him off, but instructing his posterity in succeeding ages after various manners: on whose account, in the conclusion of the world, he has sent his Son to become man for man's sake, and to undergo all human passions without sin.

5. Him, therefore, let the priest even now call upon him in baptism, and let him say: Look down from heaven and sanctify this water and give it grace and power, that so he that is baptized, according to the command of Christ, may be crucified with him, and may die with him, and may be buried with him, and may rise with him to the adoption which is in him, that he may be dead to sin and live to righteousness.

Chapter 44

1. And after this, when he has baptized him in the name of the Father and of the Son and of the Holy Spirit, let him anoint him with chrism, and say:

2. O Lord God, who are without generation, and without a superior, the Lord of the whole world, who has scattered the sweet odor of the knowledge of the gospel among all nations, grant at this time that this chrism may be efficacious upon him that is baptized, that so the sweet odor of Christ may continue upon him firm and fixed; and that now he has died with him, he may arise and live with him.

3. Let him say these and the like things, for this is the efficacy of the laying on of hands on every one; for unless there be such a recital made by a pious priest over every one of these,

the candidate for baptism does only descend into water as do the Jews, and he only puts off the filth of the body, not the filth of the soul.

Chapter 45

1. After this let him stand up, and pray that prayer which the Lord taught us. But, of necessity, he who is risen again ought to stand up and pray, because he that is raised stands upright. Let him, therefore, who has been dead with Christ, and is raised up with him, stand up.

2. But let him pray towards the East. . . .

3. But let him pray thus after the foregoing prayer, and say: O God Almighty, the Father of Christ, your only-begotten Son, give me an undefiled body, a pure heart, a watchful mind, an unerring knowledge, the influence of the Holy Spirit for the obtaining and assurance of the truth, through Christ, by whom be glory to you in the Holy Spirit for ever. Amen.

4. We have thought it proper to make these constitutions concerning the catechumens.

Gregory of Nyssa

The scene of some of St. Paul's mission journeys, Cappadocia (central Turkey) was long an obscure and tempestuous part of the Hellenistic Roman world. In the fourth century, however, it emerged from turmoil and obscurity. In part, the reason was the burgeoning prosperity centered around its major city, Caesarea. But it was also because of the intellectual and religious vitality centered around a distinguished family of Caesarea. The father, Basil, a rhetorician, had large property holdings; the mother, Emmelia, daughter of a martyr, gave birth to ten children, three of whom became celebrated bishops, Basil, Gregory, and Peter. In addition, their eldest daughter, Macrina the Younger, became the paradigm for women ascetics in the Greek-speaking East.

The dynamo of the family was the young Basil, whose parents saw to it that he had the best education the Eastern empire could supply. After study in Caesarea, Constantinople, and Athens, Basil determined to follow his father's footsteps into rhetoric. Like so many others in the fourth and fifth centuries (especially males), his baptism was delayed until he settled down (he later railed against the practice, as did Gregory). Once started on his career, he experienced a conversion, received baptism (ca. 358), gave his possessions to the poor, and sought solitude with a group of his friends. In 370 Basil became the bishop of Cappadocian Caesarea and, with his friend Gregory of Nazianzus and his brother Gregory, among others, soon established Orthodox or Catholic Christianity as a force to be reckoned with, both in and well beyond Cappadocia.

Basil was largely responsible for his younger brother Gregory's education and subsequent career. The latter, not surprisingly, sought out rhetoric as a way of life. Married, he reluctantly accepted the bishopric of the obscure town of Nyssa at Basil's insistence. When Basil died in 379, Gregory came into his own and set about completing the theological, monastic, and ecclesiastical work Basil had begun. His activities and prominence peaked about 386, after which he turned his attention to the ascetic and mystical life and to implementing his desire to give a permanent mystical orientation to the monastic movement. He is considered the architect of Eastern Christian spirituality.

The reading is taken from Gregory's extant liturgical works. Delivered most likely on January 6, 383, in Nyssa's imposing new church, it is a homily for the feast of the Epiphany, which in the East came to be the feast of the Nativity. The major themes, largely biblical, are the creation of light (thus its name, "The Day of Lights"); the baptism of Christ, who appears at the Jordan as the Light of the world (thus the name of the feast, *epiphania;* see ch. 2, especially Ephrem); and Christian baptism. The homily presents Gregory's theology of baptism in a way that his people clearly found winning.

Of special note is his treatment of the way in which the ordinary things of the earth like water and wood can, in the hands of the Holy Spirit, transform people; he seems unwilling to go so far as some (see, for example, ch. 2; also vol. 6, ch. 3) and attribute transformation to the consecration of the waters. The work is done by water and the Spirit. In addition, he provides an extended treatment of what he calls the "figures" or "types" of baptism in the Hebrew Bible. Finally, his theology of baptismal grace recapitulates well the teaching of the Greek Fathers. Like Cyril of Jerusalem, Gregory was much influenced as a homilist by Origen (vol. 6, ch. 3). There is no indication that

Epiphany was a day of solemn baptism, as it would become in some places during the sixth century (see vol. 6, ch. 1, Innocent).

Unlike contemporaries elsewhere, none of the Cappadocians comment on the rites of baptism. Although Basil was a liturgical reformer, at least as far as the Eucharist goes, there is little reason to think that baptism in Cappadocia differed much from the Antiochene tradition (see below, Chrysostom) with which the Cappadocians were thoroughly familiar.

The text is that of Ernest Gebhardt, ed., "In diem luminum," *Gregorii Nysseni Opera,* vol. 9, *Sermones Pars I* (Leiden: Brill, 1967) 221–242; the translation is adapted from H. A. Wilson, NPNF (2nd ser.) 5, 518–524.

On the Baptism of Christ: A Homily for the Feast of Lights

Now I recognize my own flock: today I behold the familiar figure of the Church, when, turning with aversion from the occupation even of the cares of the flesh, you come together in your undiminished numbers for the service of God—when the people crowd the house, coming within the sacred sanctuary, and when the multitude that can find no place within fills the space outside in the precincts like bees. For some bees are at their labor within, while others outside hum around the hive. Do likewise, my children: and never abandon this zeal. . . .

The Meaning of Baptism

The time, then, has come, and bears in its course the remembrance of holy mysteries, purifying man—mysteries which purge out from soul and body even that sin which is hard to cleanse away, and which bring us back to that fairness of our first estate which God, the best of artificers, impressed upon us. Therefore it is that you, the initiated, are gathered together; and you bring also that people who have not made trial of them, leading, like good fathers, by careful guidance, the uninitiated to the perfect reception of the faith. I for my part rejoice over both; over you the initiated, because you are enriched with a great gift; also over you that are uninitiated, because you have a fair expectation of hope—remission of what is to be accounted for, release from bondage, close relation to God, free boldness of speech, and in place of servile subjection equality with the angels. For these things, and all that follow from them, the grace of baptism secures and conveys to us.

Therefore let us leave the other matters of the Scriptures for other occasions, and abide by the topic set before us, offering, as far as we may, the gifts that are proper and fitting for the feast: for each festival has its own riches. . . .

Christ, then, was born, as it were, a few days ago—he whose generation was before all things, sensible and intellectual. To-day he is baptized by John that he might cleanse him who was defiled, that he might bring the Spirit from above, and exalt man to heaven, that he who had fallen might be raised up, and he who had cast him down might be put to shame. And marvel not if God showed so great earnestness in our cause: for it was with care on the part of him who did us wrong that the plot was laid against us; it is with forethought on the part of our Maker that we are saved. And he, that evil charmer, framing his new device of sin against our race, drew along his serpent train, a disguise worthy of his own intent, entering in his impurity into what was like himself, dwelling, earthly and mundane as he was in will, in that creeping thing. But Christ, the repairer of his evil-doing, assumes manhood in its fullness, and saves man, and becomes the type and figure of us all, to sanctify the first-fruits of every action, and leave to his servants no doubt in their zeal for the tradition.

Baptism, then, is a purification from sins, a remission of trespasses, a cause of renovation and regeneration. By regeneration, understand regeneration conceived in thought, not discerned by bodily sight. For we shall not, according to the Jew Nicodemus and his somewhat dull intelligence, change the old man into a child, nor shall we form anew him who is wrinkled and gray-headed to tenderness and youth, if we bring back the man again into his mother's womb: but we do bring back, by royal grace, him who bears the scars of sin, and has grown old in evil habits, to the innocence of the babe. For as the child new-born is free from accusations and from penalties, so too the child of regeneration has nothing for which to answer, being released by royal bounty from accountability.

Water and the Spirit

And it is not the water that bestows this gift (or in that case it were a thing more exalted than all creation), but the command of God, and the visitation of the Spirit that comes sacramentally to set us free. But water serves to express the cleansing. For since we are wont by washing in water to render our body clean when it is soiled by dirt or mud, we therefore apply it also in the sacramental action, and display the spiritual brightness by that which is subject to our senses. Let us however, if it seems well, persevere in enquiring more fully and more minutely concerning baptism, starting, as from the fountain-head, from the scriptural declaration. "Except a man be born of water and of the Spirit, he cannot enter into the kingdom of God" [John 3:3].

Why are both named, and why is not the Spirit alone accounted sufficient for the completion of baptism? Man, as we know full well, is compound, not simple: and therefore the cognate and similar medicines are assigned for healing to him who is twofold and conglomerate: for his visible body, water, the sensible element, for his soul, which we cannot see, the Spirit invisible, invoked by faith, present unspeakably. For "the Spirit breathes where he wills, and you hear his voice, but cannot tell whence he comes or whither he goes" [John 3:8]. He blesses the body that is baptized, and the water that baptizes.

Despise not, therefore, the divine laver, nor think lightly of it, as a common thing, on account of the use of water. For the power that operates is mighty, and wonderful are the things that are wrought thereby. For this holy altar, too, by which I stand, is stone, ordinary in its nature, no way different from the other slabs of stone that build our houses and adorn our pavements; but seeing that it was consecrated to the service of God, and received the benediction, it is a holy table, an altar undefiled, no longer touched by the hands of all, but of the priests alone, and that with reverence. The bread again is at first common bread, but when the sacramental action consecrates it, it is called, and becomes, the Body of Christ. So with the sacramental oil; so with the wine: though before the benediction they are of little value, each of them, after the sanctification bestowed by the Spirit, has its several functions.

The same power of the word, again, also makes the priest venerable and honorable, separated, by the new blessing bestowed upon him, from his community with the mass of men. While but yesterday he was one of the mass, one of the people, he is suddenly rendered a guide, a president, a teacher of righteousness, an instructor in hidden mysteries; and this he does without being at all changed in body or in form; but, while continuing to be in all appearance the man he was before, being, by some unseen power and grace, transformed in respect of his unseen soul to the higher condition . . . .

[Gregory here cites some biblical examples of the power of ordinary things: Moses' rod, the mantle of Elijah the prophet, the burning bush, Elisha's remains, clay, and the wood of the cross.]

Now, by a similar train of reasoning, water also, though it is nothing else than water, renews the man to spiritual regeneration, when the grace from above hallows it. And if anyone answers me again by raising a difficulty, with his questions and doubts, continually asking and inquiring how water and the sacramental act that is performed therein regenerate, I most justly reply to him, "Show me the mode of that generation which is after the flesh, and I will explain to you the power of regeneration in the soul." You will say perhaps, by way of giving an account of the matter, "It is the cause of the seed which makes the man." Learn then from us in return, that hallowed water cleanses and illuminates the man. And if you again object to me your "How?" I shall more vehemently cry in answer, "How does the fluid and formless substance become a man?" and so the argument as it advances will be exercised on everything through all creation. How does heaven exist? how earth? how sea? how every single thing? For everywhere men's reasoning, perplexed in the attempt at discovery, falls back upon this syllable "how," as those who cannot walk fall back upon a seat.

To speak concisely, everywhere the power of God and his operation are incomprehensible, and incapable of being reduced to rule, easily producing whatever he wills, while concealing from us the minute knowledge of his operation. . . .

Why Three Immersions

Let us then leave the task of searching into what is beyond human power, and seek rather that which shows signs of being partly within our comprehension: what is the reason why the cleansing is effected by water? and to what purpose are the three immersions received? That which the Fathers taught, and which our mind has received and assented to, is as follows: We recognize four elements, of which the world is composed, which everyone knows even if their names are not spoken; but if it is well, for the sake of the more simple, to tell you their names, they are fire and air, earth and water. Now our God and Savior, in fulfilling the dispensation for our sakes, went beneath the fourth of these, the earth, that he might raise up life from thence. And we in receiving baptism, in imitation of our Lord and teacher and guide, are not indeed buried in the earth (for this is the shelter of the body that is entirely dead, covering the infirmity and decay of our nature), but coming to the element akin to earth, to water, we conceal ourselves in that as the Savior did in the earth: and by doing this thrice we represent for ourselves that grace of the resurrection which was wrought in three days: and this we do, not receiving the sacrament in silence, but while there are spoken over us the names of the three sacred persons in whom we believed, in whom we also hope, from whom comes to us both the fact of our present and the fact of our future existence. It may be you are offended, you who contend boldly against the glory of the Spirit, and that you grudge to the Spirit that veneration wherewith he is reverenced by the godly. Leave off contending with me: resist, if you can, those words of the Lord which gave to men the rule of the baptismal invocation. What says the Lord's command? "Baptizing them in the name of the Father and of the Son and of the Holy Spirit" [Matt 28:19]. How in the name of the Father? Because he is the primal cause of all things. How in the name of the Son? Because he is the maker of the creation. How in the name of the Holy Spirit? Because he is the power perfecting all.

We bow ourselves therefore before the Father, that we may be sanctified: before the Son also we bow, that the same end may be fulfilled: we bow also before the Holy Spirit, that we may be made what he is in fact and in name. There is not a distinction in the sanctification, in the sense that the Father sanctifies more, the Son less, the Holy Spirit in a less degree than the other two. Why then do you divide the three persons into fragments of different natures, and make three Gods, unlike one to another, whilst from all you do receive one and the same grace? . . .

Figures of Baptism

I find that not only do the Gospels, written after the crucifixion, proclaim the grace of baptism, but, even before the incarnation of our Lord, the ancient Scripture everywhere prefigured the likeness of our regeneration; not clearly manifesting its form, but foreshowing, in dark sayings, the love of God to man. And as the Lamb was proclaimed by anticipation, and the cross was foretold by anticipation, so, too, was baptism shown forth by action and by word. Let us recall its types to those who love good thoughts—for the festival of necessity demands their recollection.

[Gregory here presents several nontraditional types of baptism: (1) Hagar and Ishmael (Gen 21:1-21): When, driven from Abraham's house they are about to die of thirst in the desert,

God leads Hagar to a well otherwise hidden from her eyes, and mother and child are saved; (2) Jacob the patriarch and Rachel (Gen 29:1-14): Jacob meets Rachel at a well dug by his father, Isaac, moves the great stone that seals it, and waters her flock of sheep; (3) the infant Moses and the Nile (Exod 2:1-10): his mother sets him adrift in a basket, and thus is he saved from death by Pharaoh's decree. The homilist then returns to develop the more traditional types in his distinctive way.]

Exodus

Again, according to the view of the inspired Paul [1 Cor 10:1-2], the people itself, by passing through the Red Sea, proclaimed the good tidings of salvation by water. The people passed over, and the Egyptian king with his host was engulfed, and by these actions this sacrament was foretold. For even now, whensoever the people is in the water of regeneration, fleeing from Egypt, from the burden of sin, it is set free and saved. But the Devil with his own servants (I mean of course, the spirits of evil), is choked with grief, and perishes, deeming the salvation of men to be his own misfortune.

Even these instances might be enough to confirm our present position; but the lover of good thoughts must yet not neglect what follows. The people of the Hebrews, as we learn, after many sufferings and after accomplishing their weary course in the desert, did not enter the Land of Promise until it had first been brought, with Joshua for its guide and the pilot of its life, to the passage of the Jordan. But it is clear that Joshua also, who set up the twelve stones in the stream [Josh 4], was anticipating the coming of the twelve disciples, the ministers of baptism.

Elijah and Elisha

Again, that marvelous sacrifice of the old Thesbite [1 Kgs 18:23], that passes all human understanding, what else does it do but prefigure in action the faith in the Father, the Son, and the Holy Spirit, and redemption? For when all the people of the Hebrews had trodden underfoot the religion of their fathers, and fallen into the error of polytheism, and their king Ahab was deluded by idolatry, with Jezebel, of ill-omened name, as the wicked partner of his life, and the vile prompter of his impiety, the prophet, filled with the grace of the Spirit, coming to a meeting with Ahab, withstood the priests of Baal in a marvelous and wondrous contest in the sight of the king and all the people; and by proposing to them the task of sacrificing the bullock without fire, he displayed them in a ridiculous and wretched plight, vainly praying and crying aloud to gods that were not. At last, himself invoking his own and the true God, he accomplished the test proposed with further additions. For he did not simply by prayer bring down the fire from heaven upon the wood when it was dry, but exhorted and enjoined the attendants to bring abundance of water. And when he had thrice poured out the barrels upon the cleft wood, he kindled at his prayer the fire from out of the water, that by the contrariety of the elements, so concurring in friendly cooperation, he might show with superabundant force the power of his own God. Now herein, by that wondrous sacrifice, Elijah clearly proclaimed to us the sacramental rite of baptism that should afterwards be instituted. For the fire was kindled by water thrice poured upon it, so that it is clearly shown that where the mystic water is, there is the kindling, warm, and fiery Spirit, that burns up the ungodly, and illuminates the faithful.

Elisha and Namaan

Yes, and yet again his disciple, Elisha, when Naaman the Syrian, who was diseased with leprosy, had come to him as a suppliant, cleanses the sick man by washing him in Jordan [2 Kgs 5], clearly indicating what was to come, both by the use of water generally, and by the dipping in the river in particular. For Jordan alone of rivers, receiving in itself the first-fruits of sanctification and benediction, conveyed in its channel to the whole world, as it were from some fount in the type afforded by itself, the grace of baptism.

[Gregory now develops a series of prophecies about baptism as an act of regeneration, citing largely Isaiah, Ezechiel, and the Psalms. The central theme is that God uses water as a source of renewal, refreshment, and rejuvenation.]

The New Way of Life of the Baptized

But do you all, as many as are made glad by the gift of regeneration, and make your boast of that saving renewal, show me, after the sacramental grace, the change in your ways that should follow it, and make known by the purity of your way of life the difference effected by your transformation for the better. For of those things which are before our eyes nothing is altered: the characteristics of the body remain unchanged, and the mold of the visible nature is nowise different.

But there is certainly need of some manifest proof, by which we may recognize the new-born man, discerning by clear tokens the new from the old. And these I think are to be found in the intentional motions of the soul, whereby it separates itself from its old customary life, and enters on a newer way of life, and will clearly teach those acquainted with it that it has become something different from its former self, bearing in it no token by which the old self was recognized. . . .

[Gregory gives his listeners two gospel models of baptismal transformation, Matthew and Zacchaeus, both tax collectors, and he urges his audience to "fashion and frame themselves to the likeness of the Father that they may be true children adopted by grace."]

Therefore, also, it is that after the dignity of adoption the devil plots more vehemently against us, pining away with envious glance, when he beholds the beauty of the new-born man, earnestly tending towards that heavenly city, from which he fell: and he raises up against us fiery temptations, seeking earnestly to despoil us of that second adornment, as he did of our former array. But when we are aware of his attacks, we ought to repeat to ourselves the apostolic words, "As many of us as were baptized into Christ were baptized into his death" [Rom 6:3]. Now if we have been conformed to his death, sin henceforth in us is surely a corpse, pierced through by the javelin of baptism, as that fornicator was thrust through by the zealous. Flee therefore from us, ill-omened one! for it is a corpse you seek to despoil, one long ago joined to you, one who long since lost his senses for pleasures. A corpse is not enamored of bodies, a corpse is not captivated by wealth, a corpse slanders not, a corpse lies not, snatches not at what is not its own, reviles not those who encounter it.

My way of living is regulated for another life: I have learnt to despise the things that are in the world, to pass by the things of earth, to hasten to the things of heaven, even as Paul expressly testifies, that the world is crucified to him, and he to the world [Gal 6:14]. These are the words of a soul truly regenerated: these are the utterances of the newly-baptized man, who remembers his own profession, which he made to God when the sacrament was administered to him, promising that he would despise for the sake of love towards him all torment and all pleasure alike.

And now we have spoken sufficiently for the holy subject of the day, which the circling year brings to us at appointed periods. We shall do well in what remains to end our discourse by turning it to the loving giver of so great a boon, offering to him a few words as the requital of great things.

Concluding Prayer

For you truly, O Lord, are the pure and eternal fount of goodness, who did justly turn away from us, and in loving kindness did have mercy upon us. You did hate, and were reconciled; you did curse, and did bless; you did banish us from Paradise, and did recall us; you did strip off the fig-tree leaves, an unseemly covering, and put upon us a costly garment; you did open the prison, and did release the condemned; you did sprinkle us with clean water, and cleanse us from our filthiness. No longer shall Adam be confounded when called by you, nor hide himself, convicted by his conscience, cowering in the thicket of Paradise. Nor shall the flaming sword encircle Paradise around, and make the entrance inaccessible to those that draw near; but all is turned to joy for us that were the heirs of sin: Paradise, yes, heaven itself may be trodden by man: and the creation, in the world and above the world, that once was at variance with itself, is knit together in friendship: and we men are made to join in the angels' song, offering the worship of their praise to God. For all these things then let us sing to God that hymn of joy, which lips touched by the Spirit long ago sang loudly: "Let my soul be joyful in the Lord: for he has clothed me with a garment of salvation, and has put upon me a robe of gladness: as on a bridegroom he has set a miter upon me, and as a bride has he adorned me with fair array" [Isa 61:10]. And truly the adorner of the bride of Christ, who is, and was, and shall be, blessed now and for evermore. Amen.

John Chrysostom

Gregory of Nyssa had a younger contemporary whose star, perhaps to Gregory's chagrin, was rising. His name was John, the Golden-Tongued *(Chrysostomos),* the incomparable Greek-speaking Christian orator of the patristic period. Unlike Gregory, whose legacy is theological and mystical, Chrysostom's consists in volumes of biblical commentaries, homilies, and sermons. As part of that legacy, he left behind two sets of baptismal instructions, both from his Antioch years (370–397). One set, delivered in 388, bears the name *Papadopoulos-Keramaeus* for the Byzantinist who found it in 1909 at the Moscow Historical Museum.

The other set, from which the reading is taken, was delivered in 390 and bears the name *Stavronikita* for the monastery of Mt. Athos, where patrologist Antoine Wenger found it in 1955. Chrysostom left Antioch in 397 to become Patriarch of Constantinople, where his fiery temperament and political naïveté occasioned his deposition and exile in 403, followed by his death in 407.

The reading is *Baptismal Homily* 2 (= *Stavronikita* 2), which Chrysostom delivered some two weeks before Easter, 390, in the Constantinian basilica consecrated in 341 and known as the "Great" or "Golden" church. It is a stenographic record (a practice that accounts for much patristic literature) and comprises, together with *Baptismal Homily* 11 (= *Papadopoulos-Keramaeus* 3), his most systematic instruction on the rich Antiochene baptismal liturgy.

Lent and Easter baptisms were by then (see above, Egeria) traditional in Christianity, both East and West. In the evening of the first Sunday of Lent in Antioch, those catechumens chosen for baptism (*photizomenoi*, "those about to be enlightened") assembled with their sponsors (2:15-16) in the church. The initial rite, called "enrollment," consisted of two parts: (1) officials inscribed the names in the baptismal registry, and (2) the *photizomenoi* heard an instruction on the meaning of the rite, on its connection with baptism, and on the Antiochene baptismal creed, which they were given to memorize (see *Baptismal Homily* 1 [= *Stavronikita* 1]). The work of preparation began the next evening, continued for thirty days (not including Saturdays and Sundays), and consisted of daily instruction in the Scriptures (primarily the Old Testament) and the creed, concluding with a solemn exorcism (2:9-14).

As Easter approached, the pace of the liturgical drama accelerated. At 3:00 P.M. on Good Friday the candidates assembled in the church (barefoot and in burlap tunic) to renounce Satan and to pledge allegiance to Christ (2:17-21). Part of the pledge seems to have been the profession of the Antioch baptismal creed. In any case, allegiance was followed with anointing the forehead in the sign of the cross (2:22-24). On Holy Saturday night the *photizomenoi* reassembled in the church, were ritually stripped and fully anointed (2:24), and then baptized by triple immersion (2:25-26). They emerged from the font reciting intercessory prayers and the Lord's Prayer, put on the white garment, received the kiss of peace and a candle, and then proceeded to the Eucharist (2:27). There was no postbaptismal anointing. The week following Easter was devoted to postbaptismal instruction (primarily biblical homilies with a strong moral application rather than instruction in the rites as in Jerusalem) and other celebrations. Elsewhere, Chrysostom adverts to the high profile of the newly baptized in their white garments.

In the selected reading, the golden-tongued orator sets baptism in the context of the history of salvation. Specifically, he joins a commentary on the Fall in the Book of Genesis with a commentary on the baptismal rites themselves, developing the theme of Paradise lost and Paradise regained.

The text is that of Antoine Wenger, ed., SC 50 (1950); the translation, Edward Yarnold, *The Awe-Inspiring Rites of Initiation* (Slough: St. Paul Publications, 1972). For study of the rite and its meaning in Chrysostom, see T. M. Finn, SCA 15 (1967).

Baptismal Homily 2

1. Today I am going to speak a few more words to those who have been enrolled among the household of Christ, to teach them the power of the weapons which they are about to receive and the indescribable goodness of the love God shows to the human race. I hope that as a result they may approach him with great faith and confidence and enjoy his generosity more liberally.

God's Generosity Even Towards Sinners

Consider, my beloved, the abundance of God's goodness from the beginning. For if, without your having worked for it nor shown any qualifications, he thinks you worthy of such a gift and pardons all the sins you have committed in your life, what return are you likely to merit from a loving God if after such great kindness you learn to be grateful and determine to make a contribution of your own?

2. In human affairs nothing similar has ever been seen. On the contrary, many men on many occasions, after undergoing many labors and troubles in hope of recompense, return home empty-handed. Those from whom they expected a return have proved ungrateful for all their exertions, or else they have themselves often been snatched away from this world before they could fulfill their own aim. But in the service of our Master we need

never suspect anything of the sort. Even before we begin our efforts and offer anything of our own, he forestalls us and shows his generosity, so that his many kindnesses may induce us to take thought for our own salvation.

3. And so from the very beginning he has never ceased to bless the human race. For as soon as he created the first man, at once he put him to dwell in the garden of Paradise and gave him a life of ease, allowing him the freedom of all that was in the garden except for a single tree. But once the man had intemperately allowed himself to be deceived by the woman, he rode roughshod over the command that was given to him and abused the great honor that had been paid him.

4. Here too you can see the extent of God's love for man. It would have been just if one who had been so ungrateful for the benefits prepared for him had been judged unworthy of any further pardon and set outside God's providence. Not only did God not do this, but he was like a loving Father with an undisciplined son. In his instinctive love for the boy, he does not measure punishment by the fault; nor does he completely let him go free, but chastises him with moderation so as not to drive him to greater evil and the shipwreck of his life. In the same way God in his goodness expelled man for his great disobedience from this comfortable way of life and condemned him to toil and hardship so as to check his pride for the future in case he should kick over the traces again.

It is almost as if God had said to him:

5. "This ample ease and freedom which you enjoyed has led you to this act of grave disobedience and has made you forget my commandments. You had nothing to do, and this has given you thoughts above your own nature ('It is idleness that is the teacher of all vices' [Ecclus 33:27]). Consequently I am condemning you to toil and hardship, so that by working the land you may have a continual reminder of your own disobedience and of the worthlessness of human nature. For since you have had great dreams and refused to remain within your own limits, I order you to go back to the dust from which you have been taken [Gen 3:19]. 'You are dust and to dust you shall return.' "

6. To increase his sorrow and make him perceive his own fall, God made him dwell not far from Paradise and walled off his entry into it, so that the continual sight of what he had forfeited by his heedlessness might serve as a perpetual warning and make him in future more careful to keep the commands

that were given to him. For when we do not remember as we should how fortunate we are in the enjoyment of some blessing, as soon as we are deprived of it the sense of loss makes us take great notice of it and increases our distress. And this is just what happened then in the case of the first man.

7. If you wish to learn of the evil demon's treachery and our Master's resourceful plan, consider what the devil has tried to effect in man by his deceit and what kindness our Master and Protector has shown towards man. That evil demon, in envy of man's home in Paradise, by promising him greater hopes, deprived him even of what he had already. In leading him to dream of an equality with God [Gen 3:5] he brought him to the punishment of death. Such are his incitements: he not only deprives us of the blessings we have, but attempts to face us with a fall from a greater height. But even so, God in his love did not abandon the human race. He showed the Devil the futility of his attempts and showed man the extent of the care he has for him—through death he gave him immortality. Just think. The Devil threw man out of Paradise; the Master brought him into heaven. The profit is greater than the loss.

8. But as I said at the start—and this is the reason for these remarks—God considered that one who was heedless of such blessings was worthy once more of his great kindness. So if you, who are the soldiers of Christ, try to be grateful for these indescribable gifts that are being granted to you and if you are vigilant to preserve them once they are granted, who can say what kindness you will win from him, if you succeed in preserving them? He it was who said: "To everyone who has will more be given, and he will have abundance" [Matt 25:29]. One who makes himself worthy of what he has already received deserves to enjoy greater blessings still.

The Need of Faith

9. I ask all of you who have been found worthy to be inscribed in this heavenly book to bring a generous faith and a firm resolve. What is performed here requires faith and the eyes of the soul: we are not merely to notice what is seen but to go on from this to imagine what cannot be seen. Such is the power of the eyes of faith. The eyes of the body can only see what falls under the sense of sight, but with the eyes of faith it is just the reverse. They see nothing that is visible, but they see what is invisible just as if it lay before their eyes. For faith is

the capacity to attend to the invisible as if it were visible. "Now faith is the assurance of things hoped for, the conviction of things not seen" [Heb 11:1].

10. What is the meaning of these words? Why have I said that one must not attend to the visible but develop spiritual eyes? I will tell you. I said it so that when you see the font with its water and the hand of the priest touching your head, you will not think that this is mere water nor that it is simply the hand of the bishop that is laid upon your head. It is not a man who performs the rites but the gracious presence of the Spirit who sanctifies the natural properties of the water and who touches your head along with the hand of the priest [priest and bishop are interchangeable in the homilies]. I was right, then—was I not?—to speak of the need we have of the eyes of faith if we are to believe in what is unseen instead of despising what our sense perceives.

11. As you know, baptism is a burial and a resurrection: the old self is buried with Christ to sin and the new nature rises from the dead "which is being renewed after the image of its creator" [Col 3:10]. We are stripped and we are clothed, stripped of the old garment which has been soiled by the multitude of our sins, clothed with the new that is free from all stain. What does this mean? We are clothed in Christ himself. St. Paul remarks: "As many of you as were baptized into Christ have put on Christ" [Gal 3:27].

Exorcisms

12. Since you are on the threshold of the time when you are to receive these great gifts, I must now teach you, as far as I can, the meaning of each of the rites, so that you may go from here with knowledge and a more assured faith. So you need to know why it is that after the daily instruction we send you off to hear the words of the exorcists. This rite is neither a simple one nor pointless. You are about to receive the heavenly King into your house. So those who are appointed for this task, just as if they were preparing a house for a royal visit, take you on one side after our sermon, and purify your minds by those fearful words, putting to flight all the tricks of the Evil One, and so make the house fit for the presence of the King. For no demon, however fierce and harsh, after these fearful words and the invocation of the universal Lord of all things, can refrain from flight with all speed. And, in addition, the rite imprints great reverence in the soul and leads it to great sorrow for sin.

13. The wonderful, unbelievable thing is that every difference and distinction of rank is missing here. If anyone happens to be in a position of worldly importance or conspicuous wealth, if he boasts of his birth or the glory of this present life, he stands on just the same footing as the beggar in rags, the blind man or the lame. Nor does he complain at this since he knows that all such differences have been set aside in the life of the spirit; a grateful heart is the only requirement.

14. Such is the effect of these marvelous, awesome words and invocations. But something else is made known to us by the outward attitude—the bare feet and the outstretched hands. Just as those who suffer bodily captivity show by the appearance they present their dejection at the disaster that has struck them, so do those men who have been captives of the Devil. As they are about to be freed from his tyranny and go beneath the yoke that is easy [see Matt 11:30], first of all they remind themselves by their appearance of their previous situation and try to understand what they are being saved from and what they are hastening to. This then becomes for them a reason for greater gratitude and thankfulness.

The Duties of Sponsors

15. Will you allow me now to address some words to your sponsors so that they may know the rewards they are worthy of if they show great care for you and the punishment that will ensue if they become negligent? Consider this, my beloved. Those who act as guarantors for money accept a greater responsibility than the debtor who receives the money. If the borrower proves generous he lightens the load of the guarantor, but if not he prepares a greater crash for him. It is for this reason that the wise man offers his advice: "If you offer yourself as surety, be concerned as one who must pay" [Ecclus 8:13]. If those who stand as surety for money are responsible for the full sum, those who guarantee that others will pay their account of virtue in matters of the spirit have an even greater duty to show vigilance, advising, counseling, correcting with a paternal affection.

16. They should not consider that what they are doing is a routine action. Rather they should be fully aware that they will share the credit if they guide their charges to the path of virtue by their advice, but that if they are negligent, then grave condemnation will fall upon them. For this reason it is the custom to call them "spiritual fathers," in order that they may learn from their office the affection they owe to their charges in giving them

spiritual instruction. For if it is a noble thing to lead those who are in no way connected with us to a desire of virtue, we have much greater duty to fulfill this obligation to one whom we have received to the position of our spiritual son. To sum up, negligence brings no small danger to those of you who are acting as sponsors.

Renunciation of Satan and Contract with Christ

17. I turn now to the sacraments and the covenant between yourself and the Lord into which you are about to enter. In business, when a man wishes to entrust his affairs to another, it is necessary for a contract to be signed between the two parties. The same is true now, when the Lord of all things is about to entrust to you affairs that are not mortal and passing away and decaying, but spiritual and heavenly. The contract is also called a pledge of faith, since we are doing nothing that can be seen but everything can be discerned by the eyes of the spirit. Meanwhile it is necessary for the contract to be signed, not with ink on paper but with the spirit in God. The words that you pronounce are inscribed in heaven, the agreement spoken by your lips remains indelibly before God.

18. Now consider once again the posture of captivity. The priests who introduce you first of all tell you to kneel down and pray with your hands raised to heaven, and by this attitude of body recall to your mind the one from whom you have been delivered and the other whom you are about to join. After that the bishop approaches each in turn and demands your contracts and confessions and instructs each one to pronounce those fearful and awesome words: "I renounce you, Satan."

19. Tears and deep sighs now force themselves upon me. I have recalled the day on which I too was judged worthy to pronounce these words. As I reckon up the weight of the sins which I have gathered from that day to this, I am confused in mind and stung in conscience as I reflect upon the shame with which I have covered myself by my subsequent negligence. And so I beg all of you to show some generosity towards me, and since you are about to approach our King—he will receive you with great alacrity, he will dress you in the royal robe [i.e., the white garment] and will grant every kind of gift that you desire, at least if you seek spiritual gifts—beg a favor for me too. Pray that God may not ask an account of my sins but grant me pardon, and for the future count me worthy of his support. I have no doubt that you will do this in your affection for your teachers.

20. But I must not allow myself to lose the thread of my argument any more. The priest then instructs you to say, "I renounce you, Satan, your pomp, your worship and your works." There is great power in these few words. For the angels who are present and the invisible powers rejoice at your conversion and, receiving the words from your lips, carry them to the common Master of all things, where they are inscribed in the books of heaven.

21. Have you seen the terms of the contract? After the renunciation of the Evil One and all the works he delights in, the priest instructs you to speak again as follows: "And I pledge myself, Christ, to you." Do you see the overwhelming goodness of God? From you he receives only words, yet he entrusts to you realities, a great treasure. He forgets your past ingratitude; he remembers nothing of your past; he is content with these few words.

Anointing with Chrism

22. Then once you have made this covenant, this renunciation and contract, since you have confessed his sovereignty over you and pronounced the words by which you pledge yourself to Christ, you are now a soldier and have signed on for a spiritual contest. Accordingly the bishop anoints you on the forehead with spiritual chrism, placing a seal on your head and saying: "N. is anointed in the name of the Father, the Son and the Holy Spirit."

23. Now the bishop knows that the Enemy is enraged and is sharpening his teeth going around like a roaring lion [see 1 Pet 5:8], seeing that the former victims of his tyranny have suddenly defected. Renouncing him, they have changed their allegiance and publicly enlisted with Christ. It is for this reason that the bishop anoints you on your forehead and marks you with the seal, to make the Devil turn away his eyes. He does not dare to look at you directly because he sees the light blazing from your head and blinding his eyes. From that day onwards you will confront him in battle, and this is why the bishop anoints you as athletes of Christ before leading you into the spiritual arena.

Stripping and Anointing with Oil

24. Then after this at the appointed hour of the night [the Easter Vigil], he strips you of all your clothes, and as if he were about to lead you into heaven itself by means of these rites, he pre-

pares to anoint your whole body with this spiritual oil so that his unction may armor all your limbs and make them invulnerable to any weapons the Enemy may hurl.

Baptism

25. After this anointing he takes you down into the sacred waters, at the same time burying the old nature and raising "the new creature, which is being renewed after the image of the creator" [Col 3:10]. Then by the words of the bishop and by his hand the presence of the Holy Spirit flies down upon you and another man comes up out of the font, one washed from all the stain of his sins, who has put off the old garment of sin and is clothed in the royal robe.

26. To give you a further lesson that the substance of the Father, the Son and the Spirit is one; baptism is conferred in this form. As the bishop pronounces the words, "N. is baptized in the name of the Father and of the Son and of the Holy Spirit," he plunges your head into the water and lifts it up again three times, by this sacred rite preparing you to receive the visit of the Holy Spirit. For the bishop is not the only one who touches your head; Christ also touches it with his right hand. This is shown by the actual words of the bishop who baptizes you. He does not say, "I baptize N.," but rather, "N. is baptized." This shows that he is only the minister of the grace and merely lends his hand since he has been ordained for this by the Spirit. It is the Father, Son and Holy Spirit, the indivisible Trinity, who bring the whole rite to completion. It is faith in the Trinity that bestows the grace of remission of sin, and the confession of the Trinity that grants us the adoption of sons [see vol. 6, ch. 2].

The Kiss

27. The ceremonies that follow are well able to teach us the afflictions from which those who have been counted worthy to receive this sacred rite have been set free and the blessings which they have been granted. As soon as they come up from those sacred waters all present embrace them, greet them, kiss them, congratulate and rejoice with them, because those who before were slaves and prisoners have all at once become free men and sons who are invited to the royal table. For as soon as they come up from the font, they are led to the awesome table which is laden with all good things. They taste the Body and Blood of the Lord and become the dwelling place of the Spirit; since they have put on Christ, they go about appearing everywhere like

angels on earth and shining as brightly as the rays of the sun
[i.e., in their white garments].

Conclusion

28. It is not without good reason and careful thought that I
have explained all these things to you in advance, my loving
people. Even before you actually enjoy them, I wanted you to
feel great pleasure as you fly on the wings of hope. I wanted
you to take up a disposition of soul worthy of the rite and, as
the blessed Paul advised you, to "set your mind on things that
are above" [Col 3:2], raising your thoughts from earth to
heaven, from the visible to the invisible. We see such things more
clearly with the eyes of the spirit than the perceptions of the
senses.

29. But since you have come near the royal entrance-hall and
are about to approach the very throne where the King sits dis-
tributing his gifts, show complete unselfishness in your requests.
Ask for nothing worldly or natural, but make a request that
is worthy of the giver. As you step out of the sacred waters and
express your resurrection by the act of coming up from them,
ask for alliance with him so that you may show great vigilance
in guarding what has been given to you, and so be immune from
the tricks of the Enemy. Pray for the peace of the Churches.
Intercede for those who are still wandering. Fall on your knees
for those who are in sin so that we may deserve some pardon.
You were once diffident; God has given you great assurance.
You were once slaves; he has enrolled you among the chief of
his friends. You were once captives; he has raised you up and
adopted you as sons. He will not refuse your demands; he will
grant them all, true again in this to his own goodness.

30. In this way too you will draw God to still greater kindness.
When he sees you showing such concern for those who are your
own members [see Eph 4:25] and anxious about the salvation
of others, because of this he will count you worthy to receive
great assurance. Nothing so warms his heart as our compassion for our members and the affection that we show for our
brothers, the great forethought we show for the salvation of
our neighbor.

31. And so, dearly beloved, in this knowledge, prepare yourselves with joy and spiritual delight to receive this grace so that
you may enjoy the gift in its abundance. And so may we all
together, living lives that are in keeping with the grace we have

received, be counted worthy to win the eternal and indescribable blessings through the grace and loving kindness of our Lord Jesus Christ with whom to the Father and the Holy Spirit be glory, power, honor now and always, for ever and ever. Amen.

Theodore of Mopsuestia

Mopsuestia (now a village on the Syro-Turkish border) was a comparatively small town about one hundred miles north of Antioch. It acquired otherwise unwarranted prominence from Bishop Theodore (393–428), friend of Chrysostom, fellow Antiochene, and the most perceptive and imaginative of Antioch's school of Christian thinkers. He was also its most controversial thinker, largely because of his approach to the long-debated issue about the way in which Christ can be considered at once divine and human. Theodore distinguished between the divine Word and the "man" Jesus, whom the Word assumed, and then proposed a union of wills between them such that they "are no longer two persons but one" (*On the Incarnation,* bk. 8, frag. 7). In so doing, according to his opponents, he taught that the Christ is a composite of two separable persons, the Word/Son and the man Jesus, thereby jeopardizing salvation. One of his disciples, Nestorius (see ch. 2, Narsai), went on to propose that the "one assumed" is the son of Mary, who could not, therefore, be called "Mother of God." The result was a controversy that led to the condemnation of Nestorius at the Council of Ephesus in 431, to the Council of Chalcedon in 451 (vol. 6, ch. 3, Cyril of Alexandria; Coptic Rite), to posthumous trouble for Theodore, and finally to his condemnation at the Second Council of Constantinople in 553.

Nevertheless, Theodore was widely revered during his life and long afterward. And Christians, often called "Nestorian" (see ch. 2, Narsai), regarded "Mar Theodore" as the great teacher of Scripture. Indeed, some modern scholars, working with new information, have rehabilitated him as an orthodox thinker and teacher.

Theodore left behind a large corpus of biblical commentaries, homilies, and controversial theological works. Unfortunately, only fragments of the Greek texts are extant. Many were translated into Syriac, however, and their recovery in the early part of this century has led to much contemporary interest in Theodore. The

initial impulse came from Alphonse Mingana's discovery and publication of Theodore's *Baptismal Homilies* in 1932. Sixteen in
number, Theodore delivered them in Mopsuestia about 420 (some
scholars date them several decades earlier and site them in Antioch). The first ten homilies are on the creed; the eleventh, on
the Lord's Prayer; the twelfth through the fourteenth, on baptism. The last two are on the Eucharist. They quickly became
something of a textbook for catechumens (like Cyril's), probably when translated into Syriac.

The liturgy on which Theodore comments is Antiochene, albeit with some differences, one of which is major: A postbaptismal anointing has been added that emphasizes the baptismal gift
of the Holy Spirit. Some think it a later addition; others detect
the influence of Cyril of Jerusalem and the *Apostolic Constitutions;* still others, the growing need to bring Syrian tradition into
line with the rest of the Church. Yet the presence of the rite in
Mopsuestia's liturgy also had much to do with the now-settled
controversies about the nature and status of the Holy Spirit by
giving the Spirit added prominence in baptism. In early Christianity, belief and worship went hand in hand.

As a liturgical commentator, Theodore is far from concise. Although three homilies on baptism survive, considerations of space
permit only the presentation of the third. The first of the three
is devoted to the preliminaries: (1) enrollment and solemn exorcism, during which the candidate stood barefoot on sackcloth and
in a penitential tunic of sackcloth (technically, it was goatskin);
(2) oral instruction on the creed, article by article; and (3) profession of the creed and promise of faithful service. The preliminaries occupied the better part of Lent. The second homily is
devoted to the renunciation of Satan and the first anointing; the
third, to the ritual stripping, the second anointing, baptism, vesting in white, and chrismation.

Although Theodore's explanation of how the baptismal liturgy
achieves its effect recalls Cyril's, his perspective is quite different
(see General Introduction, "Baptism: Symbolic Participation").
Cyril holds that baptism actualizes in the present the effects of
Christ's historical passion and resurrection. His vantage point is
the present, looking back. Theodore sees baptism as actualizing
in the present the promise of the "world to come." His vantage
point is the present, looking forward. The key to Theodore's

thinking, as noted in the General Introduction, is in his doctrine of the Two Ages. The first age is the world of space, time, choice, and sin; the second, the age of the end of time, Paradise regained, the final harvest. The two ages, however, are not discontinuous. Christ, according to Theodore, entered into the first age and bound it to the second with his death, resurrection, and ascension. Baptism is the link: In celebrating the rites the newly baptized, the bishop repeatedly says, achieve by anticipation the first fruits of immortality, resurrection, ascension, and the gifts that characterize the second age. In an inchoative way they already participate in the second age when they emerge from the font.

The text is that of Alphonse Mingana, photographically reproduced in R. M. Tonneau and Robert Devreesse, eds., SeT 145, 366–461, which has a valuable introduction and a French translation. The English translation is that of Edward Yarnold, *The Awe-Inspiring Rites of Initiation* (Slough: St. Paul Publications, 1972). Rowan Greer has done an important study of Theodore in his *Theodore of Mopsuestia: Exegete and Theologian* (London: Faith Press, 1961). For baptism see also T. M. Finn, SCA 15 (1967). In this reading, an asterisk (*) indicates compression of Theodore's thought within a sentence. Four dots (. . . .) indicate elision.

Baptismal Homily 3

[The previous day Theodore had spoken to the candidates about rites in the following synopsis, which was inserted at the beginning of *Baptismal Homily* 2 when the homilies became a manual of instruction.]

Synopsis. You stand again on sackcloth, bare-footed, with your outer garment removed and your hands stretched out to God in the attitude of prayer. First you fall on your knees, holding the rest of your body upright. Then you say, "I renounce Satan, all his angels, all his works, all his service, all his vanity and all his worldly enticements. I pledge myself by vow, I believe and I am baptized in the name of the Father, of the Son and of the Holy Spirit." Kneeling on the ground, but with the rest of your body upright, you look up to heaven and stretch out your hands in the attitude of prayer. The bishop, wearing light, shining vestments of linen, signs your forehead with the oil of anointing, saying: "N. is signed in the name of the Father and of the Son and of the Holy Spirit." Your sponsor, standing behind you, spreads a linen stole over your head and raises you to your feet.

1. I concluded yesterday's instruction at the point where you had been sealed with the oil of baptism to mark you out for service in the heavenly army as one chosen and approved. Now the kingdom of heaven was revealed in the person of Christ our Lord in his incarnate life, when after his passion and resurrection he ascended into heaven and established his kingdom there. And we, who have been called to this service, ought to have an affinity with heaven, for we are all now bound for the place where our king is, since he said himself: "I desire that they also may be with me where I am" *[John 17:24]. We hope to "reign with him," as St. Paul said, if we show our love for him by endurance [see 2 Tim 2:12], because when we are in heaven with him we shall share in his great glory. . . . So as soon as you come up from the font and receive the mark, you spread a linen cloth over your head to signify your state of freedom. Since you have been chosen to serve in the heavenly army you have been set free from all contact with earthly things and assumed the liberty of heaven. If an earthly ruler will not countenance the presence of a slave in his army, all the more should one who serves in the army of heaven be free from slavery. Our share in heavenly things has set us all free; in St. Paul's words, "The Jerusalem above is free, and she is our mother" [Gal 4:26].

2. These then are the effects of the sealing, and you know all you need to know about the ceremony, for I described it yesterday. Today I must explain the next ceremonies, for at this stage you have to come forward for baptism itself. Baptism contains the signs of the new birth which will be manifested in reality when you rise from the dead and recover all that death has stolen from you. . . . You will gain this new birth by rising from the dead to a second existence, just as when you were born of a woman you entered upon the existence that death takes away from you. You will gain this in reality when the time comes for you to rise again to your new birth; but now you have faith in Christ our Lord, and while you are waiting for the resurrection you must be content with receiving symbols and signs of it in this awesome sacrament which affords you certainty of sharing in the blessings to come.

3. You come forward then for baptism, the symbol of this birth you hope for. This is why Christ our Lord calls it a second birth in his words to Nicodemus: "Unless one is born anew, he cannot see the kingdom of God" [see John 3 for the full account].

. . . Nicodemus, taking Jesus to mean that this birth was like birth from a woman, asks: "How can a man be born when he is old? Can he enter a second time into his mother's womb and be born?" . . . So Christ our Lord says no more about the second birth that we shall receive in reality at the resurrection, for he knows that this is a truth too sublime for Nicodemus to grasp. Instead he tells him about the symbolical birth that takes place at baptism, and which believers must undergo in order to pass by means of the signs to the enjoyment of the reality. "Unless," he says, "one is born of water and the Spirit, he cannot enter the kingdom of God." He explains the means, water, and he reveals the cause, the Spirit. That is why he adds the words: "That which is born of the flesh is flesh, and that which is born of the Spirit is spirit." He says no more about the water, because it merely serves as a sacramental sign; he speaks of the Spirit because this birth is due to the Spirit's operation. This is clearly his meaning: just as one who is born in the flesh and of the flesh is by nature subject to death, pain, corruption and all kinds of change, so we are to expect that when we are born, so to speak, of the Spirit, we shall become by nature free from all these afflictions.*

4. But Nicodemus repeated the question: "How can this be?" Jesus answered: "The wind blows where it wills and you hear the sound of it, but you do not know whence it comes or whither it goes; so it is with everyone who is born of the Spirit." He does not say a word about water; he refers to the reliability and credibility of the Spirit to establish his teaching against all doubt. For the expression "blows where it wills" indicates the Spirit's power to accomplish his will in anything. . . . Therefore Christ's words are conclusive: "So it is with everyone who is born of the Spirit."

5. For the same reason St. Paul says: "All of us who have been baptized into Christ Jesus were baptized into his death. We were buried therefore with him by baptism into death, so that as Christ was raised from the dead by the glory of the Father, we too might walk in newness of life" [Rom 6:3-4]. Before Christ's coming, God's sentence enabled death to exercise sovereign power over us, and it was quite beyond our strength to break our bonds, so firm was death's hold on us. But by his death and resurrection Christ our Lord altered the sentence and undid death's hold on us, so that now the death of those who believe in Christ is like a prolonged sleep. This is implied in St. Paul's words: "Christ has been raised from the dead, the first-

fruits of those who have fallen asleep" [1 Cor 15:20]. By "those
who have fallen asleep," he means those who have died since
the resurrection of Christ, for they will rise again and cast off
their death.* So it is because Christ our Lord has abolished the
power of death by his own resurrection that St. Paul says: "All
of us who have been baptized in Christ Jesus were baptized into
his death"; we know, he means, that Christ our Lord has already abolished death. Believing this we come to him for baptism, because we wish now to share in his death so as to share
like him in the resurrection from the dead. So when I am baptized and put my head under the water, I wish to receive the
death and burial of Christ our Lord, and I solemnly profess
my faith in his resurrection; when I come up out of the water,
this is a sign that I believe I am already risen.

6. These things only happen to us in symbols, but St. Paul wishes
to make it clear that we are not concerned with empty symbols
but with realities, in which we profess our faith with longing
and without hesitation. So he continues: "If we have been united
with him in a death like his, we shall certainly be united with
him in a resurrection like his" [Rom 6:5]. He proves the present by the future, taking the splendor of what is to come as
evidence of the value of these symbols, the symbols contained
in baptism, the work of the Holy Spirit. You receive baptism
only because you hope for the blessings to come: by dying and
rising with Christ and being born to a new life, you come to
share in the reality of the signs that attracted you.* . . . This
second birth is the work of the Holy Spirit, whom you receive
in the sacrament as a kind of guarantee. So you can see what
a great sacrament this is, how awesome and deserving belief
its symbolism. . . . That is why St. Paul says: "In him we have
believed and were sealed with the Holy Spirit of promise, who
is the guarantee of our inheritance to the praise of his glory"
[Eph 1:13-14]. He calls this grace that the Holy Spirit gives us
here on earth "the Spirit of promise" because we receive it as
a promise of future gifts. He calls it also "the guarantee of our
inheritance," because it enables us already to share in the gifts
to come.

7. Similarly he says in another place: "It is God who establishes
us with you in Christ, and has commissioned us; he has put
his seal upon us and given us his Spirit in our hearts as a guarantee" [2 Cor 1:21-22]. In yet another place he says: "And not
only the creation, but we ourselves, who have the first-fruits
of the Spirit, groan inwardly as we wait for adoption as sons,

the redemption of our bodies'' [Rom 8:23]. We have the first-fruits of the Spirit, he says, on this earth, because we receive the fullness of grace only when we enjoy the reality. "We wait for adoption as sons, the redemption of our bodies," he says, meaning that in this life we receive adoption in anticipation; we shall receive the reality when we are born again and rise from the dead, becoming at once immortal, incorruptible and free from all physical evil. . . .

Second Anointing

8. Then you come forward to be baptized. First you strip completely. Originally Adam was "naked and not ashamed" [Gen 2:25] but once he had disobeyed the commandment and become mortal, he needed a covering; you, on the other hand, are to present yourself for baptism in order to be born again and become immortal in anticipation, and so you must first take off your clothes. For they are proof of mortality, convincing evidence of the humiliating sentence which made man need clothes. When you have done this, you are anointed all over with the oil of anointing in the prescribed manner; this is a sign of the garment of immortality you will receive through baptism. . . . You are anointed all over: unlike clothes, which only come in contact with part of the body, and even if they touched the whole surface of the body would still not come in contact with the internal organs, our whole nature will "put on the imperishable" [1 Cor 15:53] at the moment of the resurrection, by virtue of the working of the Holy Spirit within us.* When this anointing is conferred upon you, the bishop begins the ceremony with the words: "N. is anointed in the name of the Father and of the Son and of the Holy Spirit," and the appointed ministers anoint your body all over.

Blessing of the Font

9. Next, at the time I have already explained to you, you go down into the water that has been blessed by the bishop. You are not baptized in ordinary water, but in the water of second birth. Now ordinary water cannot become this other thing except by the coming of the Holy Spirit. Consequently the bishop beforehand pronounces a prescribed form of words, asking God to let the grace of the Holy Spirit come upon the water and make it capable of begetting this awesome birth, making it a womb for sacramental birth. For when Nicodemus asked: "Can a man enter a second time into his mother's womb and be reborn?" our Lord replied: "Unless one is born of water and the

Spirit, he cannot enter the kingdom of God.'' He means that just as in natural birth the mother's womb receives a seed, but it is God's hand that forms it according to his original decree, so too in baptism the water becomes a womb to receive the person who is being born, but it is the grace of the Spirit which forms him there for a second birth and makes him a completely new man. A seed settling in the mother's womb has neither life nor soul nor sense; but God's hand forms it so that it emerges a living man, endowed with soul and senses and a nature capable of any human action. So too here: the one baptized settles in the water as in a kind of womb, like a seed showing no sign of an immortal nature; but once baptized and endowed with the divine grace of the Spirit, his nature is reshaped completely. Once mortal, it becomes immortal; once corruptible, it becomes incorruptible; once changing, it becomes unchanging; by the almighty power of him who forms it.

10. A baby born of a woman has the potentiality of talking, hearing, walking and working with his hands, but is too utterly weak for any action of the kind; yet, in due time, by God's decree he becomes capable of these actions. So too one who is born by baptism possesses in himself all the potentialities of his immortal and incorruptible nature, but cannot use or exhibit them until the moment God has ordained for us to be born from the dead and attain full enjoyment of our freedom from corruption, death, pain and change. We are endowed with the potentiality for these things at baptism but gain the effective use of them only when we are no longer merely natural [i.e., our condition in this life] but spiritual [our condition in the next], and the working of the Spirit has made the body incorruptible and the soul immutable, holding them both in his own power and preserving them. As St. Paul says, ''What is sown is perishable, what is raised is imperishable. It is sown in weakness, it is raised in power. It is sown in dishonor, it is raised in glory. It is sown a merely natural body, it is raised a spiritual body'' [1 Cor 15:42-44]. He means that it is the power of the Holy Spirit that will make us imperishable, glorious and powerful, working upon our bodies and souls, making the former immortal and the latter immutable. The body that will rise from the dead and that man will assume will not be merely natural now but spiritual. Now it is not in the nature of water to work these effects; they are the result of the working of the Spirit at baptism by water. So first of all the bishop pronounces the prescribed words of consecration, praying that the grace

of the Holy Spirit may come upon the water and by his holy
and awesome coming endow the water with power to produce
all these effects. In this way the water becomes an awesome
womb of the second birth; in this way all who go down into
the water are formed again by the grace of the Holy Spirit and
born again in another, higher nature. . . .

Baptism

11. So the water you enter is like a crucible in which you are
reshaped to a higher nature: you lay aside your old mortality
and assume a nature that is completely immortal and incorruptible. You are born in water because you were formed originally
from earth and water [Gen 2:6-7], and when you fell into sin
the sentence of death made you totally corruptible. This is what
a potter does when a vase he is shaping from clay becomes spoilt:
he shapes it again in water and so it recovers its true form. This
is why God told Jeremiah to go to the potter; and when he had
seen the potter doing this God said to him: "O house of Israel,
can I not do with you as this potter has done?" [Jer 18:6].*
For we too were formed from earth and clay—"You too were
formed from a piece of clay, like me" [Job 33:6, LXX]. Pardon "those who dwell in houses of clay, for we too are of the
same clay" [Job 4:19, LXX]. We too fell and were corrupted
by sin. Then sentence of death involved us in complete decay,
but our Creator and Master subsequently shaped us afresh by
his immeasurable power: he abolished death by the resurrection and gave all of us hope of salvation from death and of
a better world than this, in which we shall not only survive,
but become immortal and incorruptible . . . [no. 12 elided].

13. When the potter has made a vase, he can reshape it in water,
as long as it retains the plastic quality of clay and has not yet
come into contact with the fire; but once it has been baked there
is no longer any way of reshaping it. So it is with us now: since
we are by nature mortal, we need to undergo this renewal by
baptism; but once we have been formed afresh by baptism and
received the grace of the Holy Spirit, who will harden us more
than any fire, we cannot undergo a second renewal or look to
a second baptism [i.e., a repeat], just as we can only hope for
a single resurrection, since Christ the Lord also, as St. Paul said,
"being raised from the dead will never die again; death no longer
has dominion over him" [Rom 6:9].

14. This then is the effect of the gift of baptism. But to teach you once for all who it is who is the cause of all these blessings, who is now recasting you, who is raising you to a higher nature, who is making you immortal instead of mortal, imperishable instead of perishable, the bishop stands and lays his hand on your head saying: "N. is baptized in the name of the Father and of the Son and of the Holy Spirit." He wears the same vestments as before, when he sealed your forehead while you knelt, and when he blessed the water [white]. He wears it now while performing the ceremony of baptism, because it is appropriate that he should perform all the rites of the sacrament in the same vestments which symbolizes this new world to which the sacrament transports you. He says, "N. is baptized in the name of the Father and of the Son and of the Holy Spirit," to teach you by these words who it is who is the cause of this grace. . . . This formula corresponds to our Lord's commission: "Go therefore and make disciples of all nations, baptizing them in the name of the Father and of the Son and of the Holy Spirit" [Matt 28:19]. These words show that the effects are produced entirely by the Father, the Son and the Holy Spirit, who exist from all eternity, and are the cause of all things. To them we owe our original existence, and by them we now hope to be renewed. . . . It is evident that the one who originally saw fit to make us mortal and corruptible is none other than the one who is now making us immortal and incorruptible. . . . He made us originally according to his good pleasure and in the end brought us to a state of excellence, to teach us that the first state too was his doing; the thought that we owe our attainment of excellence to him should make us realize that we would never have existed in the first place if he had not brought us into existence.

15. This is why, when the bishop places his hand on your head, he does not say, "I baptize," but "N. is baptized"; for no man, only divine grace, is capable of making such a gift.* He goes on at once to say who it is who signs and baptizes: the words "In the name of the Father and of the Son and of the Holy Spirit" show who is responsible for the effect, and proclaim that he himself is simply the obedient minister. . . . For just as Peter's words, "In the name of Jesus Christ of Nazareth, stand up and walk" [see Acts 3:6], show that Christ is the cause of the man's recovery of his powers, so too the bishop's words show that the Father, the Son and the Holy Spirit are the cause of the gifts we receive at baptism.* This is the cause of our re-

newal, of our second birth, of our reshaping as new men, free from death, decay, suffering and change, of our exchange of our former slavery for a state of liberty, in which we are free from all our ills and enjoy for ever these indescribable blessings.

16. "In the name of the Father," etc. means "at the invocation of the Father," etc. Similarly Isaiah said: "Lord, apart from you we know no other; we call on you by name" [Isa 26:13, LXX]. He meant this: We acknowledge no other Lord apart from you, the Creator of all things; you have put an end to all our ills; from you we expect to receive the enjoyment of all our blessings; it is you, the Creator of all things, whom we have learnt to invoke in all our needs; you alone can produce and give every gift at will. So at this stage the bishop says, "In the name," etc., meaning that we are baptized invoking the Father, the Son and the Holy Spirit, the cause of all things, that can accomplish whatever it wills. But he does not say: "In the name of the Father and in the name of the Son and in the name of the Holy Spirit." Each of them has his own name which he does not share with the others. . . . But the name that the bishop pronounces is not that by which the Father, the Son and the Holy Spirit are invoked individually: the name which he invokes and by which we call upon the cause of these blessings, is the divine nature existing from all eternity, the nature shared by the Father, the Son and the Holy Spirit; we call upon them in a single invocation.* We do not call upon the Father as one cause and the Son as another and the Holy Spirit as a third. The invocation is addressed to one, and towards this one we look for the enjoyment of the graces of baptism. . . .

17. Consider then that these names act as a prayer. When the bishops says, "In the name of the Father," take him to mean, "Grant, Father, these everlasting, inestimable blessings for which this man is now baptized." So too with the Son and the Holy Spirit.* When Peter said, "In the name of Jesus Christ of Nazareth, stand up and walk" [Acts 3:6], he meant, "Grant, O Jesus Christ, to this man that he may stand up and walk." So too when the bishop says "In the name," etc., all he means is: "O Father, Son and Holy Spirit, grant to this man who is baptized the grace to be born again." Peter's words, "In the name of Jesus Christ, stand up and walk," have the same meaning as his later words, "Aeneas, Jesus Christ heals you" [Acts 9:34]; in both cases he showed who was really responsible for the cure. . . .*

18. Then the bishop lays his hand on your head with the words, "In the name of the Father," and while pronouncing them pushes you down into the water. You obediently follow the signal he gives by word and gesture, and bow down under the water. You incline your head to show your consent and to acknowledge the truth of the bishop's words that you receive the blessings of baptism from the Father. If you were free to speak at this moment you would say "Amen"—a word which we use as a sign of our agreement with what the bishop says. This is implied in St. Paul's question: "How can anyone in the position of an outsider say the 'Amen' to your thanksgiving?" [1 Cor 14:16]. St. Paul's words show that "Amen" is the people's response to the bishop's thanksgiving, by which they express agreement. But since at the moment of baptism you cannot speak, but have to receive the sacrament of renewal in silence and awe, you bow your head when you immerse yourself to show your sincere agreement with the bishop's words.

19. You bow down under the water, then lift your head again. Meanwhile the bishop says, "And of the Son," and guides you with his hand as you bend down into the water as before. You make the sign of consent as before, signifying that you accept the bishop's declaration that it is from the Son that you hope to receive the blessings of baptism. You raise your head, and again the bishop says, "And of the Holy Spirit," pressing you down into the water again with his hand. You bend beneath the water again, humbly acknowledging by the same sign that you hope for the blessings of baptism from the Holy Spirit. . . . Then you come up out of the font to receive the completion of the mystery [i.e., the postbaptismal anointing].

20. Three times you immerse yourself, each time performing the same action, once in the name of the Father, once in the name of the Son and once in the name of the Holy Spirit. Since each person is named, you understand that each enjoys equal perfection, and each is able to dispense the graces of baptism. You go down into the font once, but you bend beneath the water three times in accordance with the bishop's words, and you come up out of the font once. This teaches you that there is only one baptism, and that the grace dispensed by the Father, the Son and the Holy Spirit is one and the same. They are inseparable one from the other, for they have one nature. So although each person can confer the grace, as is shown by your immersion at each of the names, we do not consider baptism to be complete until the Father, the Son and the Holy Spirit have all been

invoked. Since their substance is one and their divinity is one, it follows that it is by a single will and a single operation that the Father, Son and Holy Spirit regularly act upon their creatures. So we too can hope for new birth, second creation and in short all the graces of baptism only upon the invocation of the Father, the Son and the Holy Spirit—an invocation which we believe to be the cause of all our blessings.

21. It is in this sense that St. Paul says: "One Lord, one faith, one baptism, one body and one Spirit, one God and Father of us all, who is through all and in all" [Eph 4:4-6, adapted. For what follows, see the introduction and discussion of Theodore's Christology. See also ch. 2, Narsai]. He does not mean that the Lord is not God or Spirit, and God is not Lord or Spirit, and the Spirit is not Lord or God. For necessarily the Lord is also God and Spirit, and God is also Lord and Spirit, and the true Spirit—the Holy Spirit—is also God and Lord. No, what he is teaching us is this: the one lordship is the one Godhead. For the Substance of the Father, the Son and the Holy Spirit is one without body or limit. It is the Substance which at baptism grants us adoption, this Substance in which we believe we are baptized and become a single body by the power of the Holy Spirit at baptism. This power makes us sons of God and the one body of Christ our Lord, whom we call our head, since he shares our nature and he was the first to rise from the dead so that we might share in these blessings through him. By naming the Father, the Son and the Holy Spirit we received the cause of all blessings. St. Paul indeed would not have said that there was one faith in the Father, the Son and the Holy Spirit if he had believed that their nature was distinct; he would not have said that there was one baptism in the name of the Father, the Son and the Holy Spirit if he had believed that their will, their power and their activity were distinct. It is clear that there is one faith, because there is one Being in which we believe. There is one baptism, because those whom we invoke have one will, one operation and one power, which enables us all to be born again and to become the one body of Christ whom we call our head. In his human existence he was assumed from among us and became the first to rise from the dead, in this way assuring for us a share in his resurrection, which allows us to hope that our bodies too will be like his: "But our commonwealth is in heaven, and from it we await a savior, the Lord Jesus Christ, who will change our lowly body to be like his glorious body" [Phil 3:20-21].

22. This prediction will be fulfilled in reality at the resurrection; at baptism we merely perform the signs and symbols. For the same reason we are called, according to St. Paul's saying, the body of Christ our Lord, who is our head: Christ is the head "from whom the whole body, nourished and knit together, grows with a growth that is from God" [Col 2:19].

Our Baptism and Christ's Baptism

Our Lord himself, before his resurrection from the dead, was seen to receive baptism at the hands of John the Baptist in the River Jordan in order to present in anticipation a sign of the baptism that we were to receive by his grace. For us he was "the first-born from the dead" [Col 2:19], in St. Paul's words, "that in everything he might be pre-eminent" [Col 1:18]; therefore he chose for your sake to be the first not only in the reality of the resurrection but also in sign. . . . St. John the Baptist said to him [see Matt 3:14-15 for what follows]: "I need to be baptized by you, and do you come to me?" showing in this way the difference there was between himself and Jesus. But Jesus replied: "Let it be so now; for thus it is fitting for us to fulfill all righteousness." Righteousness, he meant, is established by the grace of baptism, and it is fitting that your hands should introduce it among those who are subject to the Law. So the Law too is publicly honored, since through it righteousness entered the world.

23. Our Lord, then, was baptized by John, but not with John's baptism. For John's baptism was a baptism of repentance for the remission of sins, and our Lord had no need of it as he was free from all sin. He was baptized with our baptism, and presented an anticipation of it. Consequently he also received the Holy Spirit, who appeared descending in the form of a dove and "remained on him" [John 1:32], as the evangelist says. For John did not have the power to confer the Spirit; he said himself: "I baptize you with water; but among you stands one whom you do not know; he will baptize you with the Holy Spirit and with fire" [John 1:26; Matt 3:11]. . . . The power to confer the Spirit belonged to our Lord. He gives us "the first-fruits of the Spirit" [Rom 8:23] now, and promises to give us the full measure at the resurrection, when our nature will be fully capable of being transformed in reality to a state of excellence.*

24. You were baptized, then, with the same baptism that Christ our Lord received in his humanity. This is one reason why you are baptized "in the name of the Father and of the Son and

of the Holy Spirit," because the very events at Christ's baptism foreshadowed your baptism in sign. When the Father said aloud from far off, "This is my beloved Son, with whom I am well pleased," he was referring in fact to the grace of our adoption, which is the purpose of baptism . . . [see Matt 3:17]. This adoption is far superior to Jewish adoption, which was subject to change. God is saying in effect: "I say, 'You are gods, sons of the Most High, all of you; nevertheless, you shall die like me' " [Ps 82:6-7]. This adoption remains firm and unshakable, because anyone who is adopted in this way will remain immortal. For these signs enable him to pass to the adoption which will take place at the resurrection, transforming him into an immortal and incorruptible nature. The Son also was present in the one who was baptized, and united with the one who was assumed, confirming our adoption as sons [see above introduction]. So the Holy Spirit too was there: he descended in the form of a dove and "remained on him." And so Christ too was baptized in the name of the Father and of the Son and of the Holy Spirit.

25. When the bishop says, "In the name of the Father," he recalls the Father's words: "This is my beloved Son, with whom I am well pleased." When he says, "of the Son," take these words to refer to him who was present in the man who was baptized, and acknowledge that he has obtained adoption for you. When he says, "of the Holy Spirit," remember the one who descended in the form of a dove and remained on him, and in short expect that your adoption too will be confirmed by the same Spirit. For, as St. Paul said, "those who are led by the Spirit of God are sons of God" [Rom 8:14]. The only genuine adoption is that granted by the Holy Spirit; but it is not genuine if the Spirit is not present to produce the effect and encourage us to receive the gift in which we have faith. And so, by the invocation of the Father, the Son and the Holy Spirit, you have received the grace of adoption.

Then you come up out of the font. You have received baptism, second birth. By your immersion you fulfilled the sentence of burial; by coming up you received a sign of the resurrection. You have been born again and have become a completely different man. You no longer belong to Adam, who was subject to change, because he was afflicted and overwhelmed by sin; you belong to Christ, who was entirely free from sin through his resurrection, and in fact had committed no sin from the beginning of his life. For it was fitting that he should have from the beginning a claim to the immutable nature that he received in full at the resurrection. So it is that he confirms for us the resurrection from the dead and a share in his freedom from corruption.

The White Garment

26. As soon as you come up out of the font, you put on a dazzling garment of pure white. This is a sign of the world of shining splendor [see Matt 13:43] and the way of life to which you have already passed in symbol. When you experience the resurrection in reality and put on immortality and incorruptibility, you will not need such garments any longer; but you need them now, because you have not yet received these gifts in reality, but only in symbols and signs. . . .

Chrismation

[See General Introduction, "Anointing and the Holy Spirit."]

27. When you have received grace by means of baptism, then, and put on this shining white garment, the bishop comes to you and puts a seal on your forehead, saying: "N. is sealed in the name of the Father and of the Son and of the Holy Spirit." When Jesus came up out of the water, he received the grace of the Holy Spirit, which came and remained on him in the form of a dove. This is why he too is said to have been anointed by the Holy Spirit: "The Spirit of the Lord is upon me," he said, "and therefore the Lord has anointed me." [see Luke 4:18; Isa 61:1]. "Jesus of Nazareth, whom God anointed with the Holy Spirit and with power" [Acts 10:38]. This shows that the Holy Spirit never leaves him, just as the anointing attaches to those who are anointed by men with oil and never leaves them. You too, then, must be sealed on the forehead. While the bishop is putting the seal on you, he says: "N. is sealed in the name of the Father," etc. This sign shows you that, when the Father, the Son and the Holy Spirit were named, the Holy Spirit came upon you. You were anointed by him and received him by God's grace. He is yours and remains within you. You enjoy the first-fruits of him in this life, for you receive now in symbol the possession of the blessings to come. Then you will receive the grace in its fullness, and it will free you from death, corruption, pain and change; your body too will last for ever and will be free from decay, and your soul will not be liable to any further movement towards evil.

28. Such, then, is the second birth which we receive at baptism, and which you are now about to approach. We hope that this baptism will enable us to pass in reality to this dread birth of the resurrection. Baptism assures us of the resurrection, a resurrection which in signs and symbols we already enjoy sacramentally by faith.* The fact that we receive a double birth, and pass from the first to the second, need not surprise us, because even in our physical existence we receive a double birth, first from a man and then from a woman. First we are born from a man in the form of sperm. Everyone knows that the seed bears no resemblance to a human being until it has been conceived, shaped and brought to birth by a woman according to the laws of nature decreed by God.* So too at baptism we are born in seed, but not yet in the immortal nature which we hope to attain at the resurrection: we do not yet bear the least resemblance to it. But if in faith and hope of the future blessings we shape ourselves by a Christian life, when the time of the resurrection comes, according to God's decree we shall receive a second birth from the dust and assume this immortal and incorruptible nature. "Christ our Savior," says St. Paul, "will change our lowly body to be like his glorious body" [Phil 3:21].

29. When you have undergone the sacramental birth of baptism in this way, you will come forward to receive the food of immortality, the food that will be in keeping with your birth. On a later occasion you will be able to learn about this food and the way in which it is offered to you. But now at the end of this instruction you are going to receive the birth of baptism; you have come forward now to share in the indescribable light by means of this second birth. So for the moment our words have, so to speak, wound you tightly in swaddling bands to keep you in mind of this birth which is about to take place. Here, then, we shall let you rest in silence; at a suitable time we shall bring you to this divine food and explain it to you. But now let us end our address in the usual way, praising God the Father, his only-begotten Son and the Holy Spirit, now and for ever. Amen.

The Ordo of Constantinople

As the "new" Rome and the imperial capital from 330 on, Constantinople gradually became the cynosure for much of Eastern Christianity. Its oldest liturgical document is the *Ordo of Constantinople,* which in effect is a catechesis on the baptismal rite of the renunciation of Satan, technically known among the Greek-speaking Syrian Christians as "breaking ranks with Satan and entering the ranks of Christ" *(apotaxis/syntaxis)*. The manuscript is the *Barberini Euchologion* (dated 790).

The rite of renunciation, although detectable in a far simpler form at least as early as the second century in Egypt, achieved high profile in the fourth and fifth centuries, especially in Hellenized Syria. Such prominence (see General Introduction; also see vol. 6, ch. 1), which had its roots in the social and legal jeopardy of Christians in the pre-Constantinian period (to 311), bespeaks a Church much at odds with its social world in spite of official state toleration (311/313) and subsequent establishment (390).

In Chrysostom's Antioch the rite began at 3:00 P.M., the traditional time of Christ's death. In Constantinople it began at noon, the traditional beginning of the crucifixion—but little else has changed. The spirit of the homily owes much to Chrysostom, who was Patriarch of Constantinople from 397 to 407 (albeit deposed and exiled). The *Ordo* may date from his patriarchy; if not from his, then from the Patriarch Proclus (434–446).

The text is that of Antoine Wenger, SC 50 (1957) 84–90, which Wenger has corrected in the light of a fuller but unpublished eleventh-century manuscript in the Vatican Library (*Ottoboni graecus* 175). The translation is T. M. Finn, SCA 115, 114–118. I have summarized the rubrics and omitted the long final prayer.

The *Ordo of Constantinople:*
The Rite of Renunciation and Adherence

[The archbishop arrives at noon Holy Friday, directs the baptizands to remove their shoes and outer clothes, and then gives the following catechesis into which the rites that compose renunciation and adherence are woven.]

Catechesis. "Thus has come the end of your catechumenate and the time of your deliverance. Today you are going to bring to Christ the letter of your faith. Let us see, then, how you are going to sign your confession. Do not linger on the side in order not to be included. Those who are going to die make their last will and testament. They appoint another to inherit their goods. But you, also, you are going, tomorrow night, to die to sin. Now, then, you make your will and you make your testament, which is this renunciation. You appoint the devil heir to sin. You leave him your sins as a paternal heritage. If, then, any of you possesses something of the devil in his soul, let him get rid of it, for he who is about to die no longer has power over his own goods. Let no one among you have anything more belonging to the devil in his soul. It is for this reason that you hold yourself erect, hands stretched towards heaven, as if the angels were searching you, in order to find out whether there was still anything belonging to the devil on you. Let no one store up hatred, let no one nurse anger, let no one approach through deceit, let no one listen with hypocrisy. Cast onto the devil all corruption and every evil growth. Take the posture of captives, because it is as captives that Christ redeems you. Let each one of you breathe on the devil, looking at him full in the face, and hating him [the rite of exsufflation]. Search your consciences, scrutinize your hearts. Let each one see what he has done, and if there is anything in you belonging to the adversary, spit it out by exsufflation.

"Let no one here be a Jew by hypocrisy [i.e., a catechumen who observes the Torah], let no one have doubts about the mysteries. The word of God pierces your hearts more incisively than a two-edge sword. The devil now stands in the West, he grinds his teeth, his hair stands on end, he rings his hands and bites his lips, he is furious and he groans from his solitude, and he is unable to believe your deliverance. Thus Christ brings you face to face with him in order that you may renounce him and you breathe on him. Then you turn towards the East and enter into Christ's ranks.

"Stand in fear, for everything here is frightening and terrible. All the powers of heaven are present here. The angels and archangels invisibly write down your words. The cherubim and the seraphim open the heavens to receive your contracts and carry them to the Master. Pay attention, then, to the manner in which you renounce the enemy and attach yourself to the Creator."

[The archbishop then directs the baptizands individually to face the West and renounce "Satan, all his works, and all his angels, and all his seduction." They repeat the renunciation three times and then, with a hissing sound (exsufflation), show their contempt for Satan. The baptizands then face the East and say, "And I submit myself to Christ, and I believe in God, the Father Almighty (i.e., the full Nicene-Constantinopolitan baptismal Creed). They also repeat this submission to Christ three times, after which they are enjoined to adore God, while the archbishop prays: "Blessed be God who wills that all men be saved and come to the knowledge of the truth, now and always and forever and ever."]

After this he says: "Thus have you renounced the devil and submitted yourselves to Christ. The contract is made. The Master keeps it in heaven. Strive to observe its conditions. For this contract will be presented to you on the day of judgment. Do not lose the principal; on the contrary, add interest to it. See to it that you do not have to be ashamed before the terrible and frightening tribunal, when all the powers of heaven shall tremble and the entire human race will present itself to be judged. The myriads of angels will be drawn up there, the armies of archangels, the ranks of the powers from on high; the river of fire will be there, the worm which never dies, the exterior darkness, and also the contract. If you have been generous and merciful, your defenders will be those to whom you have shown mercy. But if you have been inhuman, avaricious, pitiless, proud, unjust to those who have done you no harm, then the devil shall rise up as the accuser: 'Lord,' he will say, 'This man has renounced me in words only; by his works he has always been my servant.' And the angels will groan, and all the just will weep for you. The resulting sentence is hard even to speak. Here below, when someone gets into trouble, he finds some defenders, he appeals to his friends, he is helped by his parents, he is saved by his wealth. There, nothing of the sort: neither helping father, nor mother moved to the depths, nor brother who responds, nor friends who hasten to help. But every man will be naked, alone, and without resources, helped or condemned only by his works, because 'if a brother does not rescue, what man will?' [see Ps 48:8]. See that you guard yourselves. You have renounced the devil, hate him until the end. You have submitted yourselves to Christ, confess him until your last breath. Die in this orthodox confession, and do not be shipwrecked in the faith. Have pity on the poor, do not scorn those who are victims of injustice; do not steal the goods of another, do not hurt the innocent, do not listen to profitless speech, defend your priests, and be provident in every circumstance.

"I have hesitated to say these hard things to you. Henceforth, you will know how to take care of yourselves. I have done the best that is in me. I have told you these awe-inspiring things in advance that the sword may not cut into this people and carry off one soul. For from now on, the enemy observes your words, your movements, and all your actions. Be on your guard, then, so that the adversary will have nothing to say against you on the day of judgment, and so that you may be able to stand without shame before the tribunal of Christ and hear that happy and desired sentence: 'Come blessed of my Father and take possession of the kingdom, prepared from the beginning of the world' [Matt 25:34]. To him belong glory, honor, and adoration, now and always and forever. Amen."

[Prayers follow, the theme of which is the baptismal illumination, which is shortly to come. The dismissal concludes the rite.]

Dionysius the Pseudo-Areopagite

In fifth-century Syria a body of works (the *Corpus Dionysianum*) appeared that claimed as their author an Athenian convert of Paul of Tarsus named Dionysius (see Acts 17:37). The *Corpus* includes works on theology, the *Divine Names;* on mysticism, the *Mystical Theology;* on spiritual beings, the *Celestial Hierarchy;* and on the Church, the *Ecclesiastical Hierarchy.* In addition, the *Corpus* contains ten fictional letters on a variety of theological and mystical topics. Although scholars reject the author's claim to the mantle of Dionysius, they generally agree that he was a Syrian Christian convert imbued with Greek (Neoplatonic) philosophy, quite possibly a student of Proclus, the pagan Neoplatonist who headed the Platonic Academy at Athens until his death in 485.

Dionysius (which may well have been his real name) sought to integrate his Neoplatonism and his Christian faith. In the process he developed a theology that had great impact throughout the Middle Ages in both East and West. Indeed, medieval thinkers accorded him a niche higher than any other Father of the Church save Augustine (vol. 6, ch. 2), and his name is inseparable from the history of Christian mysticism.

The *Ecclesiastical Hierarchy* is devoted to the rites of the Church as Dionysius knew them: baptism (called "illumination," 2), the Eucharist (3), consecration of the oils (4), priestly consecrations ("holy orders," 5), the order of monks (6), and the rites for the dead (7). The author's method is, first, to give a brief orientation to the subject at hand; second, to describe the rite of what he calls "the mystery"; and, third, to contemplate its inner meaning. The goal, both of rites and of instruction, is to lead the candidate from the realm of the "visible" to the "invisible" and "hidden." For Dionysius, Christian initiation is at once a journey of ascent into participative union with God and a withdrawal from the sensible into the spiritual (as other Neoplatonists like Augustine put it, "the eye of the soul") to find God, who is beyond being. Baptism, as first illumination, begins the ascent that achieves full illumination in the divine darkness "where truly dwells, as the oracles declare, the one who is beyond all being" (*Mystical Theology* 1, comment 4). In his contemplations he lays down the sacramental principle that the rites before him are so perfectly adapted to the human way that they lead one step by step from the surface of things to the depths where God is found. The *Ecclesiastical Hierarchy* is the first West Syrian document to record the use of consecrated oil in the consecration of the baptismal water. Coming, as it does, later than Theodore and the *Apostolic Constitutions* (and another Syrian document, the *Testament of Our Lord Jesus Christ*), it also registers a postbaptismal anointing.

The reading comprises the second chapter of the *Ecclesiastical Hierarchy* and is divided into three sections: (1) an orientation of the candidate to baptism as the indispensable means of becoming "godlike," (2) a description of the baptismal rites, and (3) a meditation that ascends from the visible rites to the divine realities, which, although embodied in the rites, lie beyond them in the world of the spirit. Notable for its absence is biblical typology.

The text is that of Johannes Quasten, FP 7 (1937); the translation, that of Thomas L. Campbell, *Dionysius the Pseudo-Areopagite: The Ecclesiastical Hierarchy,* Studies in Sacred Theology, 2nd ser., 83 (Washington: The Catholic University of America Press, 1955) 6–13, which also contains a valuable introductory study.

The *Ecclesiastical Hierarchy:* 2:1–3
What Is Accomplished by Illumination

We have reverently asserted that the scope of our hierarchy is assimilation and oneness with God as far as possible. As the divine Scriptures teach, we shall attain this only by the loving and pious observance of the most holy commandments. It says, "if anyone love me he will keep my word, and my Father will love him, and we will come to him and will make our abode with him'' [John 14:23]. What is the beginning of the sacred observance of the most august commandments? It consists in the fashioning of the dispositions of our soul for the most suitable reception of the other divine words and operations, in the preparation of the way for our ascent to supracelestial repose, in the conferring of our sacred and most divine regeneration. As our illustrious teacher said, the first movement of the soul to divine things is the love of God; but, the very first approach to the sacred observance of the divine commandments is the utterly ineffable operation through which we are made godlike.

Since to be godlike is divine regeneration, never would one know or perform anything received from God unless he had already begun to exist divinely. Humanly speaking is it not necessary that we first exist before we do what is according to our nature? He who does not exist at all has not motion, nor even substance. Whatever in some way exists does or suffers only those things within the limits of its existence. This, I think, is evident.

Now let us contemplate the divine symbols of rebirth in God. Let no un-initiated [unbaptized] person approach this spectacle because it is not safe to gaze on the rays of the sun with weak eyes, nor is it without danger to undertake things that are above us. The hierarchy of the Law was right when it rejected Ozias for touching the sacred things, Core for attempting sacred things beyond his power, Nadab and Abiud because they did not exercise holily the functions proper to them [see 2 Par 26:16-21; Num 16:1-33; Lev 10:1-2].

The Mystery of Illumination

1. Wishing that every single man be saved by assimilation to God and arrival at a knowledge of the truth, the bishop proclaims to all the truly ''Good News'' that God, in mercy towards men on earth, out of his own inherent goodness, deigned to come to us with arms outstretched in love for man. He deigned to assimilate the unified by union with himself in the manner of fire, proportionately to their aptitude for deification. ''But as many as received him he gave them power to be made the sons of God, to them that believe in his name; who are born, not of blood, nor of the will of the flesh . . . but of God'' [John 1:12-13].

2. Whoever desires sacred participation in these truly supramundane things goes to one of the initiated and persuades him to act as his guide on the way to the bishop. Then, he

promises to follow completely all the prescriptions, and asks
his sponsor to undertake the supervision of his introduction to
all that concerns his future life. Though piously desiring the
man's salvation, when the sponsor measures human frailty
against the sublimity of the undertaking, all at once he is seized
with fear and anxiety. Nevertheless, with good grace, he finally
promises to make the petition. He takes the man in charge and
leads him to the chief of the hierarchy.

3. Joyfully, the bishop receives the two men as sheep upon
his shoulders [see Luke 15:1-10]. First of all, he expresses his
gratitude, and then in spiritual thanksgivings and bodily pros-
tration praises the one beneficent Principle by whom those to
be called are called, and those to be saved are saved.

4. Then he assembles the whole of the sacred order in the
holy place to cooperate and rejoice together in the salvation
of this man, and to give thanks to the divine goodness. He begins
by chanting with all his clergy some hymn drawn from the Scriptures [Ps 133]. After this, when he has kissed the holy table,
he advances to the candidate standing before him and asks him
for what purpose has he come.

5. When, out of love for God, the candidate has confessed
his impiety, his lack of the divine life, and his ignorance of the
truly beautiful, in accordance with the instructions of his sponsor, he asks to attain to God and divine things through his holy
mediation. Whereupon the bishop proclaims to him that he
ought to approach God wholeheartedly, since [God] is abso-
lutely perfect and unblemished. After he has explained to him
the divine way of life, asked him if he would live in this manner, and received his consent, the bishop places his hand on
the candidate's head. When he has sealed him, he orders that
the priests register the candidate and his sponsor.

6. After the registration, the bishop offers a holy prayer.
When the whole church has finished this with him, he loosens
the sandals of the candidate and disrobes him with the help of
the deacons. When he has placed him facing west with his hands
stretched out in aversion in that direction, the bishop orders
the candidate to breathe out [i.e., exsufflation] upon Satan three
times, and further, to pronounce the formula of renunciation.
After witnessing his threefold renunciation, when he has pronounced it three times, the bishop turns him towards the east
as he is, looking up to heaven with hands upraised. Then the

bishop orders him to submit to Christ and to all the sacred teachings given us by God [see the above *Ordo*].

7. When he has done this, again the bishop witnesses for him his threefold profession. After he has confessed three times, the bishop prays, blesses him and imposes hands. Then, when the deacons have stripped the candidate completely, the priests bring forth the holy oil of chrism. The bishop begins the anointing with a triple sacred sealing and gives the man over to the priests for the anointing of the rest of his whole body. The bishop himself proceeds to the mother of filial adoption, sanctifies its water by sacred invocations, and consecrates it by a triple effusion of the most holy oil in the sign of the cross. Each time he pours the sacred oil, he intones the sacred hymn uttered by the prophets when inspired and rapt in God [Ps 28], and orders the candidate to be brought forward. When one of the priests has read his name and that of his sponsor from the lists in a loud voice, he is led over to the water by the priests, conducted by their hands to the hand of the bishop. While the priests near the bishop call out three times the name of the initiate standing in the water, the bishop, standing on an elevation, plunges him into the water, invoking at each of the three immersions and emersions of the initiate the threefold personality of the divine Beatitude. Then the priests take him in charge and confide him to his sponsor, the one in charge of his introduction. With his help they put appropriate clothing around the one being initiated, and lead him once more to the bishop, who, after he has sealed the man with the oil that produces most divine effects, declares him henceforth a partaker of the most sacred and sanctifying Eucharist.

8. When this is completed, the bishop rises again from his occupation with secondary matters to the contemplation of primary things, as one who at no time or in any way turns to anything foreign to his proper functions, but who always places himself under the inspiration of the divine Spirit by unceasing advance from the divine to the divine.

Contemplation

1. This initiation in the sacred symbols of divine regeneration contains nothing unbecoming or irreverent, nor does it contain any sensible image, but it reflects through natural images suitable to men enigmas of a contemplation worthy of God. Should it seem in any way imperfect, the power of the word

of God should persuade (even though the more divine account of the ceremonies were passed over in silence), since it works diligently and holily to effect the good life of the one who approaches. At the same time, by the physical purification proper to water, it announces to him in a more material way purification from every kind of evil through a virtuous and divine life. Even if the symbolic teaching of the initiations had nothing more divine, this would not be without religious value I think, since it introduces a discipline of a well-regulated life, and naturally suggests complete purification from an evil life through the cleansing of the whole body by water.

2. Let this be a spiritual introduction for the uninitiated, setting apart, as is right, sacred and purifying things from the profane, and apportioning to the orders the elevation proper to them in due measure. However, we who have contemplated the principles of initiation in holy elevations and have been instructed sacredly in these mysteries shall recognize of what stamps they are the reliefs and of what invisible things they are the images. As is clearly shown in the treatise entitled, *On Things Spiritual and Sensible* [a lost work of Dionysius], sensible sacred things are representations of the spiritual things to which they lead and show the way, while spiritual things are the principles and explanations of the sensible forms of our hierarchies.

3. Let us affirm, then, that the goodness of divine Beatitude is always the same in condition and object, bounteously dispensing the salutary rays of its own light upon all the spiritual visions. Whether the self-determined free-will of spirits withdraws from spiritual light through love of evil, closing the faculties of enlightenment which naturally lie within it, or shuts itself off from the light present to it, the light itself does not turn away, but continues to shine on the spirit though it is purblind. The light generously pursues what turns away from it. Or, should the spirit overstep the bounds of the vision proportionately assigned it and boldly undertake to gaze upon rays superior to its own sight, the light does nothing against the nature of light. However, the spirit, as imperfectly approaching the perfect, will not attain things foreign to it, but by rebelliously disdaining due proportion will fail through its own fault.

As I said, the divine light is always unfolded beneficently to the eyes of the spirit [faith]. It is in their power to seize it when it is present. It is always most ready for the communication of its properties in a manner worthy of God. To this model the divine bishop is fashioned, generously unfolding to all the luminous rays of his own divine teaching. In imitation of God, he is most ready to enlighten whoever comes to him, not showing any ill-will or unholy anger towards former defection or excess, but always divinely shining with hierarchical light on those who approach him in order and harmony, and in proportion to the aptitude of each for divine things.

4. Since God himself is the principle of the sacred order within which are the holy spirits who know themselves, he who is moved to the proper view of his own nature will himself see what he was in the beginning, and will receive this as the first sacred gift of his elevation to the light. Now, he who has looked well upon his own condition with unbiased eyes will escape from the gloomy recesses of ignorance. But, since he is uninitiated, he will not at once of his own accord desire the most perfect union and participation of God, but he will be raised up holily and in order, step by step, to the supremely divine summit, from things closest to him to things more advanced, and, once he has been initiated, from these to things higher still.

An image of this harmonious and holy order is the modesty of the candidate, the recognition of his own state, and his having someone as sponsor and guide on his path to the bishop. The divine Beatitude receives into participation of itself the man thus conducted and communicates to him its own light as a sort of sign [see Ps 4:7], making him godlike and a sharer in the inheritance and sacred order of godly men, of which the seal of the bishop given the candidate is the sacred symbol. The registering by the priests is an image of salvation that enlists him among those to be saved and places his sponsor and himself in the sacred commemorations, himself as a true lover and follower of a godlike guide on the life-giving journey to truth, and the sponsor as the unerring guide of the disciple along the paths God has traced out.

5. However, it is not possible to participate in wholly opposed things at one and the same time, nor is it possible for one who has had a certain communion with the One to lead a divided life as long as he holds on to the firm participation in the One. He must be invincible and persistent before all division of the uniform. This is what the tradition of the symbols reverently suggests when the candidate strips off his former life as it were, and loosens himself completely from the habits that belong to that life. It places him naked and barefoot looking towards the west, his hands thrust out in rejection of all communication in the darkness of evil, breathing out, as it were, the habit of

dissimilarity he had, and affirming his entire renunciation of what is opposed to deification. When he has thus become invincible and free, he is led towards the east where he clearly proclaims that his new status will be in the divine light and complete flight from evil. When he makes the sacred promises of his complete dedication to the One, he is unified through love of truth. I think it is quite evident to those learned in hierarchical matters that those who are spiritual possess the constancy of the godlike state through unbroken and vehement striving towards one thing, and by the eradication and annihilation of what is opposed to this. It does not suffice only to renounce all evil, but a manly steadfastness against deadly submission to it is also necessary. Nor, should he ever abandon his holy love of truth, but he must with all his power persistently and continually aspire to it, always working holily for his elevation to the sublimity of divine perfection.

6. In the hierarchical rites of initiation you find the exact images of these things. The godlike bishop starts the holy anointing and the priests under him finish the sacred ceremony of the chrism, symbolically calling the initiate to the holy contests in which, with Christ as judge, he will take part. As God, he is the promoter of the contest; as wise, he sets down its rules; as fair, he determines the awards suitable for the victors. But what is still more divine, as good, he enters into the contests beside them, fighting for their freedom and their victory over the forces of death and corruption. The initiated person will enter the contests joyfully since they are divine. He will remain faithful to the regulations of the wise One, and he will contend in accordance with them without transgression in the firm hope of meriting beautiful prizes, because he is enrolled under a good Lord and leader of the combat. When he has followed in the footsteps of the athlete first in goodness, and when he has overthrown the energies and powers opposed to his deification by struggles modeled on God's, to speak mystically, he will die with Christ to sin through baptism.

7. Consider attentively with me how very appropriately the symbols are adapted to the sacred rites. Since with us death is not an annihilation of our essence, as some imagine, but the separation of things that were joined together that leads the soul into what is for us the realm of the invisible (as if being deprived of the body, it becomes unseen, while the body, hidden in the earth as it were, by some kind of bodily alteration loses all trace of human form), the complete covering by water is appropri-

ately taken as an image of the death and darkness of the tomb. The symbolical teaching, therefore, reveals that the man baptized according to sacred rites imitates by his triple immersion in the water, in so far as divine imitation is granted to men, the supremely divine death of the life-giving Jesus who spent three days and three nights in the tomb, and in whom according to the mystical and secret tradition of the Scriptures the prince of this world found nothing [see John 14:30].

8. Next they put garments as white as light on the initiated, and because of his manly and godlike insensibility to what is opposed, on account of his constant inclination to the One, the disorderly is set in order, the formless takes on form, and the man is radiant with a life full of light. The most perfective anointing with oil makes the one initiated of sweet odor, since the holy perfection of divine regeneration unifies the initiated with the supremely divine Spirit. However, the spiritual commerce which makes perfect and of sweet odor I leave to those deemed worthy of sacred and deifying communion with the divine Spirit according to the spirit to recognize spiritually since it is most ineffable. At the conclusion of everything, the bishop calls the initiated to the most holy Eucharist, and grants him communion in the perfective mysteries.

Chapter 2
East Syria

The origin and development of Syriac-speaking Christianity is many stranded. Tracing the strands, however, is at best a tentative enterprise, because the literary sources, often anonymous, are difficult to place, and the historical figures, often enigmatic, are shrouded in legend or personal reserve. Nonetheless, modern scholarship provides some points of orientation.

About origins, Syriac Christianity has long retained characteristics that point to (1) an early break with the synagogue, (2) a thoroughly Jewish Christianity in the early years, and (3) Jews and Christians socially connected until the fourth century. The Christianity we meet in the first authors who can be known directly through their works—Aphrahat (ca. 275–360) and Ephrem (ca. 306–373)—is orthodox. It may have emerged as the dominant form of Christianity in regions of Nisibis (Nusyabin, Syria) and Edessa (Urfa, Turkey) only in the fourth century. Edessa, already well populated with Christians (see below, the *Acts of Judas Thomas*), succeeded Nisibis as the center in 363. At that time many Christians fled the city (see below, Aphrahat and Ephrem) because Rome had ceded Nisibus to the Persians, and the departure of the Christians was part of the peace settlement. Whatever the dislocations, Syriac-speaking Christians and Jews continued to share traditions of biblical interpretation and piety, and Christians remained deeply Semitic in outlook and patterns of thought—a fact of considerable importance for understanding the allusive and symbolic character of Syriac Christian literature.

The fifth and sixth centuries heralded a cultural shift marked by Hellenization. The Greek Bible gained great prestige alongside the (Syriac) Peshitta in the Syriac Church, and Greek learning, especially philosophical and theological, entered the Syriac Christian schools. One important cause was the controversy about the humanity and divinity of Christ, which led to the councils of Ephesus (431) and Chalcedon (451) and ultimately to the divisions between the disciples of Theodore of Mopsuestia (ch. 1), among whom were Nestorius and Narsai (below), those of Chalcedon, and those who emphasized the divine nature of Christ (see below, Jacob of Serugh; also see vol. 6, ch. 3, Coptic Rite), sometimes called, often inaccurately, "Monophysites." The debates necessarily focused on the Greek text of the New Testament rather than the Syriac version and required the philosophical and theological precision native to the Greek-speaking Christian heritage. The resulting divisions were sealed by the Islamic invasions of the seventh century, which finally severed the Greek- and Latin-speaking Christian world from Syriac and Coptic Christianity.

Characteristics

Ancient Syriac Christianity had distinctive characteristics. Pervasive in the extant literature is an enthusiasm for the ascetic, specifically for abstinence from meat, alcohol, and sexual relations. In its more extreme forms, Syrian asceticism gave birth to encratite (self-mastery) groups like the *Aquarii,* who substituted water for wine in the Eucharist, and the Manicheans, who numbered among themselves for a period Augustine of Hippo (vol. 6, ch. 2). Their founder, Mani (ca. 216–276), was raised among Syriac Jewish Christians known as the Elkesaites, who equated matter and evil.

The heart of Syriac Christian asceticism appears to have been dedication to a life of celibacy and, for the married, renunciation of sexual relations. The second-century community reflected in the *Acts of Judas Thomas* (below) seems to have been just such a group. A similar, apparently celibate evaluation of Christian life permeates the *Odes of Solomon* (below) and the *Gospel According to Philip* (below). Aphrahat, himself a celibate, addresses at least ten of his *Demonstrations* to his ascetic colleagues. So also Ephrem, who lived in a community of ascetics.

Syriac has a term for these ascetics, "Covenanters" *(bnay qyama),* which first appears in Aphrahat. Indeed, his sixth treatise (*Demonstration* 6) might be called broadly the "Rule for the

Covenanters." In addition to virginity and continence, they were to be of firm and exemplary faith, seasoned in the right use of speech, modest and simple in dress and adornment, temperate in food and drink, reserved in social intercourse, generous with possessions, especially in almsgiving, sensitive to others and guarded of tongue, able but not ready to reprove, prepared to beg where necessary, and capable of dialogue with those outside the Church. Although not coextensive with the Syriac-speaking Church, the Covenanters appear to have been its heart. They lived at home, or away from home with a companion or two, or in small groups and larger communities. They were baptized before the ordinary people (at least in Aphrahat's time), and the sacrament was their special moment of commitment; within its complex of rites the renunciation of Satan and profession of allegiance to Christ may have constituted the liturgical moment of the covenant. Syriac Christians stood in close cultural and linguistic proximity to the biblical world and tradition, carrying on the "covenant" consciousness of Israel. They viewed the covenant as embodied first in Israel and subsequently in Christ, in the Church, and in the Covenanters. Since the extant Syriac literature is largely by and for such ascetics, it would be a mistake to conclude that marriage was not an option for Syriac Christians, the silent majority of whom were doubtless married.

A second characteristic is the symbolic poetry that pervades Syriac Christian literature. The imagery turns on axial biblical events and figures (Creation and Adam, Abraham, Moses and Exodus, crossing the Jordan into the Promised Land, priesthood and kingship), sometimes, as noted in the General Introduction ("The Bible and the Baptismal Liturgy"), called "types," sometimes "images," sometimes "symbols," sometimes "mysteries." Whatever the term, the world-view behind Syriac typology is that the "old" event (Creation or Exodus or crossing the Jordan, for instance) paves the way for the "new" (Christ's incarnation, his baptism, Christian baptism), in which the old achieves its promise. Thus, the way for the baptism of Christ in the Jordan was paved by the Spirit "hovering" over the waters at creation and turning the waters of the Red Sea and Jordan back upon themselves during the Exodus and the entry into the Promised Land. These events achieve their promise for salvation when Christ enters the Jordan with the very same Spirit hovering over him, anoint-

ing him as priest, king, and beloved Son. Further, the space and
time of history coalesce with the space and time of heaven, so
that the events of heaven (Christ's resurrection, for instance) and
those of earth intersect at baptism. The effect is that what happened at Christ's baptism in the Jordan (and in his post-Jordan
life) now happens to the newly coming-to-birth Christian in the
baptismal anointing and immersion in the font.

Like typology elsewhere in early Christianity, Syriac typological thinking invites the participant to enter into and experience
salvation. What is truly distinctive is the vehicle, that is, the hymn
and the metrical homily (see below, Ephrem, Narsai, and Jacob
of Serugh). Although these forms originate in the Semitic culture
of Mesopotamia and are conditioned by the Jewish tradition of
"oral Torah" as well as by groups like the followers of Bardaisan (155–222) and the Manicheans, the hymn and homily permeate Syriac Christian literature from Ephrem on.

A third characteristic is the role of the Holy Spirit. Although
there are a variety of terms, the usual *ruha* (spirit) is feminine.
The dominant image is that the Spirit "hovers" and is the source
of fruitfulness, whether of the water, the oil, the bread and wine,
or even of the type and the symbol. It is the same Spirit at Creation, Exodus, and the Jordan crossing who descends on Christ
in the Jordan, uniting all four events. Indeed, it is the same Spirit
hovering over the baptismal font who makes of its waters those
of the Jordan, of the Red Sea, and of Genesis. When one enters
the baptismal stream of salvation, "then" is "now" and "now"
is "then." The Spirit is link.

Baptismal Liturgy

For Syriac-speaking Christianity the pattern of salvation was
established in the baptism of Christ and is replicated in every baptism. As a result, the core of the baptismal rite is a twofold anointing, first of the head and then of the whole body, followed by
baptismal immersion and then the Eucharist. The anointing, however, is central, as in West Syria, because it replicates in sign and
symbol the Spirit's anointing of Christ as priest, king, and Son.
As a result, the newly anointed is seen as marked with the "mark"
(rushma) of Christ, just as the Israelite is marked with the sign
of circumcision. Indeed, baptism as the seal, as already noted in
the General Introduction ("Anointing and the Holy Spirit"), is

a common Syriac Christian way of speaking of the rite—the new and inner circumcision (see below, Aphrahat). Differences and developments are noted in the selected readings, but this core is invariable until the sixth century, when a postbaptismal anointing begins to appear.

Unlike Rome, Africa, and Egypt, early Syriac tradition does not address the question of infant baptism. Adult baptism is the norm, and the baptismal rites embrace those brought up in Christian as well as pagan homes (so Aphrahat and Ephrem). Occasionally, a Jew would come to seek baptism, but the evidence, at least from Egypt and West Syria, suggests that Christians were far more likely to seek out the synagogue than Jews to seek out the Church. Whichever the direction taken, however, whether toward synagogue or Church, their long-shared traditions would surely have been inviting.

An early Armenian catechism is included because Syriac-speaking Christianity appears to have been the decisive influence in Armenian institutional life, especially in its liturgy and catechesis. Although the *Teaching of St. Gregory* (below) shows wide familiarity with West Syrian Fathers, its ambience is clearly East Syrian.

Valuable studies are those of Robert Murray, "The Characteristics of Earliest Syriac Christianity," in Nina Garosian, and others, eds., *East of Byzantium: Syria and Armenia in the Formative Period* (Washington: Dumbarton Oaks, 1982) 3–16, and his *Symbols of Church and Kingdom* (Cambridge, England: The University Press, 1975); Sebastian Brock, *The Holy Spirit in the Syrian Baptismal Tradition,* The Syrian Churches Series 9, ed. Jacob Vellian (Poona, India: Anita, 1979); and Jacob Vellian, ed., *Studies on Syrian Baptismal Rites,* The Syrian Church Series 6, ed. Jacob Vellian (Kottyam: C.M.S. Press, 1973).

The Odes of Solomon

The *Odes,* a collection of forty-two hymns, constitute perhaps the earliest Christian hymnal as well as the earliest nonbiblical book in Syriac. It may, however, have first been composed in Greek. Although dates ranging from the first to the third century are given, the second century seems right. Both Antioch and

Edessa are proposed as the place of origin, with the latter preferred.

The setting of the work is worship, especially baptism, and the
distinctive themes and characteristics discussed in the introduction above abound in a number of the hymns. In the first reading (*Ode* 11), themes that recur frequently in the hymns make their
appearance: baptism as circumcision; the "Way" as a very early
name for the Christian community and reminiscent of the "Two
Ways" catechesis in the *Didache* (ch. 1); the living waters that
beget new life; stripping off the old and putting on Christ, the
new garment; baptismal enlightenment; the streams of baptism
and the return to Paradise.

In the kaleidoscope of images in the second reading (*Ode* 19),
for instance, the Holy Spirit is feminine, the Father is double
breasted, and baptism as a new begetting lies allusively beneath
the image of the conception and birth of Christ.

The final reading (*Ode* 42) is the last hymn of the collection,
chosen because its undergirding theme is Christ's death, burial,
descent into Sheol, and resurrection, which together make of baptism a saving event. From his entombment Christ descends into
Sheol, the very place of death, to liberate the just there
immersed—the celebrated "Harrowing of Hell" first broached
in 1 Peter 3:19 and addressed repeatedly in Syriac literature and
in Cyril of Jerusalem's fourth and tenth prebaptismal instructions.
Just so, Christ descends into the tomb of the baptismal waters
in which the candidates are immersed. In liberating them, he seals
them on the head with the mark of his ownership.

The baptismal liturgy that stands behind the *Odes* is difficult
to discern with any degree of clarity because of their allusive quality. Nonetheless, it almost surely consisted of catechetical instruction, the double anointing, immersion coupled with the Trinitarian
form, vesting in a white garment, and the Eucharist, in which a
cup of milk mixed with honey and a cup of water were also administered (see vol. 6, ch. 1, Hippolytus; also see vol. 6, ch. 2,
Tertullian).

The text is that of James H. Charlesworth, ed., The *Odes of
Solomon* (Oxford: Clarendon, 1973); the translation is also that
of Charlesworth, ed., *The Old Testament Pseudepigrapha* vol.
2 (Garden City: Doubleday, 1985), 752–753, 744–746, 770–771.

Ode 11

My heart was pruned and its flower appeared,
then grace sprang up in it,
and it produced fruits for the Lord.

For the Most High circumcised me by his Holy Spirit,
then he uncovered my inward being toward him,
and filled me with his love.

And his circumcising became my salvation,
and I ran in the Way in his peace,
in the Way of truth.

From the beginning until the end
I received his knowledge.

And I was established upon the rock of truth,
where he had set me.

And speaking waters touched my lips
from the spring of the Lord generously.

And so I drank and became intoxicated,
from the living water that does not die.

And my intoxication was not with ignorance;
but I abandoned vanity;

And turned toward the Most High, my God,
and was enriched by his favors.

And I abandoned the folly cast upon the earth,
and stripped it off and cast it from me.

And the Lord renewed me with his garment,
and possessed me by his light.

And from above he gave me immortal rest;
and I became like the land which blossoms and rejoices in its
    fruits.

And the Lord [is] like the sun
upon the face of the land.

My eyes were enlightened,
and my face received the dew;

And my breath was refreshed
by the pleasant fragrance of the Lord.

And he took me to his Paradise,
wherein is the wealth of the Lord's pleasure.

(I contemplated blooming and fruit-bearing trees,
and self-grown was their crown.

Their branches were flourishing
and their fruits were shining;
their roots [were] from an immortal land.

And a river of gladness was irrigating them,
and the region round about them in the land of eternal life.)

Then I adored the Lord because of his magnificence.

And I said, blessed, O Lord, are they
who are planted in your land,
and who have a place in your Paradise;

And who grow in the growth of your trees,
and have passed from darkness into light.

Behold, all your laborers are fair,
they who work good works,
and turn from wickedness to your kindness.

For they turned away from themselves the bitterness of the trees,
when they were planted in your land.

And everyone was like your remnant.
(Blessed are the workers of your water,)
and the eternal memorial of your faithful servants.

Indeed, there is much room in your Paradise.
And there is nothing in it which is barren,
but everything is filled with fruit.

Praise be to you, O God, the delight of Paradise for ever.

Hallelujah.

Ode 19

A cup of milk was offered to me,
and I drank it in the sweetness of the Lord's kindness.

The Son is the cup,
and the Father is he who was milked;
and the Holy Spirit is she who milked him;

Because his breasts were full,
and it was undesirable that his milk should be released without
    purpose.

The Holy Spirit opened her bosom,
and mixed the milk of the two breasts of the Father.

Then she gave the mixture to the generation without their
knowing,
and those who have received [it] are in the perfection of the
right hand.

The womb of the Virgin took [it],
and she received conception and gave birth.

So the Virgin became a mother with great mercies.

And she labored and bore the Son but without pain,
because it did not occur without purpose.

And she did not seek a midwife,
because he caused her to give life.

She bore as a strong man with desire,
and she bore according to the manifestation,
and possessed with great power.

And she loved with salvation,
and guarded with kindness,
and declared with greatness.

Hallelujah.

Ode 42

I extended my hands and approached my Lord,
because the stretching out of my hands is his sign.

And my extension is the common cross,
that was lifted upon the way of the Righteous One.

Christ Speaks

And I became useless to those who knew me [not],
because I shall hide myself from those who possessed me not.

And I will be with those
who love me.

All my persecutors have died,
and they who trusted in me sought me, because I am living.

Then I arose and am with them,
and will speak by their mouths.

For they have rejected those who persecute them;
and I threw over them the yoke of my love.

Like the arm of the bridegroom over the bride,
so is my yoke over those who know me.

And as the bridal feast is spread out by the bridal pair's home,
so is my love by those who believe in me.

I was not rejected although I was considered to be so,
and I did not perish although they thought it of me.

Sheol saw me and was shattered,
and Death ejected me and many with me.

I have been vinegar and bitterness to it,
and I went down with it as far as its depth.

Then the feet and the head it released,
because it was not able to endure my face.

And I made a congregation of living among his dead;
and I spoke with them by living lips;
in order that my word may not fail.

And those who had died ran toward me;
and they cried out and said, "Son of God, have pity on us.

"And deal with us according to your kindness,
and bring us out from the chains of darkness.

"And open for us the door
by which we may go forth to you,
for we perceive that our death does not approach you.

"May we also be saved with you,
because you are our Savior."

Then I heard their voice,
and placed their faith in my heart.

And I placed my name upon their head,
because they are free and they are mine.

Hallelujah.

The *Gospel According to Philip*

As the *Odes* suggest, there were many strains of early Christianity. The *Gospel According to Philip,* found in 1946 among the library of texts discovered in Egypt at Nag Hammadi, represents a very important strain. The work is an anthology of some one hundred short excerpts taken from Gnostic Christian works, largely from the Valentinian school of Gnostics. The compiler, the place of the compilation, and the purpose of the work are unknown, though some scholars have placed it in East Syria, citing Edessa as a strong possibility. The material is generally regarded as second century.

Gnostics were active from the mid-second century (some think well before), especially in Italy, Egypt, Syria, and Mesopotamia. Their self-designation was *gnostikos* (gnostic), an unusual name meaning roughly "leading to knowledge." The knowledge they sought *(gnosis)* was not information but the understanding that comes from personal encounter, specifically personal encounter with God—in short, "saving knowledge." Gnostics could be distinguished from other Christians because of their (1) distinctive myth of origins based on the myth of beginnings in the *Timaeus* of Plato and combined with the Book of Genesis; (2) strong sense of superiority and group identity; (3) intense subjectivity; (4) thoroughly allegorical approach to Scripture, ritual, and creed; and (5) deep sense of alienation from the world of matter and the physical.

Among the most influential early Gnostics was the Alexandrian Valentinus, who headed a movement within the second-century Church that took the form of a network of philosophical schools, spreading rapidly both east and west. Although the Valentinians would eventually be forced to separate from the ordinary (i.e., orthodox or Catholic) Christian congregations (ca. 200), they nonetheless were nourished by the same Scriptures, rule of faith, and sacraments and stood within the Church as a distinctive interpretation of Christianity.

Like the *Excerpts of Theodotus* (vol. 6, ch. 3), also an anthology, the *Gospel According to Philip* is Valentinian, the work of theological poets and a compiler, most likely in Syria east of Antioch. Rather than attempting to establish a consistent body of religious thought, they sought to discover the underlying and hidden meaning of their Christianity, especially of the "mysteries" (sacraments). The Valentinian view about the externals of ritual held that what one could see was but the clothing of the true. As "Philip" puts it, "Truth did not come to the world nakedly; rather, it came in prototypes and images: the world will not accept it in any other form" (59). Although one of the texts (60) speaks of five mysteries (baptism, anointing, Eucharist, the bridal chamber, and redemption), the excerpts that follow are reflections largely on anointing, baptism, and the Eucharist. The bridal chamber *(nymphon)* and redemption are very likely allegorical symbols for the advanced stages of saving enlightenment rather than for rites; enlightenment was the goal toward which the first three rites moved. With respect to the baptismal liturgy, it would have been little different, if at all, from that of the *Odes*.

The text is the critical edition of Bentley Layton, in vol. 21 of *Nag Hammadi Codex II, 27, Together with XIII, 2*, Brit. Lib. Or. 4926 (1) and P. Oxy. 1, 654, 655,* Nag Hammadi Studies (Leiden: E. J. Brill, in press). The translation is also Layton, *The Gnostic Scriptures: A New Translation with Annotations and Introductions* (Garden City: Doubleday, 1987) 329–353. The volume also contains the most recent accessible studies on both Gnosticism and Philip. The dots (. . .) indicate gaps in the text.

The *Gospel According to Philip*
Baptismal Selections

22

Baptism and chrism

By water and fire the entire place is sanctified—the visible [elements of it] by the visible, the hidden by the hidden. • Some [elements] are hidden by the visible: • there is water within water, there is fire within chrism.

37

God's dyes

God is a dyer. • Just as the good dyes called "true" dyes dissolve into the things that have been dyed in them, even so the things that god has dyed become imperishable through his colors, inasmuch as his dyes are imperishable. • Yet those whom god dips, he dips in water.

41

The pearl in the mud

If a pearl is cast into the mud, it will not be less valuable. • Also, if it is anointed with balsam it will not become more valuable. • Rather, it always has its value for its owner. • Just so, the children of god still have their value for their father, whatever the circumstances in which they live.

47

The lord's dyes

The lord entered the dye works of Levi, and took seventy-two hues and cast them into the caldron. • He brought them all out white. • And he said, "For this did the child of the human being come—to be a dyer."

51
Baptism and the name Christian

Anyone who goes down into the water and comes up without having received anything and says, "I am a Christian," has borrowed the name. But one who receives the holy spirit has the gift of the name. • Anyone who has received a gift will not have it taken away. • But one who has borrowed something will have it taken back. • So it is with us, if something comes to pass through a mystery.

58
Otherworldly fire

Soul and spirit are constituted of water and fire; a bridegroom's attendant is constituted of water, fire, and light. • Fire is chrism; light is fire—I do not mean worldly fire, which has no form, but another kind of fire, whose appearance is white, which is beautifully luminous, and which bestows beauty.

59
Resurrection an image of the return

Truth did not come to the world nakedly; rather, it came in prototypes and images: • the world will not accept it in any other form. • Rebirth exists along with an image of rebirth: • by means of this image one must be truly reborn. • Which image? Resurrection. • An image must arise by means of image. • By means of this image, the bridal chamber and the image must embark upon the realm of truth, that is, embark upon the return. • Not only must those who produce the names of father, son, and holy spirit do so, but also [those who] have acquired these. • If someone does not acquire them, the name too will be taken from that person. • But if one gets them in the chrism of [. . .] • of the force of the cross, which the apostles called right and left. • For this person is no longer a Christian but rather is Christ [anointed].

60
The five sacraments

The lord [did] all things by means of a mystery: baptism, chrism, eucharist, ransom, and bridal chamber.

67

Baptism

We are reborn by the holy spirit. • And we are born by the anointed [Christ] through two things. • We are anointed by the spirit. • When we were born we were joined. • No one can see himself in the water or in a mirror without light. • Nor, again, can you see by the light without water or a mirror. • For this reason it is necessary to baptize with two things—light and water. • And light means chrism.

68

An allegory of the Temple: baptism, ransom, bridal chamber

There were three offering places in Jerusalem: • one opening to the west and called the holy; • another open to the south and called the holy of the holy; • the third open to the east and called the holy of holies, into which the high priest alone could enter. • The holy building is baptism, the holy of the holy is ransom, the holy of holies is the bridal chamber. • [Baptism] possesses resurrection [and] ransom; ransom is in the bridal chamber. • [The] bridal chamber is within what is superior to [. . .] its [. . .] is like [. . .] those who pray [. . .] Jerusalem [. . .] Jerusalem [. . .] Jerusalem, expecting [. . .] who are called [the holy] of the holies [. . .] veil rent [. . .] bridal bedroom except for the image [. . .] above. • Thus, its veil was torn from top to bottom, because certain people from below had to ascend.

72

The arrival of Jesus in the world

Jesus appeared [. . .] Jordan, the fullness [of the] kingdom of heavens. The person who [was born] before all things was reborn; the one anointed in the beginning was reanointed; the one who had been ransomed ransomed others in turn.

78

Baptism and righteousness

[. . .] go down into the water [. . .] ransom him [. . .] those who [. . .] in his name. • For he said, "[It is thus] that we shall fulfill all righteousness."

79

One must acquire resurrection now through baptism

People who say they will first die and then arise are mistaken. If they do not first receive resurrection while they are alive, once they have died they will receive nothing. • Just so it is said of baptism: "Great is baptism!" • For if one receives it, one will live.

80
Joseph and the wood of the cross

Philip the apostle said: "Joseph the carpenter planted a paradise, for he needed wood for his trade. • It is he who made the cross from the trees that he had planted, and its seed hung from what he had planted: the seed was Jesus, and the plant was the cross. • But the tree of life is in the midst of paradise, • and from the olive tree comes chrism; and from the latter comes resurrection."

83
Chrism, baptism, bridal chamber

Chrism has more authority than baptism. • For because of chrism we are called Christians, not because of baptism. • And the anointed [Christ] was named for chrism, • for the father anointed the son; • and the son anointed the apostles, and the apostles anointed us. • Whoever has been anointed has everything: resurrection, light, cross, holy spirit; • the father has given it to that person in the bridal chamber, and the person has received [it]. • The father existed in the son, and the son existed in the father. • This [is the] kingdom of heavens.

84
Outward signs of the sacraments

Well did the lord say, "Some have gone into the kingdom of heavens laughing. • And they came out [. . .] for a Christian [. . .]. • And [. . . go] down into the water, [. . .] all [. . .] it is a trifle, but [. . .] despise [. . .] kingdom of [heavens . . .] if he despises [. . .] and he despises it as a trifle [. . .] forth laughing." • Just so are the bread and the cup and the oil, even though there are ones higher than these.

86
Consecrated water in the eucharist and baptism

The cup of prayer contains wine and contains water, • being established as a representation of the blood over which thanksgiving is offered. And it is full of the holy spirit, • and belongs entirely to the perfect human being. • Whenever we drink it we take unto ourselves the perfect human being.

The living water is a body. • It befits us to put on the living human being; • accordingly, when one is about to descend into the water, one strips naked in order to put that one on.

90

The garment of light

The perfect human being not only cannot be restrained, • but also cannot be seen—• for if something is seen it will be restrained. • In other words, no one can obtain this grace without putting on the perfect light [and] becoming, as well, perfect light. • Whoever has [put it] on will go [. . .]. • This one is the perfect [. . .] that we be [. . .] before we have come [. . .]. • Whoever receives all things [. . .] hither, can [. . .] there, but will [. . . the] midpoint, as being imperfect. • Only Jesus is acquainted with that person's end!

92

Baptism and death

Just as Jesus perfected the water of baptism, so too he drew off death. • For this reason we go down into the water • but not into death, so that we are not poured out into the wind of the world. • Whenever the latter blows, winter comes: • whenever the holy spirit blows, summer comes.

94

The fragrance of spiritual perfume

Spiritual love is wine and perfume. • Those who anoint themselves with it all have the use of it, as do also those who are outside their company so long as the anointed ones stand there. • When those anointed with ointment leave them and depart, the ones who are not anointed but are only outside their company still remain within their fragrance. • The Samaritan gave nothing to the man who had been beaten except wine and oil, which means none other than ointment. • And it healed the wounds, • "since love covers a multitude of sins."

106

Revelation of the spiritual seed

Insofar as the seed of the holy spirit is hidden, evil—though inert—has not been removed from its midst, • and members of it are enslaved to wickedness. • But when this seed is revealed, then perfect light will stream forth upon each person, • and all who belong to it will [be] anointed. • Then the slaves will be free [and] captives ransomed. • "Every plant that my father in the heavens has not planted [will be] rooted up." Those who are separated will join [. . .] will become full.

107

Reception of the garment of light

Every person who [enters] the bedroom will kindle the [light.] For [. . .] like the marriages that are [. . .] be night. • The fire [. . .] night, is extinguished. • However, the mysteries of that marriage are performed in day and light; • and that day, or rather its light, does not set. • If someone becomes a bridegroom's attendant, that person will receive the light. • If one does not receive it while here, one cannot receive it elsewhere.

Whoever receives that light will be invisible and cannot be restrained. And nothing can harass such a person even while living in the world. And, furthermore, when that person leaves this world, he or she has already received the truth in the form of images, • and the world has already become the eternal realm. • For, to this person the eternal realm is fullness • and, as such, is manifest to him or her alone—• hidden not in darkness and night but hidden in perfect day and holy light.

The Acts of Judas Thomas

A legendary figure, Didymus Judas Thomas, apostle of the East, is credited with the conversion of northern Mesopotamia and India to Christianity. His middle name, Judas, is his personal name; Didymus, which means "twin" in Greek, signals that he was thought to be Jesus' identical twin brother, to whom a body of work called the "Thomas literature" is attributed—the *Gospel According to Thomas,* the *Book of Thomas (the Contender),* the *Hymn of the Pearl,* and the *Acts of Judas Thomas.*

The literature emanated from northern Mesopotamia, most likely Edessa, in the second and third centuries, authored by the members of a group sometimes called the "school" of St. Thomas. Indeed, Edessa possessed a relic of Judas Thomas that the Western ascetic Egeria (ch. 1) saw during her late fourth-century pilgrimage. The authors appear to have been bilingual, because versions of the Thomas literature circulated in both Greek and Syriac almost simultaneously.

Originally written in Syriac, the *Acts* is one of a set of apocryphal acts, among which are the *Acts of Peter,* the *Acts of*

Paul, and the *Acts of John.* Its influence is attested by the fact that versions are extant in Arabic, Armenian, Coptic, Ethiopic, and Latin. The work is composed of thirteen "acts," which recount the missionary exploits of the Apostle Judas (Thomas) in India. They appear to be based on two cycles of the Thomas tradition, which seek to establish the authenticity of early Indian Christianity. One seems to have originated in eastern Iran and the Indus valley; the other, in southern India. The subcontinent, as legend has it, falls to Thomas' lot in the apostolic division of mission territory. He is so unwilling to go (Doubting Thomas?) that Christ has to sell him into slavery to an Indian merchant (chs. 1–2). Once launched on his mission, however, the apostle succeeds remarkably well in converting the Indian royalty who people the accounts: King Gundaphar; Mygdonia, the wife of Karish, kinsman of King Mazdai, and her slave Narkia; Sifur, the king's general, and his family; and the king's wife, son, and daughter-in-law. Finally the king, after he executes Thomas, is converted through the relic of the martyr.

The author repeatedly makes the point that Thomas embodies Jesus (he is his twin), and like Jesus, his invincible strategy, which also includes martyrdom, is a combination of miracle, message, and instructions of a predominantly moral-exhortation and wisdom-saying character. The result is conversion, which necessarily leads to baptism, of which there are five accounts (chs. 25–28, 47–50, 119–121, 131–133, 156–158). In each case a commitment to celibacy or, for the married, abstinence from sexual relations is a precondition, indicating that the Thomas school of Christianity was in the tradition from which arose the Covenanters, discussed in the above introduction.

The liturgical structure one can draw from the five accounts includes (1) preaching and teaching plus miracles (a catechumenate?), which dispose the candidate for faith; (2) struggle against powerful personal ties and obligations; (3) ritual stripping; (4) anointing of the head in the sign of the cross; (5) full anointing of the body; (6) a prayer (epiclesis) calling Jesus and the Spirit (called the "Spirit of Holiness") to effect the mystery (sometimes one precedes both the anointing and the baptism); (7) immersion in the name of the Trinity; (8) revesting (perhaps in a white garment); and (9) the Eucharist coupled with a baptismal exhortation. One account (27) hints that the newly baptized were given lighted tapers, and another (46–50) associates exorcism with baptism as a preliminary. There was no renunciation of Satan.

The first reading (Wright, pp. 256–259) recounts the baptism of Mygdonia and Narkia, whose conversions form the axis on which the work turns. The second reading (pp. 266–268), the baptism of Sifur and his family, contains a brief homily on the effects of baptism. The third (pp. 277–279) and fourth (pp. 288–290) are respectively a hortatory creedal instruction, which concludes with the Lord's Prayer and an invocation to Jesus, the Messiah, to come down upon the candidates, on the anointing oil, and on the Eucharist (an epiclesis). The Syriac text is that of William Wright, ed., *Apocryphal Acts of the Apostles* (London: 1871); his translation, which he intended to be rigorously literal, has been modernized with restraint. A helpful study is that of A. F. J. Klijn, *The Acts of Thomas: Introduction, Text, Commentary* (Leiden: Brill, 1962), which also contains Wright's translation.

The Conversion of Mygdonia and Narkia

And while Mygdonia was meditating these things, Judas came and entered in behind her. And she was afraid, and fell down from terror; and he stood over her, and said to her: "Do not be afraid, Mygdonia; Jesus the Messiah will not forsake you, and your Lord will not forsake you, to whom you have committed your soul; the Gracious will not forsake you, whose mercy is great; the Benignant will not forsake you for his kindness' sake; the Good will not forsake you for his goodness' sake; the Great will not forsake you for his greatness' sake. Rise from the ground, above which you once were (raised). Look upon the light of your Lord, for he will not let those that love him walk in darkness. Behold the Companion of his servants, to whom he is a light in darkness. Behold the Help of his servants, to whom he is a helper in afflictions."

And Mygdonia arose, and was looking at him and saying to him: "Where were you going, my Lord? And who let you out of prison to see the sun?" Judas said to her: "Our Lord Jesus the Messiah is stronger than all powers and kings and rulers; he opened the doors and lulled the keepers to sleep." Mygdonia said to him: "Give me the sign of Jesus the Messiah, and let me receive his gift from your hands, before you depart from the world." And she took him, and went and entered into her house, and awakened her nurse, and said to her: "My mother and nurse Narkia, all your deeds of help to me, and your kindnesses from my childhood until now, you have done to me in vain, and my fleeting favor I bestow upon you for them; but do me this favor which [lasts] for ever, and you shall be rewarded by him who gives everything to his, and fortune cannot deprive them (thereof)." Narkia says to her: "What do you want, my daughter Mygdonia? And what comfort can you have? For all the former honors, [which] you promised to do to me, the strange man does not let you (do), and you have made me a reproach in this country. Now, I pray you, what do you want to do anew to me?" She said to her: "Be with me a sharer in the everlasting life, and let me receive from you the perfect education. Fetch secretly for me a loaf of bread, and bring out for me a mingled draught of wine, and have pity upon me a freeborn woman." Narkia said to her: "I will fetch you bread in plenty and many flagons of wine, and I will do your pleasure [for you]." Mydonia said to her nurse Narkia: "Many flagons are of no use to me, but a mingled draught in a cup, and one whole loaf, and a little oil, even if [it be] in a lamp, bring to me."

And when Narkia had brought [them], Mygdonia uncovered her head, and was standing before the holy apostle. And he took the oil, and poured [it] on her head, and said: "Holy oil, which was given to us for unction, and hidden mystery of the cross, which is seen through it—you, the straightener of crooked limbs, you, our Lord Jesus, life and health and remission of sins, let your power come and abide upon this oil, and let your holiness dwell in it." And he poured [it] upon the head of Mygdonia, and said: "Heal her of her old wounds, and wash away her sores, and strengthen her weakness." And when he had poured the oil on her head, he told her nurse to anoint her, and to put a cloth round her loins; and he fetched the basin of their conduit. And Judas went up [and] stood over it, and baptized Mygdonia in the name of the Father and the Son and the Spirit of holiness. And when she had come out and put on her clothes, he fetched and broke the Eucharist and [filled] the cup, and let Mygdonia partake of the table of the Messiah and of the cup of the Son of God. And he said to her: "Now then, you have received the sign, and gained for yourself your life for ever and ever." And a voice was heard from heaven, which said, "Yea, Amen and Amen." And when Narkia heard this voice, she was amazed, and she too begged of the apostle that she also might receive the sign; and he gave [it] to her and said: "May the grace of Jesus be with you as with the rest of your companions." And he went to be shut up in prison, and found the doors open and the watchmen asleep.

The Conversion of Sifur and His Family: A Homily

And Judas went out from the house of Karish, and went to the house of Sifur the general, and was dwelling there. And Sifur said to Judas, "Prepare for yourself an apartment, and be teaching in it"; and he did as he said to him. And Sifur the general said to him: "I and my daughter and my wife will henceforth live purely, in one mind and in one love; and we beg that we may receive the sign [of baptism] from your hands, and may become true servants of our Lord, and may be reckoned among the number of his flock and his sheep." Judas said: "I am meditating what to say, and am afraid; and I know what I know, [but] I am not able to utter it."

And he began to speak of baptism, and said; "This is the baptism of the remission of sins; this is the bringer forth of new men; this is the restorer of understandings, and the mingler of soul and body, and the establisher of the new man in the Trinity, and a participation in the remission of sins. Glory to you, [you] hidden power of baptism! Glory to you, [you] hidden power, that communicates with us in baptism! Glory to you, [you] power that is visible in baptism! Glory to you, new creatures, who are renewed through baptism, who draw near it in love!" And when he had said these things, he poured oil upon their heads and said: "Glory to you, [your] beloved Fruit! Glory to you, name of the Messiah! Glory to you, hidden power that dwells in the Messiah!" And he spoke, and they brought a large vat, and he baptized them in the name of the Father and of the Son and the Spirit of holiness.

And when they were baptized and had put on their clothes, he brought bread and wine, and placed it on the table, and began to bless it, and said: "Living bread, the eaters of which do not die. Bread, that fills hungry souls with your blessing! You who are worthy to receive the gift and to be for the remission of sins, that those who eat you may not die! We name the name of the Father over you; we name the name of the Son over you; we name the name of the Spirit over you, the exalted name that is hidden from all." And he said: "In your name, Jesus, may the power of the blessing and the thanksgiving come and abide upon this bread, that all the souls, which take of it, may be renewed, and their sins may be forgiven them." And he broke and gave to Sifur and to his wife and to his daughter.

A Catechesis

And while Judas was saying these things, all those who were there were listening, and were thinking that his departure from the world would be at that moment.

And again Judas said: "Believe in the Healer of all pains, hidden and manifest, and the Giver of life to those souls who ask help of him; this, the freeborn and King's son, who became a slave and poor; this, the healer of his creation, and the sick because of his servants; this, the purifier of those who believe in him, and the despised and insulted by those who did not hear him; this, [who] sets free his possessions from slavery and from corruption and from subjection and from loss, and is made subject to and insulted by his slaves; this, the Father of [heaven] above, and the Lord of all creatures, and the Judge of the world; this, who came from on high, and became visible through the Virgin Mary, and was called the son of Joseph the carpenter; this, the littleness of whose body we have seen with our eyes, and whose majesty we have received through faith; this, whose holy body we have felt with our hands, and whose sad aspect we have seen with our eyes, and whose divine form on the mount we were not able to see by ourselves alone; this, who was called an impostor, and who is the True, who does not deceive, and the payer of the tax and the head-money for us and for himself; this, of whom the enemy, when he saw him, was afraid, and trembled, and asked him who he was and what was said of him, and he did not make known to him the truth, because there is no truth in him; this, [who] though he was the Lord of the world and of its pleasures and of its wealth and of all its delights, put them away from him, and admonished those who hear him and believe in him not to make use of these [things]."

And when he had finished saying these things, he stood up to pray, and spoke thus: "Our Father, who (are) in heaven, hallowed be your name; your kingdom come; and your will be [done] on earth as in heaven; and give us the constant bread of the day; and forgive us our debts and our sins, that we too may forgive our debtors; and bring us not into temptation, but deliver us from the evil [one] [Matt 6:9-13; Luke 11:2-4]. My Lord and my God, and my hope and my confidence, and my teacher and my comforter, you taught us to pray thus.

The Conversion of Visan, Tertia, and Manashar

And Judas began to pray and to speak thus: "Companion and Help of the feeble; Hope and Confidence of the poor; Refuge and Rest of the weary; Voice that came from on high, comforting the hearts of your believers; Resort and Haven of those who go forth into the region of darkness; Physician without fee, [who] was crucified among men for many, and for whom no man was crucified; you descended into Sheol with mighty power, and the dead saw you and became alive, and the lord of death was not able to bear [it]; and you ascended with great glory, and took up with you all who sought refuge with you, and did tread for them the path [leading] up on high, and in your footsteps all your redeemed followed; and you brought them into your fold, and mingled them with your sheep. Son of perfect mercy, who was sent to us with power by the Father, whom his servants praise; Son, who was sent by the supreme and perfect Fatherhood; Lord of possessions that cannot be defiled; wealthy [one], who filled your creation with the treasure of your wealth; needy [one], who bore poverty and fasted forty days; Satisfier of our thirsty souls with your blessing; Lord, be with Vizan and with Tertia and with Manashar, and gather them into your fold, and mingle them with your number, and be a guide [for them] on the path of error. Be for them a healer in the place of sickness; be for them a strengthener in the weary place; make them pure in the unclean place; and make them clean of corruption in the place of the enemy. Be a physician for their bodies, and give life to their souls, and make them holy shrines and temples, and may the holy Spirit dwell in them."

And when he had prayed thus, he said to Mygdonia: "My daughter, strip your sisters." And she stripped them, and put girdles on them, and brought them near to him. And Vizan came near first. And Judas took oil, and glorified [God] over it, and said: "Fair Fruit, that is worthy to be glowing with the word of holiness, so that men may put you on and conquer their enemies through you, when they have been cleansed from their former works,—yea, Lord, come, abide upon this oil, as you did abide upon the tree, and they who crucified you were not able to bear your word. Let your gift come, which you breathed upon your enemies and they went backward and fell upon their faces, and let it abide upon this oil, over which we name your name." And he poured it upon the head of Vizan, and then upon the heads of these [others], and said: "In your name, Jesus the Messiah, let it be for these persons the remission of offenses and sins, and for the destruction of the enemy, and for the healing of their souls and bodies." And he commanded Mygdonia to anoint them, and he himself anointed Vizan. And after he had anointed them, he made them go down into the water in the name of the Father and the Son and the Spirit of holiness. And after they had been baptized and were come up, he brought bread and the mingled cup, and spoke a blessing over it and said: "Your holy Body, which was crucified for our sake, we eat, and your life-giving Blood, which was shed for our sake, we drink. Let your Body be to us for life, and your Blood for the remission of sins. For the gall which you drank for us, let the bitterness of our enemy be taken away from us. And for your drinking vinegar for our sake, let our weakness be strengthened. And [for] the spit which you received for us, let us receive your perfect life. And because you received the crown of thorns for us, let us receive from you the crown that withers not. And because you were wrapped in a linen cloth for us, let us be girt with your mighty strength, which cannot be overcome. And because you were buried in a new sepulcher for our mortality, let us too receive communion with you in heaven. And as you did arise, let us be raised, and let us stand before you at the judgment of truth." And he broke the Eucharist, and gave to Vizan and Tertia, and to Manashar and Sifur and Mygdonia, and to the wife and daughter of Sifur, and said: "Let this Eucharist be for you life and rest and joy and health, and for the healing of your souls and of your bodies." And they said, "Amen"; and a voice was heard saying to them, "Yea and Amen." And when they heard this voice, they fell on their faces. And again the voice was heard saying: "Do not be afraid, but only believe."

Aphrahat

Aphrahat, the earliest of the Syriac-speaking Fathers and a Persian subject (modern Iran), appears to have been born toward the end of the third century. He probably embraced Christianity as an adult, very likely becoming a Covenanter at baptism. In time he emerged as a Church leader (a bishop, it seems) of considerable influence.

What can be known of Aphrahat with certainty comes from the twenty-three treatises he wrote, entitled the *Demonstrations*. He composed *Demonstrations* 1–9 in 337, 10–22 in 344, and 23 in 354, at the request of a (fellow) Covenanter who sought instruction about the faith and how to embody it in his life. In responding, Aphrahat has both Covenanters and ordinary Christians in mind and voices a variety of concerns, among them, the recently launched persecution of Shapur II (340), the Valentinian Gnostic, and other encratite Christians, who refused to allow those who "fell" in the persecution to be reconciled with the Church, and the aggressive followers of Mani, whom he calls the "Sons of Darkness" (*Demonstration* 3).

A major concern, however, is Judaism, which attests to continuing social contact between Mesopotamia's Jews and Christians. Aphrahat engages in a courteous but sustained apologetic against the Jews. The basic premises are that (1) God has rejected Israel, because Israel rejected Jesus the Messiah; (2) Israel as such would not be redeemed; (3) the Church (which he calls the "peoples") has replaced Israel; and (4) the Church's liturgy has displaced Israel's festivals and other practices. A persistent fear, found also among the Western Syrian and Egyptian Christians, was that Christians, nourished by the same biblical traditions and piety as Jews, would find the synagogue an attractive haven—in Persia, from the police of Shapur II. Nonetheless, he shows no animus toward Jews, and the treatises reveal a man deeply immersed in the ancient Syriac version of the Hebrew Bible, called the "Peshitta," originating in the first or second century very likely from the neighborhood of Edessa. He cites it extensively, interprets it historically and with restrained typology (much like the West Syrians), and treats it with both familiarity and affection.

With respect to baptism, Aphrahat considers it a mystery of life and salvation, the washing whose reality forgives sins, and the garment of immortality by which one puts on Christ, who is in the waters of baptism (see *Demonstrations* 6, 11, 12). The principal historical types that baptism fulfills are the Exodus crossing of the Red Sea and the crossing of the Jordan into the Promised Land (*Dems.* 11, 12). Baptism has a special prominence as the new circumcision (*Dem.* 11). The pattern of Christian baptism is Christ's baptism in the Jordan (*Dem.* 6), but he holds that Jesus established the rite in the passion, when he washed the feet of his disciples at the Last Supper (*Dem.* 12). Above all, however, baptism for Aphrahat enacts the passion of Christ (*Dem.* 12), which he and his Church celebrated at the Passover according to Quartodeciman custom, on the fourteenth and fifteenth of Nisan (see ch.1, Melito of Sardis), rather than on the Sunday following Good Friday as most other Churches did. These

Mesopotamian Christians appear to have continued to celebrate their Passover for the seven days following, just as the Jews celebrated the feast of Unleavened Bread (*Dem.* 12).

The liturgy of baptism seems to have differed little from that of the *Odes of Solomon, Gospel According to Philip,* and *Acts of Judas Thomas,* save that it was preceded by a nightlong vigil ending with dawn on the sixteenth of Nisan, included the renunciation of Satan and the consecration of the baptismal water, enjoined fasting, prayer, and the chanting of psalms, and was solemnized at Passover. The active force throughout baptism is the Holy Spirit. Indeed, the distinction to be made between Christians and non-Christians is that the latter have (animal or at least sentient) souls, whereas the former have the Spirit received in baptism (*Dem.* 6). The challenge of postbaptismal life is for them to live in such a way as not to grieve the Spirit, who is their advocate and the one who transforms them at resurrection.

The text is that of J. Parisot, PS 1 (1894). A valuable study of the Christianity represented by Aphrahat is Robert Murray's *Symbols of the Church and Kingdom* (Cambridge, England: The Cambridge University Press, 1975) as noted above; see also Jacob Neusner, *Aphrahat and Judaism: The Christian Jewish Argument in Fourth-Century Iran* (Leiden: Brill, 1971). Although outdated in some ways, the most comprehensive study of baptism in Aphrahat is Edward J. Duncan, *Baptism in the Demonstrations of Aphraates the Persian Sage,* SA 8 (1945).

The translation is based on J. Parisot's Latin translation in PS 1; the Gwynn English translation of *Demonstration* 6 in NPNF, 2nd ser., 13, and the Neusner translations of *Demonstrations* 11 and 12 in *Aphrahat and Judaism* have been used as points of reference and collateral verification. They do not follow the Parisot text; Neusner indicates divergent readings.

Demonstration 6:14: On Ascetics

[As already noted, Aphrahat wrote at the request of a Covenanter. In this treatise he seems almost to be composing an ascetic charter for the Covenanters. The first two chapters inculcate ascetic attitudes drawn from an abundance of New Testament texts. In the next five (3–7), the Sage addresses himself to the values and safeguards of celibacy and virginity. In chapters 8–10, he proposes Christ as the model for the ascetic, to which he adds a biblical commentary on the unity between Christ and the Father (11). The next four chapters (12–16) are devoted to an extended consideration on how Christ can be one with the Father yet dwell with humans, which leads him to develop a biblical theology of the Holy Spirit, whom he generally calls the "Spirit of Christ," particularly with reference to the indwelling of the Spirit in the baptized and to the resurrection. The final chapters discuss Satan (17) and the resurrection (18), concluding with commendation and counsel (19–20).

In the reading Aphrahat discusses what he considers the primary work of baptism, namely, rebirth through the gift of the Holy Spirit, who then guards and consummates the joyous resurrection in those who, in turn, have guarded "the Spirit of Christ in purity." If the biblical passages ring strange, one need only recall that Aphrahat's version of the Bible is the Peshitta.]

6:14. Therefore, Beloved, we have also received the Spirit of Christ, and Christ dwells in us, for it is written that the Spirit said through the mouth of the prophet: "I will dwell in you, and I will walk among them" [Lev 21:12]. Let us, therefore, prepare our temples for the Spirit of Christ, nor ought we to grieve him lest he depart far from us. Remember the word of the apostle, warning us: "Do not grieve the Holy Spirit, in whom you have been sealed for the day of redemption" [Eph 4:30]. Through baptism we have received the Spirit of Christ; for at the very hour the priests call on the Spirit heaven opens, and he descends, moves the waters [Gen 1:2: the reference is to the prayer, an epiclesis, consecrating the baptismal font], and those who are baptized put him on. For the Spirit is absent from all born from the body, until they come to rebirth from the waters; then they receive the Spirit. For in the first birth they were born, endowed with the animal spirit created in man; nor will it ever die, as it is written, "I made man into a living spirit" [2 Cor 5:8]. But in the second birth, namely, baptism, they receive the Holy Spirit immortal from divinity himself. When, therefore, people die, the animal spirit [soul] is hidden, with the body sensation taken away [as a result]. However, the heavenly Spirit, whom they received according to its nature, returns to Christ. For again the apostle teaches, saying: "The animal body is buried, and the spiritual rises" [1 Cor 15:44]. And the Spirit, according to his nature, comes back, for the apostle again says: "When we have left the body, we will be with the Lord" [2 Cor 5:8].

The Spirit of Christ, whom the spiritual receive, returns to the Lord; the animal spirit, however, is buried in its own nature, and sense is taken away from it. When someone has preserved the Spirit of Christ in purity, the Spirit of Christ returns to him [Christ] to say to him: "The body to which I came and which I put on through the waters of baptism has served me in holiness." The Holy Spirit will urge Christ that the body by which he was preserved rise; the Spirit makes the case that he be joined again to it and that this body rise with praise. However, as for the man who has grieved the Spirit received in baptism, the Spirit has already departed from him before he dies; going according to his nature to Christ, he accuses the man by whom he was grieved. When the time has come for the final consummation and the hour of resurrection is at hand, the Holy Spirit, who had been kept in purity, receives great power from his nature and will go to Christ. Awaiting all, he will stand before the doors of the tombs where the people who had kept him in purity were buried. And when the angels of the heavenly gates have appeared before the King, he [the King] will immediately sound the horn and they will send for the voice of the trumpet. The Spirit, who was waiting to hear the sound of the trumpet, when he hears it, will quickly throw open the tombs, raise up the bodies buried in them, and vest them with the very glory that he brought with him. The Spirit himself will dwell within, so that the body may be raised up, while the glory with which the body is adorned is wrapped around it. The animal spirit, which belongs to the body, will be absorbed by glory and the body by the Spirit. Seized by the Spirit, that person will fly to a meeting with the King, who will receive [her or] him with joy. Moreover, Christ will show himself beneficent to the body that kept the Spirit in purity.

Demonstration 11:11–12: On Circumcision

[In the first ten chapters of this treatise, Aphrahat argues that although Israel claims to be the children of Abraham, anyone who acts with righteousness is a child of Abraham, for circumcision without faith is useless. God had made many covenants and signified each in a different way; circumcision signified only one of them. Indeed, circumcision, he argues, was widely practiced among the ancients and mandated for the Israelites only to distinguish them from their ritually impure neighbors (the Canaanites). In fact, they were uncircumcised in the desert and circumcised only when they entered the Promised Land under

Joshua. But from then on, because they were Israel and had the Law, they could not claim to be without guilt when they broke it.

Aphrahat then goes on to argue that baptism is the true circumcision, and that Christians are the true children of Abraham, the first believer. He concludes with an extended typology between Joshua, son of Nun, who leads the Israelites across the Jordan into the Promised Land (Jos 1–12), and Jesus, the Savior, who, inaugurating the new and permanent covenant, leads the Gentiles (the "peoples") into the "promised land of life." In this Joshua-Jesus typology, both names are spelled the same in Hebrew and its dialects, of which Syriac is one, Aramaic. The first Christian writer of record to develop the typology is Origen (vol. 6, ch. 3): coupled with other similarities between the East and West Syrian and Alexandrian interpretive traditions, Origen's treatment of Joshua suggests that a common Semitic tradition lay at the root of Syrian and Alexandrian Christian biblical and liturgical traditions.]

11:11. Moreover, in every way the Law and covenant have been changed. For from olden times [God] changed the pact with Adam, and imposed a different one on Noah; he gave still another to Abraham, which he changed, in order to give a new one to Moses. And when the Mosaic covenant was not observed, he gave still another pact in the final generation [the messianic generation of Jesus], a covenant that will not be changed.

For [God] established the law for Adam that he was not to eat of the tree of life; for Noah it was the rainbow in the clouds; for Abraham, chosen because of his faith, [God] gave circumcision, an identifying mark of his posterity. For Moses [the sign of the covenant] was the [Passover] lamb, a propitiation for the people. However, each of these covenants differed from the others. Further, the circumcision that he approved as the covenant [of Abraham's posterity] is the very one about which Jeremiah spoke: "Circumcise the foreskin of your hearts" [Jer 4:4]. Now if the pact that God constituted for Abraham was sound, also sound and faithful is this one [the new covenant]: for [once giving it] he is not able to give still another law, as though starting all over again, whether to those outside the Law or to those subject to the Law. For he gave the Law of Moses with its observances and commandments once, and when [the people] did not observe [the Law], he annulled both Law and its commandments. He determined to give a new testament, about which he did not speak as he had before [i.e., through Jeremiah], although he was the giver of both. For this is the testament that he determined to give: "That all might know me, from the least of them even to the greatest" [Jer 31:34]. And in this testament there is circumcision no more nor the [distinctive] mark of the people. For surely we know, Beloved, that God has established laws in [every] generation; they apply as long as it pleases him, after which they are obsolete, since the apostle says that "in former times the kingdom of God existed in many [different] ways, each according to its own proper time" [Heb 1:1]. Moreover, it is open and obvious to the wise and those who understand that all who are of the [new] covenant, should they fall victim to lust and wantonness after circumcision [baptism], that they indeed are the circumcised, though they do not understand the words of the apostle: "Would that those who disturb you cut off their genitals" [Gal 5:12]. Further, our God is true and his commandments most faithful; and each of the covenants has proved firm and true in its time. Those who are circumcised in heart, and are circumcised again in the true Jordan [the baptismal font], and are baptized for the remission of sins, find life.

11:12. Joshua, son of Nun, circumcised the people a second time with a stone knife, when he crossed the Jordan with his people. Joshua, our Savior, circumcised those Gentiles who believed in him and were washed by baptism with the circumcision of the heart: they were circumcised "by the sword, which is his word, sharper than any two-edged sword" [Heb 4:12]. Joshua, son of Nun, led his people across to the Promised Land; Joshua, our Savior, promised the land of the living to all who crossed the true Jordan, who believed, and who had the foreskin of their hearts circumcised. Joshua, son of Nun, built a stone monument as a witness for Israel; Joshua, our Savior, gave Simon the name Peter (the solid rock) and constituted him a faithful witness for the Gentiles. Joshua, son of Nun, celebrated the Passover in the camps at Jericho, the cursed [city], and the people ate the bread of the land; Joshua, our Savior, celebrated the Passover with his disciples in the city of Jerusalem, which he had cursed, saying: "A stone upon a stone will not remain in it" [Matt 24:2]; and [in that land] he gave [them] the mystery of the bread of life. Joshua, son of Nun, condemned the avaricious Achan, who stole and hid [what he stole]; Joshua, our Savior, judged [guilty] the avaricious Judas, who stole and hid the money from the purse he held [i.e., over which he had charge]. Joshua, son of Nun, wiped out the despised Gentiles;

Joshua, our Savior, wiped out Satan and his army. Joshua, son of Nun, made the sun stop in the sky; Joshua, our Savior, made the sun go out, when they crucified him. Joshua, son of Nun, was savior of the people; Joshua, the Savior, is called the Savior of the Gentiles. Blest, therefore, are those who are circumcised in the foreskins of their hearts and are reborn from the water of the second circumcision; they receive inheritance with Abraham, the head of believers and father of all Gentiles, for his faith was reckoned for him as justice.

Here ends the treatise concerning circumcision.

Demonstration 12: On the Passover

[Araphat's interlocutor in the *Demonstrations* seems to be in discussion with Jews about the Passover, both Jewish and Christian—there was a good deal of communication between the two communities. A divisive issue was why Christians, if they were true Israelites, did not celebrate the Passover on the evening of the fourteenth of Nisan as the Law commands. Their custom was to celebrate their Passover on the fifteenth, the day, as they understood it, of Jesus' death, burial, and sojourn with the dead.

The nub of Aphrahat's response is that the Israelite covenant is invalidated by the true Passover: the passion, death, burial, and resurrection of Christ—now rendered in mystery by baptism. The appointed time for the new Passover, then, was the fifteenth, when the passion had been consummated. Aphrahat indicates that the night of the fifteenth was spent in vigil, accompanied by fasting, prayer, and the chanting of psalms, all of which culminated in baptism, the administration of which seems to have coincided with daybreak.]

12:1. The Most Holy One commanded Moses that the Passover be celebrated on the fourteenth day of the first month. So he said to Moses: "Command the assembly of the children of Israel that they take for themselves a lamb of one year, a lamb unblemished. They will take it from the sheep or goats, and the children of Israel will have a Passover [feast] for the Lord" [Exod 3:5-6]. Then he told Moses that [the children of Israel] should take this lamb on the tenth of the month and watch over it until the fourteenth. At sunset they will sacrifice it, sprinkling its blood on the doors of their homes against the destroying [angel], lest he strike them as he passes through the land of Egypt laying waste [to the firstborn of the people]. Then the whole assembly [of Israel] will eat the lamb in haste this

way: loins girt, shod, and holding their staffs. [Moses] warned
and commanded them to eat quickly and to eat it neither raw
nor boiled in water, but roasted over a fire. Likewise, he ordered them not to take any of it out of the house nor to break
any bone in it. The children of Israel acted accordingly, and
ate the Passover on the fourteenth of the first month, which
is Nisan, the month of [budding] flowers, the first month of
the year.

12:2. Now understand, Beloved, the mysteries which the Most
Holy One established in the celebration of the Passover, when
he taught [the children of Israel] all his precepts, saying: "You
will eat in one house, nor will you take any of it outside" [Exod
12:46]. Thus, Moses commanded them: "When you have entered the land which the Lord will give you, you will celebrate
the Passover in its proper season. You are not to celebrate the
Passover in just any of your settlements, but only in the place
which the Lord your God will show you; you and your household shall rejoice at your festival" [Deut 16:5-8]. He also commanded them: "Neither a foreigner nor a hired hand may eat
the Passover; but the slave you own, purchased with your
money, may eat the Passover, after the flesh of his foreskin
has been circumcised" [Exod 12:44-45].

12:3. Marvelous are these great mysteries, Beloved. While Israel lived in its own land, the Passover could not be celebrated
save in Jerusalem; Nowadays, [the people] are dispersed among
all peoples and tongues: they eat their bread in uncleanness
among the unclean and uncircumcised, among the Gentiles, just
as [the Lord] said to Ezekiel when he showed [the prophet] a
sign that he would eat his bread in uncleanness [signifying
Jerusalem's impending ruin]. For [Ezekiel] prayed, saying: "O
Lord of Lords, my spirit [has never been] polluted; nor has unclean flesh ever entered my mouth" [Ezek 4:14]. [The Lord]
said to Ezekiel that this will be as the sign: "Thus will the children of Israel eat their bread in contamination among the Gentiles in the midst of whom I will disperse them" [Ezek 4:13].

If therefore, as I said above, while Israel dwelled in its own
land it was not lawful for them to sacrifice the Passover lamb
save before the one altar in Jerusalem, how is it possible in our
time for them to celebrate the Passover mystery when they are
dispersed among alien people? They no longer have the authori-
zation: and indeed [God] has testified about them through the
prophet: "For many a long day will the children of Israel live

apart from sacrifices and the altar, without him who wears the ephod and offers incense" [Hos 3:4]. Again, he said to Jerusalem: "I will put a stop to her merry-making and to her festivals, and to new moons, and to her Sabbath" [Hos 2:11]. And about the ark of testimony [Scripture] says; "No longer shall they say 'Ark of the Testimony of the Lord'; nor remember it, nor will it be rebuilt" [Jer 3:16]. Since [the Lord] has said that neither will they remember it nor will it be rebuilt nor will it enter their [affections] again, why do they dare attempt to restore it? For Moses said about them: "I will provoke them among a people that is not a people, and among a foolish people I will enrage them" [Deut 32:21]. Now I ask of you, wise debater of [Israel], who does not understand the words of the Law, show me when [this Scripture] was fulfilled, namely, that God provoked the people through a people that was not a people, and when did he enrage them through a foolish people? But if you are [the one] stirred to zeal by the Gentile peoples, you fulfill these very words of Scripture which Moses long ago signified in his book. For if you enact the Passover wherever you wish among strangers, you do so against the commandment: truly a bill of divorce has been lodged against you.

12:4. If you do not believe [such is the case], listen to the prophet Jeremiah saying: "I have abandoned my house, I have cast off my inheritance [i.e., people]; I have given the beloved of my soul into the hand of her foes, and a painted bird has been made my inheritance [my people]" [Jer 12:7, 9]. What is this painted bird, I ask you? The painted bird is the church of the Gentiles. And consider why he calls it "painted": clearly because it has been assembled from many tongues, and drawn from distant peoples. If up to this point you are not persuaded that the Gentiles have not been made God's inheritance, listen again to Jeremiah, calling the Gentiles and rejecting Israel. For he says: "Stand at the crossroads, look, and inquire about the footpaths of the world; see what the best way is and walk on it. But you said, 'We will not walk' " [Jer 6:16]. Again, he says: "I have appointed watchmen over you, that you may hear the sound of the trumpet. And they said: 'We will not listen' " [Jer 6:17]. Since the children of Israel did not heed him, Jeremiah, he turned to the church of the Gentiles. For he said: "Hear, you nations and understand, you, the assembly among them" [Jer 6:18].

David also said: "Remember your assembly that you have had from the beginning" [Ps 74:2]. And Isaiah: "Listen, people, to what I have done, and understand my power, you who stand afar off" [Isa 33:13]. He said the same thing about the church set in the future among the Gentiles: "In the last days the mountain of the house of the Lord will be placed at the crown of the mountains, higher than the hills, and all the nations will gaze upon it" [Isa 2:2]. For this reason Isaiah said: "Listen, you nations, to what I have done, and understand my power, you who stand afar off: the sinners in Sion are terrified, and trembling has seized the impious" [Isa 33:13-14].

Why does he require that his deeds be heeded and why does he manifest his power to those who are afar off; why are sinners in Sion terrified; why does he instill fear into the impious? He summons the people [Gentiles] through them to enrage the people [Israel]; to those who are afar off he shows his power; when he displays his wrath, he will judge his people; he terrifies the sinners of Sion, which was called the "Holy City" [Isa 52:1]; he strikes fear in the godless, the lying prophets, about whom he says of the prophets of Jerusalem: "From them godlessness has spread into the whole earth" [Jer 23:15].

12:5. Beloved, you have heard what I have explained to you about this Passover, [namely] that it was given as a mystery to an earlier people, but that its reality is made plain today among the [new] people. Unfortunately, the minds of the simple and foolish are much exercised about the celebration and observance concerning the day of this great feast. Once again, our Savior is the true year-old lamb without blemish. The prophet says about him: "In him there is no sin nor is grief to be found in his mouth; indeed, the Lord willed to turn him over to terror and to hand him over to suffering" [Isa 53:9-10]. And he designated him "year-old"; recalling that an infant is free from sin, he [Jesus] said to his disciples: "Unless you have turned and become as these little ones, you will not enter into the kingdom of heaven" [Matt 8:3]. And Isaiah says about the [suffering] just one: "The child who has sinned, like the son [who has lived] a hundred years will die and as a result be cursed."

[Following a different reading here, Neusner translates: "A child who sins will die like a hundred-year-old, and be cursed." The citation is Isaiah 65:20, on the subject of the new Jerusalem. The New English Bible reads: "There no child shall die an infant . . . every boy shall live his hundred years before he dies, whoever falls short of a hundred shall be despised (or cursed).''
]

12:6. Therefore, our Savior ate the Passover with his disciples on the holy night of the fourteenth day [of Nisan]. When he had finished, he disclosed for his disciples the reality behind the sign. For after Judas had left them, he took bread, blessed and gave it to his disciples, saying to them: "This is my body; take and eat it, all of you." Also over the wine he blessed it as follows and said to them: "This is my blood, the new testament, which is poured out on behalf of many for the forgiveness of sins. When you assemble do likewise in commemoration of me" [Matt 26:26-28; Luke 22:19-20]. Not yet, of course, had the Lord been arrested. When he had said these words, he rose from [the seat] where he had celebrated the Passover and gave [them] his body as food and his blood as drink; then, he went out with his disciples to the place where he was arrested.

Now, whoever has eaten his body and drunk his blood is numbered among the dead. The Lord, however, with his own hands offered his body to be eaten, and before he was crucified gave his blood to be drunk. He was arrested on the night of the fourteenth. In addition, he was tried before the sixth hour [noon of the fifteenth], and they condemned him at the sixth hour, and raised [him] up on the cross. When they judged him, indeed he said nothing, nor did he offer a word to his judges. He was, of course, able both to speak and to reply; but it is impossible for one who is numbered among the dead to speak. From the sixth hour to the ninth, darkness covered [everything], and at the ninth hour he commended his spirit to the Father. Thus, when dawn of the fifteenth day broke, he dwelled among the dead, so [also] on the night of the Sabbath, and the whole of the [Sabbath day as well], and for three hours into the evening. During the night which ended at dawn of the first Sabbath, the very hour at which he gave his body and blood to his disciples, he rose from the dead.

12:7. Now truly show us, Sage, what is the meaning of these three days and nights during which our Savior sojourned among the dead. For we indeed see the three hours in the evening, the night before the Sabbath's dawn, and the entire day of that Sabbath, and finally the night of the first day after the Sabbath [Sunday, when] he rose [from the dead]. So explain to me about these three days and nights, how they are arranged. For he seems to have remained there [among the dead only] for complete day[s] and night[s], as the Savior has said: "Just as Jonah, son of Amathi, was in the belly of a whale for three days and three nights, so the Son of Man will be in the bosom of the earth"

[Matt 12:40]. [Thus it was that] three days and nights pass from the time he gave his body as food and his blood as drink. For it was nighttime when Judas left their midst, and the eleven disciples ate the body of the Savior and drank [his] blood: behold, therefore, the first night, the one that ended with dawn Friday. Up to the sixth hour they tried him; behold, therefore, one day and one night. Then came the three hours when darkness fell— from the sixth to the ninth hours [noon to 3:00 P.M.]— plus the three hours after the darkness [had lifted]—which makes two days and two nights. Finally, [with] the full night that ended in the Sabbath's dawn and the full Sabbath day, the three days and three nights were completed for the Lord: on the night before the first day after the Sabbath [Sunday] he rose from the dead.

12:8. The Passover of the Jews is celebrated on the fourteenth day [of Nisan], reckoned as a full day and night. However, our [Passover], the day of the solemn passion, is celebrated on Friday, namely, the fifteenth day—a full night and day. After Passover, Israel eats unleavened bread for seven days, up to the twenty-first day of the month [Exod 12:18]. We also observe [the feast of] Unleavened Bread, the feast of our Savior. They eat unleavened bread with bitterness [i.e., bitter herbs]; but our Savior rejected the cup of bitterness, and bore all the bitterness of the [new] people, when he tasted and did not wish to drink [the reference is to the sponge soaked with bitter wine just before Christ died on the cross: see Matt 27:46]. The Jews recall their sins from year to year [Lev 16:21: the rite of the scapegoat at Passover]; but we commemorate the crucifixion and disgrace of our Savior. On the [original] Passover they fled the slavery of Pharaoh; on the day of the crucifixion we were redeemed from the captivity of Satan. They sacrificed a lamb from the flock, and by his blood were saved from the destroying [angel]; we, by the blood of the chosen Son were redeemed from the works of corruption that we were pursuing.

[For them] Moses was the leader; [as for us] we have Jesus as our leader and Savior. For them Moses divided the sea, and made them cross over; our Savior opened and divided the underworld, breaking its gates, when, opening them, he penetrated into the depths and trampled out an [escape] route for those who would have believed in him. Manna was given them as food; the Lord gave us his body to eat. For them [God] caused water to gush from a rock; for us the Savior made living water flow from his side [Exod 17:6; John 19:33]. To them [God] promised the land of Canaan as their inheritance; to us was given the land of life he promised. For them Moses raised up the bronze serpent, so that whoever looked at the serpent would be cured. For us Jesus fastened himself to the cross, so that looking on him we might flee the sight of the serpent, Satan. For them Moses built a sacred dwelling for the covenant that they might offer sacrifices and offerings to expiate their sins; Jesus restored the sacred dwelling of David, which had fallen and is [now] raised. For he said to the Jews: "This temple which you see, when you have destroyed it, I will rebuild it in three days" [John 2:19]. And his disciples understood him to be speaking of his body, namely, that when [the Jews] had destroyed it, he would rise after three days. He promised us life in this sacred dwelling; in it our sins are expiated. He called their sacred dwelling a temporary dwelling, because he gave it for them to use for a short time; but he called ours the sacred dwelling of the Holy Spirit forever [1 Cor 3:16; 4:19].

12:9. Now, then, Beloved, hear about the Passover lamb, how the Most Holy commanded that it be eaten in one house rather than in many. This house is the one church of God. Again he said: "The hired hand and the foreigner shall not eat of it" [Exod 12:45]. Who are the hired hands and the foreigners, if not [the sectaries who teach] dogmas of the devil: indeed, for them it is not lawful to enact the Passover. Concerning them the Savior says: "The hired hand is he who does not own the sheep: when he sees the wolf coming, he leaves the flock and flees" [John 10:12].

Next he said: "You shall not eat it raw or boiled in water" [Exod 12:9]. This is to be known and made clear: this is the sacrifice which is offered in the church of God—to be roasted in the fire, but neither boiled in water nor offered raw.

Likewise, he said: "Thus will you eat it: you will bind up your loins; you will have sandals on your feet and your staffs in your hands" [Exod 12:11]. These mysteries are deeply sublime. For, indeed, he who wishes to eat of the true Lamb, Christ [i.e., the Messiah], binds up his loins by faith, puts sandals on his feet, that is, the preparation of the gospel, and holds in his hand the sword of the spirit, which is the word of God [see Eph 6:15-17].

Again, [Scripture] said: "A bone of it will not be broken" [Exod 12:46]. This was fulfilled on the very day of crucifixion, when [the executioners] broke the legs of those who were crucified with him; but his they did not break. And it added: "That the word of Scripture might be fulfilled: no bone in him will be broken" [John 19:36].

Further, [Scripture] said: "The slave bought for money, when the flesh of his foreskin has been circumcised, then let him eat the Passover" [Exod 12:44]. The purchased slave is the person who sins but repents and has been redeemed by the blood of Christ. When such a person has circumcised his heart from evil deeds, then he proceeds to baptism, the fulfillment of true circumcision. He is joined to the people of God and participates in the body and blood of Christ. Thus, also, [Scripture] says: "Eat [the lamb] in haste" [Exod 12:11], an injunction thus observed in the church of God. For they eat the lamb in haste, standing, in fear and trembling, because they hasten to eat the life which they have received from the gift of the Spirit [or "spiritual gift," thus Neusner].

12:10. Moreover, Israel was baptized in the middle of the sea on Passover night, the day of salvation; likewise, our Savior washed the feet of his disciples on Passover night, which is the mystery of baptism. For you know, Beloved, that the Savior gave the true baptism on this night. As long as he traveled about with his disciples, they were baptized in the baptism of the law with which the priests were baptizing, the baptism about which John said: "Repent of your sins" [Matt 3:2]. But in that night he disclosed to them the mystery, the baptism of his suffering death, of which the apostle spoke: "You were buried with him in baptism for death, and you rose with him through the power of God" [Rom 6:3-4; Col 2:12]. Understand, then, friend, that the baptism of John had no value for the remission of sins, but only for repentance. Moreover, the Acts of the Twelve Apostles reports [about this that] when the disciples asked those who were called from the Gentiles and from Israel, they said to them [see Acts 19:1-7, the Ephesian converts]: "Are you baptized?" they replied, "We were baptized with the baptism of John." Then they [Paul's companions] baptized them with the baptism of truth, the mystery of the passion of our Savior. For about this the Savior gave [his own] testimony, when he said to his disciples: "John baptized with water; but you will be baptized with the Holy Spirit" [Acts 1:5]. Later, when our Savior took water, pouring it into a basin, he hitched up his under garment and began to wash the feet of his disciples [see John 13:4-15]: "When he came to Simon Peter, the latter said to him: 'Lord, are you washing my feet? Never ever will you wash my feet.' But Jesus replied to him: 'Unless I wash you, you will have no place with me.' Simon said to him: 'You will wash not only my feet but also my head.' When, however, he had washed his disciples' feet, he put his clothes back on, and said to them: 'Behold you call me Master and Lord. For so I am. If I, your master and Lord, have washed your feet, all the more you ought to wash one another's feet! I have given you this example so that what I have done you may also do.' " And after he washed their feet and resumed his place, he gave them his body and blood. It was the reverse with the people of Israel: after they ate the Passover, they were baptized in a cloud and in the sea, just as the apostle says: "All our fathers were under the cloud, and all crossed over through the sea" [1 Cor 10:1].

12:11. I have written these few words of encouragement to you as a defense against the Jews, because they celebrate the customary feast of the Passover outside the Law and illicitly . . . [Aphrahat cites other instances of what he considers actions that he considers violations of the covenant].

12:12. I have taught you so that you might teach the children of your church, who are exercised on account of the Passover. Indeed, those who have sound minds [ought to be] concerned about knowing at least what follows.

If Passover, when our Savior suffered, should occur for us on the first day after Sabbath [Sunday], according to rule we ought to celebrate it on the second day [Monday], so that the whole week might be devoted to the passion of the Lord and to observing his unleavened bread. For there are seven days of unleavened bread after the Passover, extending to the twenty-first [of Nisan]. But should the day of the passion fall on any other day of the week, we should not be at all concerned, for our solemn day is Friday.

As the month is reckoned, the day of the crucifixion, when our Savior suffered, [i.e.,] the night and day he spent among the dead, was the fifteenth, [counting] from the sixth hour [noon] on Friday to dawn of Sunday, [for on that day], the sixteenth, he rose. At dawn on the fourteenth he ate the Passover with his disciples according to Israel's Law; and on that day, Friday, the fourteenth, his trial took place, lasting to the sixth hour [noon]; then he was fastened to the cross for three hours. Next he went down to [the abode of] the dead during [that] night before the dawn of the fifteenth. On the Sabbath, the fifteenth, he sojourned with the dead; during the night that preceded Sunday, the sixteenth, he rose and appeared to Mary

Magdalen and to two of the disciples walking on the road [to Emmaus, Luke 24:13-27].

Let anyone who is exercised by the controversy surrounding [how] these days [are reckoned] understand that the Lord celebrated the Passover and ate and drank with his disciples at dawn of the fourteenth. Indeed, from cockcrow on he neither ate nor drank anymore, because they arrested him and inaugurated his trial. Then, as I have shown you above, he passed the fifteenth—a full day and night—among the dead.

12:13. Now, so that the feast may be observed each year at the established time, the following things are enjoined on us: fasting with purity, prayer in faith, praise with diligence, also the chanting of psalms whenever appropriate; the giving of the seal with baptism according to the [proper] rite, the prayers of consecration at their proper time—thus, everything will be accomplished according to custom. "For the Lord suffered and rose; and will not die again; death will no more have dominion over him. Indeed, because he died, sin likewise died; moreover, because he lives, he lives with God" [Rom 6:9-10]. And so, we who were dead, he has given us life together with him.

Now if we are troubled about these things, especially if we are concerned more about the fourteenth and less about the way in which the feast ought to be celebrated, may it please us to observe the fourteenth of every month, and also to mourn [fast?] on Friday of every week. In addition, it is even more important to spend each day of the week in pursuing those things that are right before the Lord God.

May you be instructed, then, by these [words] which we have briefly addressed to you. You ought not to be troubled by the machinations of words [presumably, the rabbinic interpretations about the Passover], for they offer nothing profitable, indeed [they] offend against [keeping] a pure heart, which is a matter of precept. So let us be on our guard by observing this solemn day at the appointed time.

The demonstration is finished.

Ephrem

Born in Mesopotamia near Nisibis about 306, probably to Christian parents, Ephrem came early under the influence of the city's celebrated bishop, Jacob (303–338), was baptized as an adult, and became a Covenanter. He very likely lived with other Covenanters, serving the bishop and his two immediate successors as deacon, Scripture teacher, and advisor. When Nisibis was ceded to the Persians (363), Ephrem fled to Edessa, where, for the last decade of his life, he served Bishop Barsai (361–378) much as he had served Jacob of Nisibis. He died in 373, with a reputation for holiness, eloquence, and erudition.

Ephrem left behind him a considerable body of work, including biblical commentaries, controversial treatises, and correspondence. But his fame rests on his didactic poetry, for which he is considered a theologian-poet of the highest stature. Actually, his poetry is catechetical. Standing in the tradition inaugurated by Bardaisan and shared by Mani and his followers, Ephrem composed instructional hymns *(madrashe),* written in stanzas and intended for choral singing, and metrical homilies *(memre),* nonstanzaic and intended for recitation. Some eighteen collections bearing a variety of titles and totaling over three hundred hymns have come down to us. The verse homilies are less numerous but are also grouped in collections.

Ephrem's allusive style makes it difficult to select works specifically baptismal. Nonetheless, the readings chosen offer three hymns from collections respectively on virginity, the Church, and faith. In addition, two hymns have been chosen from another collection, *Hymns for the Epiphany,* attributed to Ephrem. Although it is not certain whether the hymns are authentic, they reflect Syriac baptismal tradition later than Ephrem only by a little and exude his spirit.

Although Ephrem's baptismal vision is difficult to fathom, the hymns selected, with the help of brief introductory commentary, disclose its spirit and principal themes. At this point, however, the reader may find a few notes useful. For instance, unlike Aphrahat, who sees the institution of baptism in Jesus washing the disciples' feet at the Last Supper, Ephrem finds it in Christ's descent into the Jordan. It is an axial event on which all the events of salvation turn—those of the old covenant as well as the new. And John the Baptist stands as the link between the covenants, because he transmits the ancient priesthood, which brings justification, makes expiation, and initiates sanctification (see below, the *Teaching of St. Gregory*). Thus, for Ephrem baptism is a high-priestly act celebrated by the bishop.

Further, there is focus on the nativity, for the human Christ born from Mary's womb is reborn from the baptismal womb of

the Jordan, where he emerges as king, priest, and Son. As at Jesus'
conception in Mary's womb, the Holy Spirit descends upon the
womb of the Jordan's waters. Baptism is empowered to be this
kind of event for the Christian at the crucifixion, when the soldier's spear causes blood and water to gush from the side of Christ
(see John 19:34-36). For Syriac tradition generally the spear recalls
the sword that bars Paradise (see Gen 3:24); but now the soldier's
spear opens it.

With respect to forgiveness, according to Ephrem, John's baptism purified from sin. Precisely what sins is not a matter much
on Ephrem's mind, for the baptism that Christ brought perfected
John's. Clearly, actual sins are forgiven. More important, in
Christian baptism everything that Adam lost is restored. In their
second birth, according to Ephrem, the baptized even acquire a
new body, one like Adam's before the Fall and Christ's after the
resurrection. Baptism in Ephrem, then, is Paradise regained—
thus, the symbolism of the postbaptismal vesting in a white garment, followed by the gift of the baptismal candle and the recitation of the Lord's Prayer.

One final note. For Ephrem faith and baptism are inextricable.
Nonetheless, in the normal order of things baptism follows faith,
which, in turn, is stabilized by it; but valid baptism requires an
informed and orthodox (Nicene) faith. Ephrem was, as a matter
of fact, the first of the Syriac Fathers to encounter the Arians,
and he did so in cosmopolitan Edessa. Their baptism was invalid,
he reasoned, because they denied the divinity of Christ. That he
knew of a Lenten catechumenate with its creedal instructions
seems assured, because he required those orthodox Christians who
embraced Arianism and then returned to enter the catechumenate
before reconciliation, presumably shortly before Easter.

A helpful introduction to Ephrem's work is contained in the
introduction to Sebastian Brock's *The Harp of the Spirit: Eighteen Poems of Saint Ephrem,* 2nd ed. enlarged (London: Fellowship of St. Alban and St. Sergius, 1983). See also his *Luminous
Eye: The Spiritual World Vision of St. Ephrem* (Rome: The Center for Indian and Inter-Religious Studies, 1985). For a treatment
of Ephrem's life in the Church, see Sidney Griffith, "Ephraem,
the Deacon of Edessa, and the Church of the Empire," *Diako-
nia: Studies in Honor of Robert Meyer,* eds. Thomas Halton and

J. William (Washington: The Catholic University of America Press, 1986) 22–52.

Hymns on Virginity 7

The title of this collection is based on the subject of its first three hymns. The next four (4–7) explore the theme of oil *(mesh-cha)* and anointing as a type of Christ the Anointed One *(meshicha)*. The reading is the last of these "anointing" hymns, and in Ephrem's allusive way it discloses the importance of the prebaptismal anointing that gives baptism its name, "seal" *(rushma)*.

The background to the first two stanzas is the human lot, namely, to be inhabitant of two worlds: October, this world, and April, the world of the Easter mystery. The allusions in stanzas 3–4 are to events in the life of Elijah, especially 1 Kings 17. Stanzas 5–7 underscore aspects of the baptismal oil, and the eighth gives an overall view of baptism. The concluding stanzas are in praise of oil and involve an interplay between *mescha* (oil) and *meschicha* (Christ), which leads Ephrem to a striking conclusion: "From whatever angle I look at the oil, Christ looks out at me from it" (st. 14). In the final stanza (15) the oil, which cannot sink, buoys up the anointed one.

The text is that of E. Beck, CSCO 94 (1962); the translation, that of Sebastian Brock, *The Harp of the Spirit,* cited above, which also contains helpful commentary.

Hymn 7

1. Repentance and diligence are requisites for both worlds:
    for working the land the diligent are needed, for spiritual toil the repentant.
    Though the diligent may not become rich, his diligence stands by itself,
    and though the penitent may still sin again, he belongs to those who have conquered,
    whereas the sluggards and sinners have clothed themselves in a name that is utterly evil:
    there is reproach for the idle, and reproof for the sinners.

2. October gives rest to the weary after the dust and dirt of the summer,
    its rain washes, its dew anoints the trees and their fruit.

April gives rest to the fasters, it anoints, baptizes and clothes
in white;
it cleanses off the dirt of sin from our souls.
October presses out the oil for us, April multiplies mercies
for us;
In October fruit is gathered, in April sins are forgiven.

3. Because Jezebel defrauded Truth [1 Kgs 21:5ff.], the earth
refused its produce,
the womb of the earth held back, as a reproof, the seeds
that the farmers had lent it,
the earth suffocated the seeds within itself, because its in-
habitants had deceitfully held back truth.
The earth, whose nature is to bear, became barren against
her custom [1 Kgs 17:1 (drought)],
while the cruse and the horn gave birth and bore fruit
against their nature [1 Kgs 17:16].
The same prophet's voice that had deprived the earth [1
Kgs 17:1 (Elijah)] also caused barren wombs to be
fruitful.

4. Famine took its course in the land, and the flow of corn
to the granaries stood still;
the grain stores that had been full were emptied, the oil-
cellars became bare.
But Elijah joined together flour and oil as with a yoke,
and he who was lifted up in the chariot and conquered death
[2 Kgs 2:11]
conquered the famine, using these two symbols. The rain
provided the bounds for the course of his life [1 Kgs
18:45]
when the Lord of the clouds stretched out to him a crown
of plenty from his flood-waters.

5. A royal portrait is painted with visible colors,
and with oil that all can see is the hidden portrait of our
hidden King portrayed
on those who have been signed: on them baptism, that is
in travail with them in its womb,
depicts the new portrait, to replace the image of the former
Adam [1 Cor 15:45]
who was corrupted; it gives birth to them with triple pangs,
accompanied by the three glorious names, of Father, Son
and Holy Spirit.

6. This oil is the dear friend of the Holy Spirit, it serves him,
   following him like a disciple. With it the Spirit signed priests
   and anointed kings;
   for with the oil the Holy Spirit imprints his mark on his
   sheep.
   Like a signet ring whose impression is left on wax,
   so the hidden seal of the Spirit is imprinted by oil on the
   bodies of those who are anointed in baptism; thus are
   they marked in the baptismal mystery.

7. With the distinctive oil bodies are anointed for forgiveness,
   bodies that were filled with stains are made white without
   effort [Isa 1:18]:
   they go down sordid with sin, they go up pure like children,
   for baptism is a second womb for them.
   Rebirth in the font rejuvenates the old, as the river rejuve-
   nated Naaman [2 Kgs 5:14].
   O womb that gives birth without pangs to the children of
   the kingdom!

8. The priesthood ministers to this womb as it gives birth;
   anointing precedes it, the Holy Spirit hovers [Gen 1:2] over
   its streams,
   a crown of Levites surrounds it, the chief priest is its
   minister,
   the angels rejoice at the lost who in it are found [Luke
   15:10].
   Once this womb has given birth, the altar suckles and nur-
   tures them:
   her children eat straight away, not milk, but perfect Bread!

9. Oil, the beneficial fountain, accompanies the body, that
   fount of ills;
   for oil wipes out sins, just as the flood wiped out the
   unclean;
   for the flood, acting in justice, wiped out the wicked:
   those who had not subdued their lusts drowned, having
   brought on the flood through these lusts;
   but oil, acting in goodness, wipes out sins in baptism,
   for sin is drowned in the water and cannot live with all its
   desires.

10. Oil in its love accompanies the baptized in his need,
    when, despising his life, he descends and buries himself in
    the water;

oil by nature does not sink, but it accompanies the body
it has sunk its mark into.
Once baptized it raises up from the deep a wealth of riches.
Christ by nature cannot die, yet he clothed himself with
a mortal body,
he was baptized, and so raised up from the water a treasure of life for the race of Adam.

11. The oil gave itself for sale in place of the orphans, to pre-
vent their being sold [2 Kgs 4:1-7];
it acts as a pillar to the fatherless, having restrained the fate
that had tried to sever
the two brothers, like shoots, from the stock of freedom
and graft [cf. Rom 11:17] them on to the stock of slavery.
The price of the oil made an end of the bonds of debt that
cried out against the debtors;
it tore up the bonds that had come to deprive a mother of
her sons.

12. Oil in its love, like Christ [Col 2:14], pays debts that are
not its own.
The treasure that of its own accord turned up for the debtors in the pottery vessel
is like the Treasury that also turned up for the gentiles in
a body made from earth.
The oil became a slave for a time to free the freeborn,
but Christ became a slave for a time to free those enslaved
to sin.
In both name and deed does the oil depict Christ.

13. Let oil in all its forms acknowledge you in your entirety,
for oil gives rest to all.
The olive served Christ, who gives life to all, depicting him
in its abundance, its branches and its leaves:
with its branches it praised him—through the children [John
12:15; Matt 21:16]; with its abundance—through Mary,
[John 12:3];
with its leaf again, through the dove it served Noah his type
[Gen 8:11];
with its branches it depicted the symbol of his victory, with
its abundance it depicted the symbol of his dying [John
12:7],
with its leaf it depicted the symbol of the resurrection: the
flood disgorging it, as death disgorged Christ.

14. The face that gazes on a vessel filled with oil
    sees its reflection there, and he who gazes hard sets his spiritual gaze thereon
    and sees in its symbols Christ. And as the beauty of Christ is manifold,
    so the olive's symbols are manifold.
    Christ has many facets, and the oil acts as a mirror to them all:
    from whatever angle I look at the oil, Christ looks out at me from it.

15. Who has overwhelmed me in my weakness with these insistent waves?
    —for when the waves of oil lift me up, they hand me over to the sayings about Christ,
    and then the waves of Christ bear me back to the symbols of oil.
    The waves meet each other, and I am in their midst:
    I will say as Simon said: "Draw me up, Lord, as you did Simon,
    for the innumerable waves have worn me out; O compassionate one, draw me out who am so feeble! [see Matt 14:30].

    Refrain: However great our wonder for you is, O Lord,
    Your glory exceeds what our tongues can express.

Hymns on the Church *36*
On Christ as Light in Mary and in the Jordan

In spite of the title of the collection, this hymn looks to the birth and rebirth from which the Church springs. It falls into three sections: stanzas 1–5, 6–11, and 12–15.

The first section, especially stanzas 3–4, provides a key but requires some perspective from Syriac tradition. When Christ entered the Jordan he consecrated all baptismal water in advance, making it a womb capable of rebirth. When the baptismal water is consecrated the rite reenacts Christ's entry into the Jordan, Christ's conception in Mary's womb, and the Christian's rebirth from the womb of the baptismal font. Indeed, lurking just below the surface is the allusion to the Son's eternal birth from the Father. Thus, Christ's conception in Mary's womb is her baptism; his baptism is his emergence (rebirth) as the Father's Son;

and the Christian's baptism is rebirth in Paradise. Ephrem's allusions have many storeys in them.

Nor is the temporal and spatial horizon only that of the Jordan. Sacred and profane space and time intersect, enabling the
poet to see the whole of Christ's life, even the ascension, present
by anticipation in his Jordan experience (st. 5): Descent into the
Jordan is descent also into Mary's womb and into the tomb from
which he is reborn to rise and ascend. It is but a step from such
an intersection to understanding the baptism of the Christian as
a reenactment of the Jordan, the nativity, the passion, and the
resurrection. Tertullian (vol. 6, ch. 2), and Cyril of Jerusalem (ch.
1) are quite faithful to this tradition when they call the newly baptized "christs." The theme of light that permeates the hymn is
a metaphor for transformation and suggests that the setting of
the hymn is the feast of the Epiphany in Edessa or Nisibis.

The text is that of E. Beck, ed., CSCO 198 (1960) 90–92; the
translation is that of Sebastian Brock, "St. Ephrem on Christ as
Light in Mary and in the Jordan: *Hymni de Ecclesia* 36," *Eastern Churches Review* 7 (1975) 137–144. Brock's article has a valuable study of the hymn as well.

Hymn 36

1. When it is associated with a source of light
   an eye becomes clear,
   it shines with the light that provisions it,
   it gleams with its brightness,
   it becomes glorious with its splendor,
   adorned by its beauty.

   Refrain: Blessed is the Creator of light.

2. As though on an eye
   the Light settled in Mary,
   It polished her mind,
   made bright her thought
   and pure her understanding,
   causing her virginity to shine.

3. The river in which he was baptized
   conceived him again symbolically;
   the moist womb of the water
   conceived him in purity,
   bore him in chastity,
   made him ascend in glory.

4. In the pure womb of the river
   you should recognize the daughter of man,
   who conceived having known no man,
   who gave birth without intercourse,
   who brought up, through a gift,
   the Lord of that gift.

5. As the Daystar in the river,
   the Bright One in the tomb,
   he shone forth on the mountain top
   and gave brightness too in the womb;
   he dazzled as he went up from the river,
   gave illumination at his ascension.

6. The brightness which Moses put on
   was wrapped on him from without,
   whereas the river in which Christ was baptized
   put on Light from within,
   and so did Mary's body, in which he resided,
   gleam from within.

7. Just as Moses gleamed
   with the divine glory
   because he saw the splendor briefly,
   how much more should the body
   wherein Christ resided gleam,
   and the river where he was baptized?

8. The brightness that the stammering Moses
   put on in the wilderness
   did not allow the darkness
   to darken the inside of his dwelling,
   for the light from his face
   served as a sun that went before his feet—

9. like the heavenly beings
   who need no other source of light
   for their eyes to see,
   for their pupils
   flow with light, and they are clothed
   in rays of glory.

10. For if the sun chases out darkness
    without using light
    apart from its own
    —for the sun needs
    no luminary for light,
    seeing it is the source of its own rays—

11. so too at the resurrection
    the righteous are light,
    for their clothing is splendor,
    their garment brightness:
    they become their own light,
    providing it themselves.

12. Save me, Lord, on that day
    when the wicked put on
    the garment of all their sins,
    clothing full of stains,
    whence spring for them
    darkness and torment,

13. just as from the body
    in times of sickness
    there spring up
    bitter pains and fever,
    as fetters for its wrongdoing
    and a rod to chastise it.

14. O Good One, who prepared for us
    the sun by day
    and by night the moon
    with the candelabra of the stars,
    may your glorious comfort
    reach me through your grace.

15. Give thanks to the Creator of the light
    wherein is depicted
    the heavenly Light;
    give praise to the Maker of the light
    that is a symbol
    of the Light of our Savior!

Hymns on the Faith *10*
To Christ on the Incarnation, the Holy Spirit, and the Sacraments

This collection of hymns on the faith date most likely from Ephrem's Edessa years, the last decade of his life (363–373), when he encountered Arianism face to face. He has the Arians in mind, for instance, when, in the first four stanzas, he speaks of the many levels of apprehending God's nature and seeks the lowest level. Veiled as it is in imagery, the "lowly part" counters Arian rationalism.

The text is that of E. Beck, CSCO 154 (1955); the translation is that of Robert Murray, "A Hymn of St. Ephrem to Christ on the Incarnation, the Holy Spirit, and the Sacraments," *Eastern Churches Review* 3 (1970) 142–150, which also contains a valuable study of the hymn. About content and structure, he comments (p. 137):

> The hymn first refers to the difficulty of speaking about Christ's nature (sts. 1–4) and contemplates gospel examples of timidity in approaching Christ (5–6). From Christ's bodily actions Ephrem passes to consider the Eucharist, in which "fire and Spirit" are active and are received (7–9). This reception is contrasted with Old Testament examples (10–15). The altarcloth, like the table-cloth in the Upper Room, is the place where the mystery is realized (15–16). The Holy Spirit's consecrating action is considered in Mary's womb, in the Eucharist, and in baptism (17–21), and the hymn ends by picking up several earlier images (19ff.), concluding, as usual, with a personal "signature" by the author (22).

The image of the Spirit as a mother bird "hovering" (16) is characteristically Syriac, as is the figure of fire, which is especially connected to Christ's baptism. Nonetheless, the "Fire and Spirit" evoke Origen (vol. 6, ch. 3), who appears to be touched by the same tradition.

Hymn 10

1. Lord, you have had it written: "Open your mouth and I
     will fill it" [Ps 81:10].
   See, Lord, your servant's mouth and his mind are open to
     you!
     Fill it, O Lord, with your gift,
   that I may sing your praise according to your will.

   Refrain: Make me worthy to approach your Gift with awe!

2. For speaking of you there are different levels;
   in my boldness I approach the lowest step.
     Deep in silence your Birth is sealed;
   what mouth dare venture to deal with it?

3. Though your nature is one, its expressions are many;
   they find three levels, high, middle, and lowly.
     Make me worthy of the lowly part,
   of picking up crumbs from the table of your wisdom.

4. Your highest expression is hidden with your Father,
   your middle riches are the wonder of the Watchers [i.e.,
        angels].
    A tiny stream from your teaching, Lord,
    for us below makes a flood of interpretations.

5. For if even the great John cried out,
   "I am not worthy, Lord, of the strap of your sandals"
        [Mark 1:7],
      then I like the sinner-woman must flee
   to the shade of your garments, to start from there [see Luke
        7:36-50].

6. And like her who feared yet took heart when she was healed,
   heal my fear of terror, let me take heart in you;
      let me pass from your garment to your body,
   that to the best of my power I may speak of it.

7. Your garment, Lord, is a fountain of healing.
   In your visible dress dwells your hidden power.
      A little spittle from your mouth
   was a mighty wonder, for light [was] in the clay it made
        [John 9:6-7].

8. In your Bread is hidden a Spirit not to be eaten,
   in your Wine dwells a Fire not to be drunk.
      Spirit in your Bread, Fire in your Wine,
   a wonder set apart, [yet] received by our lips!

9. When the Lord came down to earth, to mortals,
   a new creation he created them, like to the Watchers [see
        2 Cor 5:17; Gal 6:15].
      He mingled fire and spirit in them,
   to make them fire and spirit within.

10. The Seraph touched not the coal with his fingers [see Isa
        6:6-7];
       only Isaiah's lips did it touch.
       He neither held it nor ate it;
    but to us, see! our Lord has granted both.

11. Bodily food for angels of spirit [see Gen 18:8-9]
    did Abraham bring, and they did eat;
       New wonder! Our mighty Lord gives to bodily creatures
    Fire and Spirit as food and drink.

12. Fire came down in anger on sinners and ate them up [Gen
        19:24; 2 Kgs 1:10ff.];

the Fire of Mercy has come down on bread, to stay.
　　Instead of that fire eating men up,
you have eaten Fire in the Bread and found Life.

13. Fire came down on Elijah's sacrifice and ate it up;
　　the Fire of Love has become our living sacrifice.
　　　Fire ate up the offering;
　　in your Offering, Lord, we have eaten Fire.

14. "Who has ever grasped the wind in his hands?" [Prov 30:4].
　　Come and see, Solomon, what your father's Lord has done!
　　　[Ps 110:1].
　　Fire and Spirit, against their nature,
　　he has mingled and poured into his disciples' hands.

15. "Who has ever," he asked, "gathered the waters in a
　　　cloth?" [Prov 30:4].
　　See, a cloth, in the lap of Mary, the Fountain!
　　　Enclosed in a cloth, your handmaids take
　　from the Cup of Life, a drop of Life!

16. See, Power concealed in the cloth of the sanctuary,
　　a power which no mind has ever conceived.
　　　His love bent down, descended, and hovered
　　over the cloth on the altar of reconciliation.

17. See, Fire and Spirit in the womb that bore you!
　　See, Fire and Spirit in the river where you were baptized!
　　　Fire and Spirit in our Baptism;
　　in the Bread and the Cup, Fire and Holy Spirit!

18. Your Bread kills the Devourer [death] who had made us
　　　his bread,
　　your Cup destroys death which was swallowing us up.
　　　We have eaten you, Lord, we have drunk you,
　　not to exhaust you, but to live by you.

19. The strap of your sandal was dread to the discerning;
　　the hem of your cloak was fearsome to the understanding.
　　　By prying into you, our foolish generation
　　has lost its reason, drunk with new wine.

20. How wonderful your footsteps, walking on the waters!
　　You subdued the great sea beneath your feet [see Matt
　　　14:25].
　　　[Yet] to a little stream you subjected your head,
　　bending down to be baptized in it.

21. The stream was like John who baptized in it,
    in their smallness each an image of the other.
       To the stream so little, the servant so weak,
    the Lord of them both subjected himself.

22. See, Lord, my arms are filled with the crumbs from your
       table;
    there is no room left in my lap.
       As I kneel before you, hold back your Gift;
    Keep it in your storehouse to give us again!

Hymns for the Epiphany *1 and 6*

A number of Epiphany hymns are attributed to Ephrem, four-
teen of which have been translated in NPNF 13 (2nd series). Their
liturgical setting is the feast of the Epiphany. The principal theme
is light, specifically, Christ the Light of the world, who dawns
among humans at his birth, appears in the full light of day at his
baptismal birth in the Jordan, and recapitulates at his baptism
key events in the history of salvation, among them Creation (Gen
1:3), the healing of Namaan the Syrian (2 Kgs 5:1-27), the Passover and Exodus (Exod 12-14), and the wilderness years (Exod
15-20). For the poet these constitute the traditional types about
which he sings. His perspective, however, is the Jordan, and he
moves from John the Baptist to the Holy Spirit to the "baptized
who have come up from the water" (6:9). All four Gospel accounts of the Baptist and the baptism of Christ have provided
the strands out of which he has woven his hymns (see Mark 1:9-12;
Matt 3:13-17; Luke 3:21-22; John 1:29-34).

As already noted they breathe the spirit of Ephrem, reflect a
baptismal liturgy little different from his, and doubtless come
from Edessa, probably within a decade or two of his death. They
presuppose that solemn baptism was administered on the feast.
The text is that of E. Beck, CSCO 187 (1959) 1-12, 50-55; the
translations are those of Sebastian Brock, who kindly provided
them to the author privately.

Hymn 1

Refrain: Praise to you from your flock on the day of your
Epiphany.

1. He has renewed the heavens—because foolish men had worshiped all sorts of luminaries; he has renewed the earth that

had grown old in Adam. There was a new creation in his very spittle: the All-Sufficing has restored bodies, along with minds.

2. Gather together, you lepers, and come to receive cleansing without any toil, for there is no need, as in Elisha's case, to be baptized in the river seven times over; nor again is there the weariness which the priests imposed with all their sprinklings.

3. Seven times over did Elisha cleanse Naaman, symbolizing seven evil spirits. The hyssop and blood serve as a powerful type: there is no place now for being kept apart, for the Lord of all's Son is not kept apart from the Lord of all.

4. Moses made sweet the waters at Mara, for they had been bitter, and the people had complained and murmured. Moses gave them a sign of baptism, that his Lord would go down and make sweet those who are embittered.

5. The cloud overshadowed and held back the heat from the Israelite camp, thus delineating the type of the Spirit of Holiness who overshadows you in the baptismal font, turning back the flame from your bodies.

6. The Israelite people crossed over the sea of old, delineating baptism's type in which you are now washed; the people crossed over it but failed to believe; the peoples are baptized in it, having believed and so received the Spirit of Holiness.

7. The Word sent the Voice to proclaim, prior to his advent, so that John might prepare for him the way by which he would travel, arranging the Bride's betrothal while he was on his way, so that she might be ready for him to come and receive her in marriage from the baptismal water.

8. The voice of prophecy goaded on the child of barren parents: he went forth wandering and preaching in the wilderness, "Behold there comes the royal Son. Prepare the way so that he may enter and reside in your abodes."

9. John cried out, "He who comes after me was prior to me; I am the voice, and not the Word; I am the lampstand, and not the Light; I am the star which rises before the Sun of Righteousness appears."

10. In the wilderness did John cry out and say, "Repent, O sinners, of your evil deeds. Proffer fruits of repentance,

for behold there is coming one who will separate the wheat from the tares.''

11. The luminary has prevailed, marking out a symbol on the steps he ascended. There are twelve days since he ascended, and today is the thirteenth—a perfect symbol of him and his twelve.

12. The darkness was vanquished—in order to indicate that Satan had been vanquished; and the light prevailed in order to acclaim the First Born's triumph. The Dark One was vanquished along with the darkness, and our Light has prevailed along with the luminary.

13. In the heights and in the depths the Son had two heralds: the star of light acclaimed him on high, while John too made proclamation below—two heralds, one belonging to earth, the other to heaven.

14. The star of light, contrary to its nature, blazed out all of a sudden—smaller than the sun, yet greater than the sun: smaller than it in its visible light, yet greater than it in its hidden power, thanks to him whose symbol it was.

15. The Epiphany star cast its rays amongst those in the dark, leading them like the blind, and as a result they came and received that great Light: they presented their gifts—and received Life. They worshiped and then returned home.

16. The heavens are opened, the Jordan water exults, the Dove is resplendent, the Father's voice, stronger than thunder, makes utterance: "This is my beloved." The Watchers gave tidings and children shouted out with their Hosannas.

Hymn 6

1. The Spirit descended from the heights
   and sanctified the water as it hovered.
   When John baptized Jesus
   it left all others and settled on one,
   but now it has come down and settled
   upon all who are reborn in the water of baptism.

2. Of all those that John baptized
   the Spirit dwelt on one alone,
   but now it has flown down
   to dwell upon many.
   Running to meet the First who went up from the Jordan
   it embraced and dwelt upon him.

3. It is a wonder that the Purifier of all
      should have gone down to the water to be baptized:
   the seas declared the river blessed
      in which you, Lord, were baptized;
   the waters that are above, in the heaven, too
      were envious that they had not been held worthy to wash
         you.

4. It is a wonder, Lord, now as well
      that, though the springs are full of water,
   only the baptismal font
      can wash clean:
   the seas may be mighty with all their water,
      but they have not the power to wash.

5. If your power, Lord, resides
      in something insignificant,
   then it grows, as part of the Kingdom;
      if you reside in the wilderness, it receives peace.
   through your power water has conquered sin,
      for Life has drowned it.

6. The sheep leapt with joy to see
      the hand in readiness to baptize.
   O lambs, receive your marking,
      enter in and mingle with the flock:
   today the angels rejoice in you
      more than in all the rest of the sheep.

7. Angels and Watchers rejoice
      at the birth effected by Spirit and water:
   beings of fire and spirit rejoice
      since those in the body have now become spiritual;
   the seraphs who cry "holy" rejoice
      because the number of those who sing "holy" is
         increased.

8. Since the angels rejoice
      at the single sinner who repents,
   how much more do they rejoice
      when at each feast and gathering
   baptism gives birth
      to heavenly beings out of earthly.

9. The baptized who have come up from the water are
         sanctified,
      those who went down to it have been cleansed;

those who have come up have been robed in praise,
those who went down have stripped off sin.
Adam stripped off his glory all of a sudden,
you have put on glory all of a sudden.

10. A house made of mud bricks, when it gets old,
can be renovated by using water;
O Adam's body, made a muddy earth,
grew old and was renovated by water.
The priests are like builders, you see,
making new your bodies once more.

11. It is a great wonder that the wool
which can receive every dye
—like the mind that receives all kinds of thoughts—
takes on the very name of the dye:
—just as you were baptized "hearers"
and have now been named "partakers."

12. Elisha, using the hidden name,
sanctified ordinary water
and the leper [Naaman] who visibly dipped in them
was cleansed by the hidden power:
leprosy was destroyed in the water,
just as sin is destroyed in baptism.

13. Today your debts are wiped out
and your names are written down;
the priest wipes them out in the water,
and Christ writes your names in heaven.
By the two actions
is your joy redoubled.

14. Today mercy shines forth,
stretching from extremity to extremity.
The Sun [of Righteousness] was baptized: Mercy shone
    forth and Justice withdrew her anger;
Grace stretched forth her love,
giving mercy and salvation freely.

15. The older sheep within the fold
ran to embrace
the new lambs that have been added.
You are white now, put on white garments,
white both within and without,
your bodies, like your clothes.

16. "Blessed are you," cries every mouth—
     for in every respect are you blessed:
   sin has been chased from you,
     the Holy Spirit has resided upon you.
   Gloom fills the Evil One's face,
     joy the face of Him who is good.

17. You have received the gift freely
     —cease not in your watch over it,
   for if the pearl be lost
     it cannot be sought out again:
   it resembles virginity,
     once lost it cannot be recovered.

18. May the power of your white garments
     keep you pure from all stain.
   Tears can wash him
     whose freewill has defiled him.
   May the supplications of the community gain pardon
     for me who am the community's servant.

19. For the poet who has toiled with words,
     may there be pardon through mercy;
   for the preacher who has toiled with speaking,
     may there be forgiveness through grace;
   for the priest who has toiled in the baptismal rite,
     may there come a crown through justice.

20. From the mouths of all, equally,
     both those on earth and those above,
   watchers, cherubs and seraphs,
     baptized, the anointed and catechumens,
   —let us all cry out aloud
     "Praise to the Lord of the Feasts."

Narsai

Born in the early fifth century, Narsai quickly rose to prominence in Syriac Christianity. Although his life is shrouded in legend and his work lies largely buried in unedited manuscripts and little-known editions, a sketch is still possible. He was first a student in the school in Edessa and then its director *(Rabban)* for two decades (451–471). The controversies about the nature and person of Christ, however, which led to the councils of Ephesus

(431) and Chalcedon (451) and numbered such important adversaries as Nestorius (d. 451), Eutyches (ca. 378–454), and Cyril of Alexandria (vol. 6, ch. 3) also engulfed Edessa, especially its school and director.

Eventually (471), Narsai, as a disciple of the Antiochene school of biblical interpretation and an ardent student of the thought and writings of Theodore of Mopsuestia (ch. 1), fled to the east. Barsauma (ca. 420–490), bishop of Nisibis, himself a Theodoran, prevailed on Narsai to remain in the city, where Narsai founded the celebrated school of Nisibis, from which flowed the Churchmen, scholars, and doctrines that shaped the Church of the East, whose members are sometimes called, often inaccurately, Nestorian Christians. He died about 503.

As a writer, Narsai is revered as a master of the Syriac tongue. Tradition credits him with over three hundred metrical homilies (see above, Ephrem). Intricately structured and balanced, they employ a variety of rhetorical devices, which he uses with delicacy to enrich and unify his thought. Contemporary Western interest in him originated with Alphonse Mingana's publication (1906) of forty-seven of his metrical homiles. Subsequently, publication has moved at a measured pace because of the difficulty of producing critical editions.

Two extant baptismal homilies, 21 and 22, published by Mingana in 1906, reveal that his baptismal liturgy is strikingly similar to that of Mopsuestia, save for the absence of a postbaptismal anointing, and that his commentary owes much to Theodore. The reading, however, is taken from a small, recently published collection of Narsai's festal homilies, *A Homily on the Epiphany of Our Lord,* which, like those of his predecessors, revolves around the baptism of Christ. The homily is of special value because it explicitly integrates his Christological and his baptismal thought.

For Narsai, Adam is pivotal. God created him to bear the image of the divine nature and to be the bond between the worlds of spirit and matter. Adam's distinctive characteristic, his rationality, consisted precisely in his integrated nature of body and spirit. This corporeal nature, as a concretely existing entity, constituted Adam in Paradise. When the Fall spoiled everything, God determined to send one who was the exact equal of the first Adam in nature, exceeding him only in honor and accomplishment. Such is the Second Adam, in whom dwells the Word of God. As Second Adam he is constituted of two integral, concretely existing entities, or natures: One is "Adamite," namely, Jesus, the son of Mary; the other, divine, namely, the Word, the Son of God. Both entities, or natures, are the source of personal acts, but neither is the source of the personal acts of the other. Thus, the Word cannot suffer and die, nor can Jesus create, nor, more important, re-create.

Narsai insists on the distinction between the Word and the man Jesus and on the integrity and autonomy of each nature because he is convinced that only in this way can one assure the salvation of humankind. He sharply contests any and every position which seems to merge Jesus' humanity into the Word's divinity. As Narsai sees the matter, Eutyches, who fell afoul of Chalcedon (see vol. 6, ch. 3), not only did not accord Jesus a full humanity but despoiled his humanity by merging it into divinity. So also Cyril of Alexandria, whom Narsai calls "The Egyptian" in the reading. He considers the issue at stake a matter of life and death—salvation.

Narsai insists on the unity between the Word and the man Jesus, whom the Word assumed. Unfortunately, he is unable to explain to his adversaries adequately how Jesus and the Word are one, and, in their view, he jeopardizes salvation by severing the human and the divine.

Nonetheless, Narsai's "diophysitism" is important for baptism. Because he holds that there is an equality between the two Adams, he insists that the man Jesus is truly and fully baptized, and that what happened to him in his baptism happens also to the candidate for baptism. Unlike his adversaries, he remains untroubled by Christ's apparent need for baptism: The first and Second Adams are equal in nature—both require the ever-deeper indwelling of the Word, the Spirit, and the Father.

The text and translation (abridged) are those of Frederick G. Mcleod, *Narsai's Metrical Homilies on the Nativity, Epiphany, Passion, and Resurrection,* PO 182 (1979) 72–105; the introduction contains a valuable study of Narsai's thought. See also his "Man as the Image of God: Its Meaning and Theological Significance in Narsai," TS 42 (1981) 458–468.

A Homily on the Epiphany of Our Lord

Refrain: Blessed be the "Spring" [Christ] that flowed into
the Jordan and [from which] Adam drank and
his thirst was quenched.

My brothers:

A rational image the Creator willed to fashion for Adam
[i.e., Adam's corporate nature of body and spirit];
and he mixed a spirit with the colors of his lowly clay.

He fashioned, first of all, an earthen vessel from dust and
anointed it with a spirit; and the whole became a living being [Gen 2:7].

He depicted limbs on the colored visible clay and breathed
an invisible spirit into [this] visible being.

5. O Painter who has concealed his artistic power and set
the beauty of his fair image within a tablet [of clay]!

Acccording to mortal art, exterior [qualities] charm and
show viewers the beauty of their fashionings.

According to divine art, interior [qualities] charm; and the
exterior are but a covering for the interior.

A twofold vessel the Fashioner of the universe made for
our nature: a visible body and a hidden soul—one
man.

10. He made the exterior from dust that is lowly to look upon
and fashioned the interior from the secret [recesses]
of his majestic power.

He placed the precious [part], that contains life, in the
mortal and lowly [clay], in order to give life to mortality by the power of its vitality.

15. The interior [part], containing intelligence, vibrated on the
strings of [man's] body; and the clay became pleasing because of the melodious sound of the living
spirit.

The living one chanted in the temple of clay a hymn of
praise; and there assembled and came rational and
dumb beings at the

20.   sound of its [melodies].

The mortal one stood like a statue within a palace;
and over his features marveled spiritual and corporeal
[beings].

The Corruption of Adam's Image

25. For a short time, there remained the beauty of the temporal image;

but there arose a vile-like iniquity over its features
[Adam's fall].
The beautiful colors of his soul faded because of [his] desire for fruit;
and he acquired the color of mortality by [his] eating
of it.
Sin effaced the name of life [belonging to] the royal image
and inscribed on his name corruption, and death upon
his limbs.
[The image] became tarnished and wasted away for a long
time in [his] mortal condition;
and death trampled him and corrupted the beauty of
his rational being.
His ill-wisher mocked and also laughed at his humiliation;
and he lost hope that he would be renewed from his corruption.

The Renewal of Man

35. The King who saw that the evil ones mocked his foremost
image
took pity upon his image lest it be [further] outraged
by the insolent.
The image proclaims the royal authority by his visible
[aspect]
and, by his features, shows the beauty of the one who
constituted him.
In Adam's image was shown the authority of his Lord;
and, in his features, was signified the power of his hidden [divine nature].
And because Adam fell and death corrupted the image
[function] of his features,
the King sent "Pity" and "Mercy" to raise him up
[John the Baptist and Jesus].
Two messengers of peace he sent to honor his image,
and he proclaimed on earth a message of renewal for
mortality.
In his fashioning, he revealed to creatures the power of
his hidden [divine nature],
[while], in his renewal, he showed them the wealth of
his love.
He exalted much more the name of his renewal than his
fashioning,
so that he might make the heavenly ones marvel over
how much he loved him.

50. In his fashioning, [the angels] were bound [in kinship]
    from the beginning;
    and in his renewal, he gladdened those who were sad
    [man as the bond of the universe].

The Fashioning of the Second Adam

His [good] pleasure descended on [one] whom he fashioned in fitting love;
and he depicted on the tablet of Adam's body, a Second Adam.
In the [same] order as Adam, he depicted a [Second] Adam
with the color of [his divine] will,
and renewed Adam and his offspring through [this] Son
of Adam.

55. The Second Adam came forth from the womb as from
    the earth;
    and he is entirely like that First [Adam] whom the earth
    bore.
    In body and soul, the Second Adam is equal with the [first]
    Adam;
    but in authority, he is the Lord of Adam and his off-
    spring.
    He is equal in nature, but greater in honor than all those
    who have come to be;
    and the witness is the vigilant one [Gabriel, in Luke
    1:26-38], who announced his conception and called
    him "Lord."

60. In many [ways], the Second Adam is greater than Adam;
    and the rank that he attained [can] not be compared
    with that of [other] creatures.
    His conception is exalted because it has had no connec-
    tion with human seed;
    and his birth is glorious because heavenly beings were
    its heralds.
    He alone has received and inherited the name of lordship,

65. so that heavenly and earthly beings might obey him.
    His nature testifies that he is an adamite from earthly
    beings;
    but the name of his authority cries out and proclaims
    that he is divine.
    He is earthly because of [his] human body and soul,
    and he is heavenly because he has become the dwelling
    place for the God of the universe.

[Ll. 71-109. Narsai recounts and reflects on the birth and
conception of John the Baptist and then continues:]

John the Baptist in the Desert

[See Mark 1:4-11; Matt 3:11-17; John 1:24-34 for the basis of Narsai's rendition, vv. 111-334.]

110. John went forth [in the role of the] messenger who [comes]
before the King;
and the [divine] will drew him to a spiritual training.
For thirty years in the outer desert he continued to grow,
while meditating on the secrets of proclamation.
With this intent the [divine] will drew him away from an
inhabited region,
that by a spiritual intimacy he might instruct his life.
115. Away from men, he continued to grow in [his understanding of] the intent of [God's] wise plans,
until the Spirit of revelation called him to his preaching.
He dawned suddenly like the radiant sphere [of the sun]
120. and drew the [Jewish] people [to follow] after the light
of his preaching.
At the River Jordan, he opened the treasury of his Sender,
while crying out: "Come, sinners! Receive forgiveness!"
With [the promise of] forgiveness for iniquity, he roused
those sleeping in iniquity;
and those immersed [in iniquity] were startled by [this]
voice [proclaiming] a forgiveness without toil.
125. His message [sounded forth] as a trumpet in the ears of
the people;
and he gathered them with his message promising forgiveness for iniquity.
In a womb of water he was promising to beget them
and, as in a crucible, to renew them by [their] repentance.
He cast a net of spoken words over all stations [of life]
and enclosed them within [as they were] listening to his
preaching.

John's Foretelling of the Messiah

130. Through forgiveness he lured them as though [it were] bait,
and then signified what was the reason for the promise
that he made.
He cried out suddenly and altered his message to the
people:

"I am the servant and minister of the one who has chosen me.

I am the messenger who [comes] before [that] King of whom it is written [that he is the one] who comes;

135.   and he has sent me to preach; and behold, he is at hand according to expectation!

By water only he commanded me to give forgiveness for iniquity,

until he himself comes and gives the Spirit with forgiveness.

With fire and the Spirit, he will destroy the [thorny] growth of mortality

and bring forth the spiritual seed of a [new] life for the dead.

In the crucible of the Spirit, he will mold the image that iniquity has rendered odious,

140.   and impart the beauty of heavenly beings to earthly ones.

In a womb of water, he will generate men in a spiritual way,

as they are enrolled with a new name [as] first-born of the Spirit.

He will free the body from the slavery of mortality

and redeem the soul from the enticements of [sinful] desires.

He will forgive iniquity and give the Spirit as a pledge,

145.   so that his co-heirs may not doubt concerning his promises.

Behold! Within your midst he stands, but [he is] hidden from your eyes;

and not even I who proclaim him know him.

The [divine] will has revealed to me that I should proclaim his dawning among those in darkness,

so that through my words they might see the "Light of Justice."

I am the lamp, not the sphere of the majestic sun;

and the radiance of my words [can] not be compared with his majesty.

155. I am inferior to him in [every] comparative and measurable way;

and I am not worthy even to loosen the sandal[s] on his feet.

From the gift of his great wealth he has given me a little;
 and my senses have grown rich from the treasures of
 his hidden love.
Of a small portion of the Spirit who is from him my
 thoughts were deemed worthy;
 and I have acquired power for the preaching of his
 secrets.
To an extraordinary manner of preaching revelation has
 compelled me;
160. and from the womb, I was eager to go forth and accomplish its words.
And even though he set me apart for an apostolate of
 preaching,
 he has willed not to show me the splendor of his countenance except in mystery.
[It is] not under the appearance of external senses [that]
 I know him;
 by the Spirit he gave me a manifest sign so that I might
 learn who he is.
That one who said to me that I should preach the birth
 of baptism
165. depicted [and] showed me by the Spirit of revelation
 a figure of a dove.
This he revealed to me in mystery as one of the household:
 that whoever you see receiving the Spirit is the Lord.
And also the very reason that I have preached and baptized is
 to open up the way so that men might proceed to his
 revelation.
Behold! He has come to him, and therefore there is at hand
 the dawning of his light. . . .
[Ll. 174–194. The poet presents John's message of repentance and reflects on the him as "Pity." He then turns
 his gaze to Jesus.]

The Appearance of Jesus

195. He cried out suddenly in the Spirit of revelation who spoke
 with him:
 "Behold the Lamb who purifies the stains [of sin] and
 takes away iniquity!
This is he who I have said comes after me and [yet] is prior
 to me;

and I do not know how to call him who is older and
[yet] younger.

Younger than my own is his conception and his birth according to his bodily structure,

200.   but older than my own as regards the things that are
to come and the mysteries [that are] awaited."

[Ll. 203–224. Narsai replies to opponents who argued that
the Son "has descended and been embodied and become flesh" to "purify our iniquity," arguing that
the "Divine Essence" (the Son) put on "corporeal
being" (Jesus) with the result that the "Assumer"
conquered through him. He then returns to Jesus' encounter with John.]

Jesus' Appearance Before John

225. The Spirit revealed him [Jesus], and [John] saw him coming and he longed to meet him;

and he rejoiced because he saw the hope that prophets
and kings had desired [to see].

He saw that, as everyone [else], he was coming to him in
order that he might receive baptism from him;

230.   and he began to entreat [Jesus] that he baptize him and
not he [be baptized] by him.

"I am in need by you to be baptized as [I am] deficient;
you should not be coming to a poor one who has been
enriched by you.

You are the Spring who enables mortality to drink [the
water of] life!

Why do you need to be fulfilled by a mortal?

235. You are the holy one, and by you are purified the unclean
of soul.

And how [is it that] you are seeking purification of soul
[if you are] the one who purifies the stains [of sin]?

Yours is the treasury of all wisdom and secrets.

What does a skilled master learn from his disciple?

You are the luminary who enlightens the universe by the
light of his countenance.

What use to you is the feeble flame from the lamp of
my words?

Yours is the abundant sea of mercy that scours away iniquity.

240. Why do you bathe your majestic glory in ordinary water?"

Jesus' Reply

"Let it be so now!" the King replied to the herald.
"It is thus fitting that justice be fulfilled in me.
Let it be so! Do not reveal my majesty and my honor in
the sight of on-lookers,
until I perform and fulfill everything that is written.

245. Let it be so! I am being baptized as one deficient and in
need of mercy, .
so that I may fill up in my person [what is] lacking to
the human race.
From the [same] race that has succumbed to sin I am also.
Let it be so! I am paying for the bond that Adam wrote
in Eden.
From the [same] clay that passions have overwhelmed is
my structure.

250. Let it be so! I am heating our weak clay in the water
of the Spirit.
I am from the [same] lineage that death has swallowed
and defrauded of its life.
Let it be so! I am descending in mystery into the water
and raising it up.
I am a member of the race that is captive to the evil one
on its own accord.
I will go forth [to] bring back our captive race from the
rebel.
A bond of death my [fore] fathers wrote out and succumbed to sin;
and I have made an agreement that I will pay for it in
mystery first of all.

255. The comely image of our bodily structure has been tarnished and worn away.
I will descend [to] scour away the filth of iniquity from
its features.
In a crucible of water, I will mold our supreme image;
and instead of fire, I will breathe in it a spirit of life.
If I do not scour away its filth in my own person, it will
not be purified;
and if it does not descend with me to baptism, it will
not receive pardon.
As the first-fruits, the Creator chose me from [among]
mortals

260.   and appointed me to be as the ransom for their life.
    With me as the sacrifice he willed to reconcile himself to
        his servants;
      and he accepted my oblation and conferred through me
        peace upon the universe.
    And because he willed [to] set me apart from the universe
      · for [the sake of] the universe,
      it is right that I should pay the debt for all to the God
        of the universe.
265.   By a second birth, I will open the way of peace
    and I will proceed ahead before all [those] who will come
        in the mystery of renewal.
    Because of my coming the [divine] command chose you
        and called you 'the voice,'
      so that you might call men to the birth that will come
        to pass through me.
    Let it be so! I will be baptized by you in water as in a grave;
270.   and I will bring mortality down with me and up [again].
    I shall now be baptized as one who is in need of purifi-
        cation;
      and after a while, I will show my power by purifying
        those unclean.''

Jesus' Baptism

The herald yielded to his sender in what he heard;
    and the priest agreed to set his hand upon the high priest.
275.   Hail to John, who was ministering in the outer sanctuary,
    because he was deemed worthy to enter the Holy of Ho-
        lies which was forbidden!
    Hail to the member of [our] race that was deficient and
        in need of forgiveness,
      because he has opened the treasury that was hidden from
        all generations!
    [It was] not to the sanctuary of the high priests [that] John
        entered;
      [it was] to that of heaven [where] he opened an entrance
        in mystery.
285.   He concluded the rite that he was administering accord-
        ing to the Law
    and began to serve spiritually in a higher order.
    He abandoned the baptismal service [current] among the
        Jews
    and began to proceed according to the canon that
      [brings] atonement to the Gentiles.

He drew near to baptism, [that] great sea which washes
sinners;

and he opened the gates that were closed before men.

The high priest descended into the water and bathed and
sanctified it

290.   and conferred upon it the power of the Spirit to give life.

The holy one drew near to the weak and inanimate element
and made it a womb which begets men spiritually.

He descended and was plunged into the womb of water
as in a grave;

and he rose and was raised [to life] and raised Adam
in mystery.

The Anointing of the Spirit

295.   He ascended from the womb of a new mother that is not
[such] by nature;

and the Spirit descended and anointed him with divine
power.

[It was] with the Spirit [that] he anointed him—not with
the legal [Mosaic] ointment

[that was] the chosen ointment far superior to that of
[all] others.

Under the figure of a dove the Spirit had descended and
remained with him;

and by [this] open appearance, he signified concerning
his hidden [divine nature].

300.   By the dove, he showed that he has received the entire
wealth of the Spirit;

and he remains with him without departing according
to the [regular] order of his indwelling.

Through [this] peace-loving bird, he depicted the
manifestation

of that one in whom the peace of the universe will remain unshaken.

Under the sign of the dove, there descended [and] abode
in him hidden power;

305.   and the Father confirmed [this] through [his] declaration that "this is my beloved."

With the Spirit, he anointed him as an athlete [so as] to
engage in wrestling;

and he made [his] voice audible to the viewers of the
contest.

The viewers heard only the declaration which the Father
proclaimed;

but the anointing under the likeness of the dove they
did not observe.

310. In secret, he anointed him before only the one who was
administering [baptism];
for thus demands the great rite of anointing. . . .

315. To priests only is it permitted to sanctify oil,
since they discern, as householders, the greatness of its
power.

Also John, as minister and friend of the bridegroom,
through a revelation was deemed worthy to observe the
Spirit descending.

He alone saw the gift under the likeness of the dove
and bore witness and said that the vision is true and [its]
significance great.

320. "I saw the Spirit, a hidden nature, under the mystery of
a bird

descend [and] abide hidden in a visible one in perfect
love."

The mediator, who was administering [the baptism], gave
witness that the Spirit descended;
and the Father has subscribed by his declaration to the
mystery of our restoration.

[Ll. 323–368. The poet replies to those (Chalcedonians)
who hold that Jesus, who, as Son, is consubstantial
with humans, is, as Son, also consubstantial with the
Father. He argues that his very need for baptism
shows that he is a created human "essence," and not
a divine "essence." He then returns to baptism.]

The Renewal of Baptism

The image which was tarnished with the filth of iniquity
because of [Adam's] desire for fruit

370.   is the very one which the Spirit molded in the crucible
of baptism.

The lowly vessel of soft clay the Potter took
and remade it [into] a vessel that is useful for glorious
things.

The nature of Adam's clay the Creator took
and fashioned it in water and heated it in the Spirit; and
it acquired beauty.

Our nature had succumbed [and] also been pledged as a
hostage to death and the evil one;
and by our [same] nature, the Creator paid the debt for
our race.

375. Because of the hatefulness of our iniquity, there was tarnished the beauty of our [comely image];
   but he depicted us again in spiritual colors.
Evil envy had effaced our outward features;
   but he has now changed and engraved them within the
   tablet [of man's body].

The Divine Plan of Renewal

380. Our race was cast into exile as [being] vicious;
      and after it was humiliated, the voice that cast it out
      took pity upon it in mercy.
It was imprisoned in Sheol, and there were laid upon it
   the fetters of death;
   but Mercy which had fashioned it took pity on its fallen
   state and descended [to] redeem it.
It was entirely putrid and being torn asunder by the diseases of iniquity;
   but Pity [John the Baptist] bandaged it and washed
   away from it the stink of its iniquity.
385. One limb [God] chose from the whole body of men
   and taught him in the Spirit to heal the diseases of the
   members of his race.
One man he chose anew in an extraordinary manner
   and renewed through him [our] nature which had worn
   away in mortality.
He did not depict him with the colors of human seed.
   He mixed in the color of the Spirit [and] depicted him
   in body and soul.
In body and soul he structured [and] made him in the likeness of Adam,
390.   so that he might thereby renew the body and soul of
       his companions.
As a comely dwelling he structured and made him for the
   [good] pleasure of his love,
   so that in his structure he might bind the universe in
   love to himself.
In the temple of [Jesus'] body, he willed to receive the worship of men;
   and in his visible [nature], to show the universe the
   power of his hidden [nature].
395. For thirty years, he reared him in body and intimacy of
   soul,
   while he was growing up in the sight of on-lookers and
   before his own countenance.

After a time when there was completed [his] bodily growth,
  he willed to signify the renewal which will be fulfilled
  in him.
He chose from his race a herald and sent [him] before him;

400. and he went forth [and] proclaimed the "voice" of
  whom it is written in prophecy.
He [John] gathered and brought [together] the sons of
  Jacob who were scattered
  and announced to them the news of the King whom they
  were awaiting.
He invited them to the banquet of the spiritual
  bridegroom;
  and under coaxing, they took [his] advice, although un-
  willingly.

405. He gave him the name of the "Lamb" and called him "the
  sacrifice who makes atonement for all";
  and he depicted by his baptism death and life and the
  renewal of all.
He compared him to a bridegroom [John 3:29] because
  of his love for men;
  and he called the bride, the members of his race who
  adhered to him.
[This one] fulfilled [the role] of the bridegroom at the marriage feast of faith
  and took to himself the church of the Gentiles [as] his
  betrothed of holiness.
Instead of purple, he covered her with the garment of
  baptism

410. and placed on her [head] a crown wholly plaited with
  the seals of the Spirit.

415. With great adornment, [the Spirit] showed his glory to on-
  lookers,
  because, although he is earthly, he gave him the crown
  of the Kingdom on high.
The voice of the Father was exalting him to an honor
  greater than anyone [else's]
  by testifying: "This is my beloved, and he fulfills my
  will!"
The Father cries out and the Son is baptized and the Spirit
  descends:

420. three witnesses who have subscribed to the authority of
  the King.

A Man Was Baptized

It is a member of our race who was baptized and acquired
the name of sonship;

and to him has been given the sovereign power and the
crown on high.

He is the one whom the Spirit anointed with power and
with whom he remained

[and] about whom the Father has borne witness by his
declaration that his love is true.

425. He is the one who was deemed worthy [to] become the
dwelling place for the Word of the Father;

and he was honored with the name of the [divine] essence, [a name] that is the most exalted of all.

He also testifies concerning the things that have come to
pass in his regard,

which were done to a man who is like to [other] men:

[Namely] a human baptism and a body that was baptized
by corporeal beings,

430. and [the fact that] he opened the way to renewal for
the fellow members of his race.

The rank and the name which he inherited cry out that
he is from mortals

[and] that he became by grace heir and lord in the height
and the depth.

The Spirit which he received under the sign of a dove has
revealed and signified to us

that he is also from the [same] race that is deficient and
in need.

435. Through the gift [of the Spirit], he has fulfilled and perfected [what was] deficient in him

and has made the fellow members of his race share in
the wealth of the Spirit.

He was baptized as every corporeal being in ordinary
water,

but the womb of baptism generated him in a spiritual
way.

In the name of the [divine] essence, the three names [of
the Trinity], he was baptized and sanctified:

440. the Father in the voice [from heaven], and the Son in
love, and the Spirit in the ointment.

The Word and the Body Are the One Son of God

The three names [of the Trinity] fulfilled for him the name
which he received;

and he was exalted in name and in reality and began
to reign over all.

At the annunciation of his conception, he [God] promised
him the name of sonship;

and he brought it to pass in mystery by means of a spiritual birth.

445. "The Son of the Most High," the vigilant one said, "He
is going to be"; and this was fulfilled for him by the
declaration that the Father has sealed.

Behold! The things that have happened to him cry out as
heralds

that it was a man who received the Spirit under the figure of a dove.

He was a man whom the Spirit anointed with hidden
power,

so that by the power of the Spirit he might banish demons and cure diseases.

450. He was a man in body and soul, save for iniquity;

and [God] anointed him with the Spirit; and he became
in power the God-man.

By the name of "man," I call him because of his body;

and the name of "God," I give him because of his rank.

One I call the Word and the Body, the Son of God:

one in the [divine] essence because he [can] not be parted
by a division.

The natures I have distinguished by the name of two. It
was not sons!

455.   As one I know the Son of the [divine] essence and the
son who is from us!

"Messiah" and "Son" I call him because of the two [facts]

that the Spirit anointed him and he became in love the
Son with the Word.

The Word and the body—when I say [that they are] two
according to nature,

it is like the body and the soul within it [being] one man.

The soul with the body and the body with the soul are
separate but co-[partners];

and everyone testifies that they are two but called one.

460. The Word with the body [is] in the [same] order as reason within the soul,

which is in the soul and [yet] outside of it in-
discriminately.

In this order [of union] is set the edifice that [forms] the
confession of my discourse,

when I join two that are separate into one whole.

And if the heretics wrong me with calumny,

465. let these show who it is who was baptized and [whom]
the Spirit anointed.

[Ll. 466–524. With some bitterness, Narsai rejects his opponents, who seem to be both Chalcedonians and
(Eutychian) Monophysites. He cites heresiarchs of the
past like the extreme Arians, Paul of Samosata, Eu-
nomius, Eutyches, and Arius as their teachers. In the
process, he singles out Cyril of Alexandria (vol. 6,
ch. 3) whom he calls "The Egyptian," who conquered
by "impudence"—a reference to the councils of
Ephesus and Chalcedon.]

A Concluding Exhortation

525. An image of the King my thoughts have depicted on a tablet of words;

and by my words I have wanted to show it to viewers.

He has permitted me to depict an image of the promise
[he made] in words:

that he has granted forgiveness to the members of his
household by the seal of his name.

He gave his word and promised a renewal of the body and
redemption of the soul,

530. and he wrote these out on the two tablets of water and
the Spirit.

The goal of life he set in baptism for his forces,

so that they might aim at the fashioning of the kingdom on high.

In water he fixed the new goal of spiritual birth,

because everyone who willingly does likewise receives
freedom.

Behold the promise of the King on high which [can] not
be broken!

Come! Let us strive to receive gratis the wealth of the
Spirit!

Behold! The goal is fixed before [his] disciples so that they
might imitate him.

535. Let the heart believe and the mouth confess and the
faculties take aim [at the goal]!

This [is] the road [that] the King has traversed for us in
his own person.

540.   Come! Let us travel on it to the end as long as there
is light.

Behold! There is opened the womb which begets men
spiritually.

Bury mortality in baptism and acquire life!

Let everyone hear that declaration [of the Father]: "This
is my beloved";

and let us acquire love for that one who holds men in
his love.

With John, let us cry out in one voice the confession:

This is the Lamb of the God of the universe who purifies
the stains [of sin]!"

Jacob of Serugh

A younger contemporary of Narsai, Jacob was born about 449
at Curtam (Turkey) on the Euphrates. He studied at the school
of Edessa toward the end of Narsai's directorship (ca. 470) and
was ordained a priest. Whether he became a monk is not certain,
but he quickly acquired a reputation for both holiness and wisdom, was named bishop (*chorepiscopos,* i.e., local auxiliary
bishop) of Hauran (Syria) in 502, and finally bishop of Batnan
in the district of Serugh (Turkey) in 518. He died in 521.

Although Jacob studied under Narsai, he took a position op-
posite the master's in the controversies about the human and divine natures of Christ, which led to Chalcedon. As the reading
demonstrates (cf. his reasoning about Christ's need for baptism
with Narsai's), his heart was with those often but inaccurately
called "Monophysites" (see vol. 6, ch. 3), and he numbered
among his friends and colleagues the leaders of the movement,
especially Philoxenus of Mabbug (d. 523) and Severus of Antioch
(d. 538). Nevertheless, he was a man of irenic dispostion who tried
always to avoid Christological controversy, a man, as one scholar
has put it, "full of nostalgia for the unity of the preceding century." Jacob is revered especially among Syrian Orthodox and
Maronite communities.

Although the bishop's congregations were comparatively rural
they were not uncultured, as his literary legacy testifies. Nonetheless, his mission was principally catechetical. At the heart of his
catechetics was the metrical homily of his predecessors. More than
three hundred of his homilies are extant in a variety of languages

including Syriac, Armenian, Georgian, Arabic, and Ethiopian. Unlike Narsai, he left no commentaries on the baptismal rites; nevertheless, baptism is the express subject of three homilies. Because of their length, only one has been selected for the reading.

The catechetical tradition in which Jacob stands is clearly inspired by Ephrem and his heirs: The Jordan is center stage; baptism's power flows from the pierced side of Christ; the sacrament is a mystical marriage; the Spirit and adoptive sonship are its principal gifts; the radiance of transformation is its primary effect; and baptism is a return to Paradise.

There is no reason to suppose that the liturgy had changed in any substantive way from that of Narsai and his Edessene predecessors, save that the recitation of the Lord's Prayer seems now to be part of the postbaptismal ritual. Nor is there any indication that a postbaptismal anointing had been added.

The text is that of Paul Bedjan, *Homiliae selectae Mar Jacobi sarugensis,* vol. 1 (Paris/Leipzig, 1905) 153–167; the translation is that of Sebastian Brock, which he has kindly supplied to the author in correspondence. Space requires some abridgement. For a valuable study see his "Baptismal Themes in the Writings of Jacob of Serugh," *Orientalia Christiana Analecta* 205 (1976) 324–347.

Memra 7: On the Baptism of the Law
the Baptism of John,
and the Baptism Our Lord Gave the Apostles

At the Son's Epiphany creation, which had been darkened, was illumined,
the blind world that could not see before now saw the Light:
the Radiance from the Essence shone out in the world which thus grew light;
like daylight he drove out the shadows from every quarter.
5. Our Lord showed himself as Light amidst the darkness,
while the night, with which the entire world had been covered, took to flight;
He flew down from the Father and shone forth in the virgin daughter of Abraham,
commencing on the path he had set himself to walk in the world.
In holy fashion did the Light reside in the Virgin's womb,

10. making there the starting point for his journey in the body.
    He came forth from the womb without losing the seals
        of virginity when he was born—
    a novel action, the like of which the world had not seen
        before.
    He went forth into creation to uproot the thorns from the
        ground
    and to sow peace on the earth that the great serpent had
        ravaged:
15. he went forth to renew the old order that had been cor-
        rupted,
    to establish on earth a new creation that would never come
        to dissolution;
    he became a child so that he might play with the basilisk,
    and he trod down the snake that had bitten Adam among
        the trees.
    From one staging post to the next did he travel, like a
        merchant
20. carrying Life to distribute amongst mortals.
    He resided in that first staging post, which is Mary,
    and came to birth so that he might visit the world as man;
    to the second staging post, which is baptism,
    he came and resided there, so as to clothe warriors in
        armor.
25.   John was the voice in the wilderness, preparing the way:
    he opened the gate that brings man into the house of God.
    Where there was water he stood up, like a fisherman,
    so as to catch men for the new world, by means of
        repentance.
    John came so as to betroth the Bride to the Son of God;
30. he made ready to wash off her filth, so that she might then
        be betrothed;
    he took her down to the water and made her clean with
        repentance,
    so that, once pure, she might then see the royal
        Bridegroom.
    In the river he burnished her, removing from her her
        shame,
    so that the Bridegroom, who loves beauty, might not look
        upon her all dirty.
35. In baptism did he make her pure and radiant,
    and then, all holy, he brought her into the bridal chamber.
    It was for this reason that the Levite's son [John] ran to
        the river,

so that he might make ready the Bride, full of beauty, from the water.

He washed her and burnished her, making her holy,

40. he caused her to shine so that the Bridegroom might behold her all beautiful.

He announced to her the greatness of the King, his master,

proclaiming to her, without hesitation, that he came from heaven;

he said to her: "I am not worthy, even of his sandals,"

so that, by his own humility, he might depict the true greatness of his master:

45. he prefers the Bridegroom's sandals to his own head,

so that the Bride might hear and feel pride in him to whom she was betrothed.

As he proclaimed to her, he instructed her how he himself was of earth,

but concerning his master, he told her how he was from heaven.

He fired her with love for him each day, so that she might wait expectantly for him—

50. but the Bridegroom was hidden and the Bride did not know who he was:

that he was great and glorious she had learnt from John,

but the Messiah was hidden, and creation burned with love to see him;

the crowds questioned one another in great agitation:

"Where is he? Where is he who has been announced by John?"

55. John in his preaching resembled the thunder,

and the Bride lay drunk with love for the Son of God.

The crowds asked questions about him, seeing that he was hidden,

and Baptism yearned to acquire from him sanctification.

  Then the Bridegroom shone forth like the sun, a great light;

60. John trembled to show the Bride His beauty,

the Levite worshiped, bowing his head in great wonder,

for he saw the Light, the Son of Majesty, come towards him.

The radiance from the Essence shone forth beside John,

64. with His rays He threw consternation on the Bride, so that she wondered at Him.

[Ll. 65–94. The poet sings about the hidden years of both John and Jesus, repeatedly making the point that

apart from their encounter in utero, John had never
seen Jesus. The poet continues:]

[But] the moment he did see him he pointed him out to
the Bride, saying, "Here is the Bridegroom."

95. The resplendent John was filled with the Holy Spirit who
reveals all mysteries

and by the Spirit was he stirred at the appearance of the
Son of God.

"This is the Bridegroom," he told the Bride, "to whom
you are betrothed;

this is the Lamb who takes away the sin of Adam,

this is he who causes the levitical sacrifices to pass away,

100. himself becoming the sacrifice on behalf of sinners."

John trembled as he saw his Lord approach

and ask to be baptized along with the penitent in baptism.

The servant said: "Lord, it is I who should be baptized
by you,

for you are the provider of sanctification and forgiveness
for the whole world;

105. You give sanctification to priests, seeing that you are holy,

and baptism looks to you to be sanctified by you."

Then our Lord silenced the servant, telling him not to
speak,

but to fulfill all righteousness in baptism.

"Leave off, for now is not the time for me to reveal the
mystery,

110. lest the ruler of the air perceive whose Son I am;

for I do not wish the demons to know whose Son I am

before I reach the great moment of the crucifixion.

Be quiet now and let me be baptized along with the
repentant

so that the Accuser may erroneously suppose I am feeble.

115. The way of birth has put me in a position to come to
baptism,

since I have been born, I shall now be baptized. Be quiet
and baptize me."

John kept silent, guarding the mystery as he had been
bidden,

and the Bridegroom went down so that baptism might be
sanctified by him.

The Son of the Rich One hid his wealth in poverty,

120. walking humbly like a poor man on his road.

John kept silent, since he was bidden to keep the mystery
hidden,

but the Father spoke, to reveal to the crowds concerning
   his Beloved;
the Holy Spirit flew down and descended upon the Only-
   Begotten,
so that the Father and the Spirit might be witnesses for
   the baptism.
125. The Spirit did not come down to sanctify the water so
   that the holy Son
   might be baptized, for it was from the Son that sanc-
      tification proceeded.
It was after Christ had washed and gone up from the water
that the Spirit descended, to show who he was, and not
   to sanctify,
for it was not in order to be sanctified that Christ came
   to baptism:
130. his path is clear for him who wishes to walk in it.
   The baptism of John is of repentance:
he called sinners to baptism to bring them forgiveness.
What sin or blemish did Christ have
so that baptism might bring him forgiveness when he went
   down to the water?
135. The Son of God did not resemble us in sin,
   so as to receive forgiveness in baptism like a sinner.
This is clear: that although he had no need he came to
   baptism
so that the justice in the Law might be fulfilled in him;
he came traveling along the path of birth, according to
   the Law,
140. and in the midst of his course baptism met him.
   Had he turned aside and not gone down as he passed by,
he would have brought confusion upon the ordered path
   on which he had commenced:
it would not have been "just" not to finish what he had
   begun.
And so our Lord was baptized to repay to justice what
   belonged to her.
145. He was baptized in the water—not to gain anything or
   to be sanctified,
but to fulfill that justice which was in the Law.
   John did not baptize in "the Spirit and Fire,"
nor did his baptism give the Holy Spirit.
He baptized in water for repentance, as it is written,
150. and his baptism was straightforward for those who went
   down to it.

The Son of God gave his apostles his own baptism
in which there is Fire and the Holy Spirit for those who
   go down to it;
in it there is a power and it gives birth to spiritual children,
and after being born by it they may call upon our heavenly
   Father.

155. This baptism which the Son of God opened up,
it gives birth to new and immortal children for the Father;
it burns with Fire and the Spirit, giving birth in divine
   fashion,
so that as a result of it men may become sons of God.
[Ll. 159–174. The poet now describes the baptisms of the
   Law to distinguish between those of the Law, of
   John, and of the "Son of God."]

175. The baptisms in the Law are a shadow,
while the baptism of John is of repentance,
whereas the baptism of the Son of God gives birth to the
   "first born,"
providing sons to be brothers to the Only-Begotten.
Moses in the wilderness depicted the image of baptism,

180. John opened it up, so that it might be for repentance,
then Christ came and kindled it with the Holy Spirit and
   Fire,
so that it might be giving birth to new and immortal
   children.
The great Moses with his baptism marked out
the baptism wherein the whole world is to receive forgiveness;

185. John cleansed off the filth of his own people in baptism
in order to sanctify them and so they might then see the
   Son of God.
Christ came and opened up baptism on his cross
so that it might be, in place of Eve, a "mother of living
   beings" for the world;
water and blood, for the fashioning of spiritual children,

190. flowed forth and so baptism became the mother of Life.
No baptism had even given the Holy Spirit
except this one which the Son of God opened up on his
   cross.
With water and blood does it give birth to children in spiritual fashion,
and, instead of a soul, the Holy Spirit is breathed into
   them.

195. Neither Moses nor John, the Levite's son,
were capable of giving the Spirit at baptism,
but the Son of God, of whom the Holy Spirit partakes,
is he who gave the Spirit so that baptism might be sanctified by him.
Although he had no need, he came to John for baptism
200. —for the baptizing which did not perfect those going down
to it. . . .
Let us now see why this baptism of repentance
210. was opened up by John.
This man was set aside to go before the face of the Son
of God
to prepare a way before his coming,
and so he began to summon men to repentance. . . .
[Ll. 214–235: The poet weaves from gospel threads John's
message and concludes:]
So it was that the son of the Kingdom stirred on his way,
washing in water all who came to baptism,
announcing to them that the Savior had arrived.
The daughter of the Hebrews was asleep and the Bridegroom had come
240. —the sleep of wickedness weighed heavy on her, and she
did not perceive him.
John, like a trusty intermediary,
awoke her and announced to her that the Bridegroom had
come;
and, because she was filthy, he washed her in baptism
so that the Bridegroom might not see her all befouled when
she received him.
245. He brought her down to the river and washed off her the
smokiness
of holocausts, with which her face reeked, by which she
was stained.
He adorned her like a free-born woman in fine clothes
so that she might stand all beautiful in the bridal chamber of the Only-Begotten.
His voice acted as herald between the Groom and the
Bride,
250. so that the Bride might be aware that the Groom had arrived in splendor.
He served, as it were, as the voice between mouth and ear,
accompanying the words so that they might reach the hearing in due array.

In an empty space the voice sounds out to make itself
known,
seeing that it has no place either in the womb or inner
chamber;
255. so too John, who is the voice in an empty space
—the wilderness—sounded out, and the crowds of Judah
heard him.
The Levite sang, and the Bride rejoiced at his songs;
the desert echoed with the good tidings of the royal
Bridegroom.
The guests are gathered, awaiting the royal Son,
260. and the Bride sits in eagerness and fear as she looks for
his arrival.
Our Lord shone out like daylight in the midst of darkness,
the voice was stirred to utterance at the Epiphany of the
Word.
He pointed out to the Bride, the daughter of light, the man
to whom she was betrothed,
and the Father acted as witness to his Son with the loud
voice.
265. The Father with his voice was a witness to his Only-
Begotten
and the Holy Spirit manifested himself beside the Savior;
in the form of a dove he fluttered down and descended
in straightforward fashion
after Christ had washed and gone up from the baptismal
water.
The Spirit waited, to show clearly that our Lord had no
need
270. for the water to be sanctified before he washed in it:
only after he had gone up from the water did the Holy
Spirit descend,
leading him out from the crowds to a desert region.
The Bride saw that the Groom had come, and recognized who he was.
Straightway he went forth to fight with the Evil One;
275. leaving the Bride proudly knowing who he was
he went off to engage battle with the lord who guards the
air;
he set his face to make battle with the ruler,
so that, having once bound him, he might come and show
his riches to the Bride.
Against him who had taken mankind captive from the
Father's domain

280. did he direct his steps, and then he shone forth in the syn-
    agogues,
    so that, once he had been tempted, had engaged in battle
    and brought the foe to the ground,
    he might manifest himself with the miracles that he might-
    ily wrought.
    Once the enemy had fallen, like lightning,
    then the Son of God began to work with signs;
285. the Bride recognized who the Bridegroom was, but he did
    not stay for her
    to rejoice with him, but instead he went off to fight,
    so that he might destroy the rebel who had taken captive
    the Bride,
    overthrowing his rule, and take off the daughter of day
    for himself.
    The Spirit led him off to be tempted and to engage in
    battle,
290. and then victorious he would manifest himself in the syna-
    gogues.
    He made battle, and the adversary fell like lightning,
    and then he began to travel on the road of mighty deeds.
    The entire path of the Only-Begotten is full of wonder:
    blessed is the Epiphany of him at whose arrival all cre-
    ation was illumined.

The Teaching of St. Gregory
(An Early Armenian Catechism)

Armenia lay restlessly on the borders of the Roman and Sas-
sanid (Persian) empires, in continual jeopardy from one or the
other. Toward the end of the third century (ca. 280) it became
the first officially Christian state in the ancient world. The key
figure in its conversion was Gregory, surnamed the "Illuminator," who seems to have been of Parthian stock. Most likely born
in Armenia, he was raised at Caesarea in Cappadocia, where he
was converted and baptized. He returned to his homeland, eventually converting the king and aristocracy, through whom the new
religion quickly spread throughout the country.

The natural result was that Gregory became the first bishop
of Armenia *(Catholicos),* an office that was handed down from
father to son thereafter. Bishops Nerses (364–374) and Shanak
(390–420/439) consolidated their ancestor Gregory's work, estab-

lishing the kind of climate needed for men like the erudite Mesrob (Mastoch) and the historian Agathangelos and their scholarly colleagues to set on its foundation a Christian national culture. Agathangelos, a pseudonymous Armenian Christian (ca. 450), gave the Armenians a foundation history. Mesrob, his contemporary, elaborated a new alphabet and set in motion the translation of the Scriptures, patristic commentaries, and the liturgy into Armenian. Included in the Agathangelos *History of the Armenians* is an early Armenian catechism entitled The *Teaching of St. Gregory,* the work of one of a group of intellectuals under the leadership of Mesrob who were sent to centers of Greek and Syrian Christian culture to learn the languages. The author composed the *Teaching* about 440 as an epitome of traditional Christian teaching, and the text shows familiarity with a wide range of Christian Fathers, especially Cyril of Jerusalem, Chrysostom, and the two Cappadocian Gregorys (ch. 1, Nyssa). Nonetheless, he records baptismal teaching that goes behind the fourth-century renaissance to an earlier Syriac-speaking tradition.

The central theme of the work is salvation, the history of which stretches from the generation of the world and humankind to their regeneration. The link that assures the continuity of salvation history is John the Baptist, who delivers to Christ at his baptism the ancient Israelite tradition. In the Savior's life, then, the key event is the gospel scene at the Jordan: (1) he is revealed as the Son of God; (2) his encounter with the river consecrates all water as an instrument of salvation; and (3) the descent of the Spirit through John's agency anoints him with Israel's tradition of prophecy, priesthood, and kingship, which he then passes on to his disciples and the Church, which he identifies as the "church of the Gentiles." Individual access to the stream of salvation history is baptism, and Christ's is the event that is the pattern.

Based on the Epiphany tradition (Nyssa; also see above, Ephrem and Jacob), the author's baptismal teaching is unfolded in his commentary on the Jordan scene as he narrates the life of Christ. What happens to the Son of God happens to the sons and daughters of men, whose baptism, like the Son's, is the central event of their lives. Given the longstanding dependency of Armenia on both Syrias, it is difficult to say whether the West or the East Syrian baptismal liturgy stands behind the catechism. The nod might best be given to the West, since the Eucharistic liturgy attributed to Gregory's brother, Basil, was translated into Armenian about the same time as the *Teaching*. The ambience of the work, however, is closer to Syriac-speaking Christianity and, as noted, reflects an earlier catechetical tradition. The liturgy, therefore, is most probably that of Edessa and Ephrem.

The reading comprises the author's commentary on Christ's baptism in the Jordan, which is contained largely in sections 409–447. The requirements of space necessitate abridgement. Taken in its entirety, however, the *Teaching* seems to have been a catechism for catechumens. Woven together are doctrinal instruction based on the baptismal creed, exposition of the baptismal types and prophecies in the Hebrew Scriptures, and moral exhortation to repentance. The text is Agathangelos, *Patumthiwn Hayoch,* critical edition by G. Ter Mkrtchean and St. Kanayeanch (Tiflis, 1909) reprinted without apparatus in *Lukasean Matenadaran* (Tiflis, 1914); the annotated translation is that of R. W. Thomson, *The Teaching of Saint Gregory: An Early Armenian Catechism,* Harvard Armenian Texts and Studies 3 (Cambridge, Mass.: Harvard University Press, 1970), which contains a valuable introduction. See also "Armenia," "Armenian Christian Literature," and "Armenian Rite," NCE 1:825–838.

On the Baptism of Christ

409. So also John came and washed the people with repentance, in order that when the Son of God should appear they might be ready to approach with worthiness and hear the teaching of the same, to build a road in their hearts, that they might be able to receive the Lord of all in gentle and humble lodging.

410. Then [Christ] came and was himself baptized by John; undertaking to write an eternal covenant and sealing it with his own blood [Heb 13:20], to give life to all by the illuminating and life-giving baptism, he ordered all men born from the earth, all humans, to imitate the divine image of salvation. Then he came to the seal-giver John to be baptized by him, who, seized with awe, refused: "I must be baptized by you" [Matt 3:14]. He heard and answered and boldly commanded him to baptize him: "Suffer it now, for thus it is fitting to occur, that we fulfill all righteousness" [Matt 3:15].

411. And what is the righteousness except what the father of the same John, Zecharia. cried by the Holy Spirit: "He remembered, he said, the oath which he swore to our father Abraham, that he would give us without fear salvation from our enemies and from the hands of all who hate us, to serve him with holiness and righteousness" [Luke 1:71-75]. In the same way the Psalmist also says: "He remembered his covenant with Abraham and his oath with Isaac, and he established for Jacob his commandment, and for Israel his covenant for ever" [Ps 104:9-10]. By the faith of the fathers he blessed the whole earth, he blessed and fulfilled the promises, and for the same reason he himself came down upon the waters, and made the waters at once purifying and renovating [see below, 413-414].

412. And because he made the first earth emerge from the waters [Gen 1:9] by his command, and by water were fattened all plants and reptiles and wild animals and beasts and birds, and by the freshness of the waters they sprang from the earth; in the same way by baptism he made verdant the womb of generation of the waters, purifying by the waters and renewing the old deteriorated earthy matter, which sin had weakened and enfeebled and deprived of the grace of the Spirit. Then the invisible Spirit opened again the womb by visible water, preparing the newly born fledglings for the regeneration of the font [Titus 3:5], to clothe all with robes of light who would be born once more.

413. For in the beginning of the creation of time, the Spirit of the Deity moved over the waters [Gen 1:2], and thence set out the order of the creatures, and commanded the coming into being and establishing of the creatures. He also ordered to be established the firmament of heaven [Gen 1:8], the dwelling of the fiery angels, which appears to us as water. In the same way he came and completed the covenant which he made with our fathers [Gen 17:7; Luke 1:72]. He came down to the waters and sanctified the lower waters of this earth, which had been fouled by the sins of mankind.

414. Treading the waters with his own footsteps, he sanctified them and made them purifying. And just as formerly the Spirit moved over the waters, in the same way he will dwell in the waters and will receive all who are born by it. And

the waters massed together above are the dwelling of the angels. But he made these waters just as those, because he himself came down to the waters, that all might be renewed through the Spirit by the waters and become angels, and the same Spirit might bring all to adoption [Rom 8:15, 23; 9:4; Gal 4:5; Eph 1:5] by the waters forever. For he opened the gates of the waters below, that the gates of the upper waters of heaven might be opened, and that he might elevate all men in glory to adoption. . . .

415. The true Son of God humbled himself and descended to the waters of baptism, that he might fulfill the promises of the fathers and the gospel. Before this, he also took upon himself circumcision [Luke 2:21], that he might bestow grace and blessings on both parties; that by his own circumcision he might complete the basis of the promises, and for the encouragement of the invitations of those worthy of the inheritance of adoption. And at his baptism he vivifies all the baptized by having himself received baptism, and he made baptism honorable by his own descent to baptism. . . .

418. And the Spirit came down over him in the likeness of a dove [Matt 3:16; Mark 1:10; Luke 3:22; John 1:32]. Why then should the Holy Spirit of God appear in the likeness of a dove? To teach those watching that in no other respect can one approach the Son of God, except in sinlessness and righteousness and holiness; that taking from the likeness of a dove, they might bear in themselves that form. . . .

420. For this reason the Spirit came down in the form of a dove, to teach those watching to approach the Son of God with pure minds, and to receive the grace of the blessing of the Spirit, and to become pleasing to the Father. For this reason the Son of God came and fulfilled the covenant of the fathers, since they had called him "son." The Son of God, therefore, came and was baptized, to establish the baptism of all who would be baptized, that handing on this tradition he might reveal salvation to all, and be understood and known, and that by this he might open his life-giving teaching of truth to be revealed to the world. As the prophet says in the name of the Lord's Son: "Come near to me and hear this: not from the beginning did I speak anything in secret, nor anything in a place of darkness in the earth. For when he was, then was I. And the

Lord has sent me and his Spirit" [Isa 48:16]. Do you see
the unity of being? "When he was, I then was," he says,
demonstrating the consubstantial hypostasis of the Trinity, acting together in establishing and united in renewing.

[421–428. The catechist calls on a variety of prophetic and gospel
texts to support the consubstantiality of Christ in what he calls
the "mystery of the Father and the Spirit."]

429. [John the Baptist passes on to Christ the Old Testament
traditions.] Then came the great John, son of the high
priest Zacharia. Here came the companion of the temple
[3 Macc 2:15], not a stranger. Here was the heir and inhabitant of Sion, of the same ephod-wearing priesthood,
wearing a tiara of the honor of the robes of holiness,
bearer of the tradition of the commandments, not a
foreigner but suitably girded, the descendant of Moses and
the branch of Aaron and the evangelist of Sion, worthy
of anointing; he received the honor of the priesthood of
his forefathers. And completing the prophecy of the
prophets, going out into the desert because of the divine
commands to those dwelling on mountains, the evangelist
of Jerusalem, going up, raised his voice, for he was the
sound of a voice in the wilderness [Isa 40:3; Matt 3:3; John
1:23], and said: "Behold our God, behold the Lord" [Isa
25:9; 40:9], and the same is king of Israel.

430. So all the grace of the tradition of the prophecy of the
race of Israel, which the keeper of the tradition of the
blessing of the covenants and the anointing bore, the
priesthood, with the kingship, was entrusted [to him]
through the tribe of Levi.

431. For at the time when the Lord called Moses in the midst
of the fire and cloud to the top of the mountain of Sinai,
and the vision of the glory of the Lord was burning like
fire, when Moses took the commandments of the laws
from the hands of God [Exod 19], and saw God was
beneficient from his answer to him: "I am merciful and
compassionate" [Exod 34:6], then he received the tradition of the authority of the priesthood, kingship, and
prophecy from God. Then he gave him a type of the
anointing of Christ, that first might occur examples and
then the truth might come—he who is [Exod 3:14]. Then
he ordered him to make the horn of anointing and the thurible of incense [Exod 31:11].

432. The horn was the type of the anointing of Christ, and the thurible the type of the holy virgin Mary. For as the former was full of the odor of sanctity, so also the virgin was full of the Holy Spirit and the power of the Highest [Luke 1:35]. The horn of oil was the type of the anointing of Christ, for who were anointed once in his example were anointed from it. Thence also Aaron was anointed to the priesthood of the Lord [Exod 40:13], and he took the crown of priesthood, to anoint according to the same type, to place on them the veil, to serve the holiness of the Lord, and to order the daily bread on the table [Lev 24:5-91], which bore the type of the flesh of the Son of God.

433. Then Moses made the silver horn of his anointing from which were anointed the priests, prophets, and kings. Thence proceeded in order the unction in succession according to the command of the authority of the commandment, which proceeded in order by seniority. The mystery was preserved in the seed of Abraham, because they passed on the tradition to each other until John, priest, prophet, and baptist. And coming to him, it remained on him as on an heir. For it came to him from the first forefathers, the kings, prophets, and anointed priests, as to a keeper of tradition. And he gave the priesthood, the anointing, the prophecy, and the kingship to our Lord Jesus Christ.

434. And the prophecy of Jacob was fulfilled in the saying to the sons of his race: "There will not lack leadership of authority until he shall come, whose is the kingdom; for he is the hope of the Gentiles" [Gen 49:10].

435. The first fathers were his type, in whom the forms of God were represented, for all creatures obeyed them because they saw the forms of the Creator in them. But how did irrational, voiceless, mute creatures obey mortal men, unless they saw the signs of God in them and the forms of the Creator? And thus in succession the traditions were handed down to John, and John gave the tradition of his trust to his Lord.

436. And then the Lord himself came forward, and John bore witness: "I am not the Christ, but I am sent before him. He who has the bride is the bridegroom, and he who is the friend of the bridegroom stands with him and obeys him; he also has great joy in his rejoicing for he hears the bridegroom's voice. This joy of mine is fulfilled and com-

pleted; he must increase and I must decrease. He who comes from above is over all. Who is from the earth, speaks of the earth; he who comes from heaven, bears witness to what he has heard and seen, and his witness no one receives. But who receives his witness has secured and sealed that indeed God is true. For he who has been sent by God speaks the words of God; for the Spirit was not given him by measure. The Father loves the Son and has given all things into his hand. Who believes in the Son receives everlasting life; and who believes not in the Son does not see eternal life, but the wrath of God dwells on him" [John 3:28-36].

437. Behold, the messenger John came to prepare the ways for his Lord. For as Gabriel was the harbinger of his birth, so he was of his revelation, and coming first said: "I am sent before him, but whose the bride is, he is the groom" [John 3:28-29].

438. But who is the bride, or who is the bridegroom, except he of whom the prophet said: "Thus says the Lord, 'I shall betroth you to me for ever, and I shall betroth you to me in righteousness and justice and mercy and compassion. And you will know that I am the Lord your God, and you will abandon your beloved of wood and stone and will say, I shall return to my first husband' " [Hos 2:19-20].

[The catechist again summons numerous biblical texts about the bride to make a point central to his catechesis, namely, that the regal, priestly, and prophetic traditions of Israel flow through John to Christ, the bridegroom, and from Christ to the bride, whom he now identifies.]

441. Who is the bride except the church of the Gentiles, or who the groom except Jesus Christ the Son of God, who descended from heaven and subdued everything to the worship of the Father? And what are the two abundant breasts except the testaments of God, which give drink to all the ignorant with the spiritual milk of knowledge? And what is the saying "the odor of your perfume more than all incense of sweetness," and "your name is perfume poured out"? It reveals the anointing of Christ and his name. And the kiss is the sign of love, because the church is Christ's, and Christ is the Son of God.

442. "He must increase and I decrease" [John 3:30], that is, he means the time of decrease. For the baptism which he

gave to the crowd was the baptism of repentance. "Who has come from above, he said, is above all" [John 3:31], indicating his coming from the bosom of the Father to us. "But I, he said, spoke from earth, taking my knowledge from heaven" [John 3:31]. But he who came from heaven speaks the Father's [words] and works the Father's works. As the Lord himself said to the Jews: "I am in the Father and the Father in me. Whatever I see that the Father does, the same I do also. For this very reason I have come, to do the will of my Father, and to complete his works" [John 5:19; 10:38; 14:10].

[443-445. The catechist then draws on a variety of biblical texts to fix his hearers' attention on baptism, the womb in which the Church conceives and from which it brings to life the Bridegroom-Savior's children. He concludes with a strikingly paternal image of the Savior:]

446. He, the Savior, came and was revealed in taking and gathering the children in his divine arms [Mark 9:36; 10:15]. And as an example to all [he said]: "Unless you are converted and become like this child, you are not able to enter the kingdom of God" [Matt 18:3]. He orders [us] to renew ourselves [Titus 3:5] and to strip off the old manhood [Col 3:9] through the bath of baptism. For although one may be greatly oppressed and laboring, bearing a heavy weight of sins according to the saying: "Behold he was in labor for injustice, conceived pains and gave birth to unrighteousness" [Ps 7:15], yet opening the doors to repentance, coming into our midst, stands the Savior crying out: "Come to me all who are laden and in travail, and whoever have heavy loads, and I shall give you rest. And take my yoke upon you and learn from me; for I am gentle, calm, and humble in heart, and you will find rest for yourselves. For my yoke is gentle and my load is light" [Matt 11:28-30].

447. But if anyone should ask who it is who will be so compassionate to those in travail, let him hear the prophecy of Isaiah who this may be; he says: "Who has measured all the waters with his fist, and all the earth with his span? Who has placed the hills in the balance, and weighed the plains with scales? Who has known the mind of the Lord, or who has been companion of his counsel?" [Isa 40:12-13]. He who learnt from the Father the sentence of

judgment, the same came, was made man and preached to the world, joining in his love all men to the Deity. And therefore came the light, coming to our midst "to illuminate every man who was to come into the world" [John 1:9]. He preached and said: "Repent, for the kingdom of God is nigh. The times are fulfilled; believe in the gospel" [Matt 4:17; Mark 1:15].

Suggestions for Further Reading

Certain key studies are cited at the end of each chapter introduction and with the introduction of each author or work. Preference has been given to accessibility and to works in English. The following is a select general bibliography. The reader is also directed to standard reference works, especially dictionaries and encyclopedias, and in particular to Quasten, cited in the abbreviations.

Aland, Kurt. *Did the Early Church Baptize Infants?* Trans. G. Beasley-Murray. Philadelphia: Westminster Press, 1963.

Bedard, Walter M. *The Symbolism of the Baptismal Font in Early Christian Thought.* Studies in Sacred Theology 45, 2nd series. Washington: The Catholic University of America Press, 1951.

Collins, Adela Y. "The Origin of Christian Baptism," SL 19 (1989) 28–44.

Crehan, Joseph. *Early Christian Baptism and the Creed.* London: Burns & Oates, 1950.

Daniélou, Jean. *The Bible and the Liturgy.* Liturgical Studies 3. Notre Dame: Notre Dame University Press, 1956.

_____. *From Shadows to Reality: Studies in the Biblical Typology of the Fathers.* Westminster, Md.: Newman, 1960.

Davies, J. G. *The Architectural Setting of Baptism.* London: Barrie and Rockliff, 1962.

Dix, Gregory. *The Shape of the Liturgy.* New York: Seabury, 1982. First published in 1945.

Dujarier, Michael. *A History of the Catechumenate: The First Six Centuries.* Trans. Edward J. Haasl. Chicago: Sadlier, 1979.

Eliade, Mircea. *The Sacred and the Profane: The Nature of Religion.* New York: Harper & Row, 1959, reprinted 1961.

Every, George. *The Baptismal Sacrifice.* London, 1959.

Finn, Thomas M. *The Liturgy of Baptism in the Baptismal Instructions of St. John Chrysostom.* SCA 15. Washington: The Catholic University of America Press, 1967.

Fisher, John D. C. *Christian Initiation: Baptism in the Medieval West.* London: SPCK, 1965.

_____. *Confirmation Then and Now.* London: SPCK, 1978.

Gavin, Frank S. B. *The Jewish Antecedents of the Christian Sacraments.* London: SPCK, 1928; New York: Ktav, 1969.

Grant, Robert M. *Gnosticism and Early Christianity.* New York: Columbia University Press, 1959; New York: Harper & Row, Torchbook ed., 1966.

Jeremias, Joachim. *Infant Baptism in the First Four Centuries.* Trans. D. Cairns. Philadelphia: Westminster, 1962.

Kavanagh, Aidan, and others. *Initiation Theology.* Toronto: Anglican Book Centre, 1978.

_____. "The Origins and Reform of Confirmation." *St. Vladimir's Theological Quarterly* 33 (1989) 5–20.

_____. *The Shape of Baptism: The Rite of Christian Initiation.* New York: Pueblo, 1978.

Kelly, Henry Ansgar. *The Devil at Baptism: Ritual, Theology, and Drama.* Ithaca: Cornell University Press, 1985.

Lampe, G. W. H. *The Seal of the Spirit: A Study in the Doctrine of Baptism and Confirmation in the New Testament and the Fathers.* London: SPCK, 1976.

Made Not Born: New Perspectives on Christian Initiation and the Catechumenate. Notre Dame: (Murphy Center for Liturgical Research) University of Notre Dame Press, 1976.

Meyer, Martin W., ed. *The Ancient Mysteries: A Sourcebook.* San Francisco: Harper & Row, 1987.

Mitchell, Leonel L. *Baptismal Anointing.* London: SPCK, 1966.

Neunheuser, Burkhard. *Baptism and Confirmation.* Trans. John J. Hughes. New York: Herder and Herder, 1964.

Riley, Hugh M. *Christian Initiation: A Comparative Study of the Interpretation of the Baptismal Liturgy in the Mystagogical Writings of Cyril of Jerusalem, John Chrysostom, Theodore of Mopsuestia, and Ambrose of Milan.* SCA 17. Washington: The Catholic University of America Press, 1974.

Schmemann, Alexander. *Of Water and the Spirit: A Liturgical Study of Baptism.* New York: St. Vladimir's Seminary Press, 1974.

Talley, Thomas J. *The Origins of the Liturgical Year.* New York: Pueblo, 1986.

Thurian, Max, and Geoffrey Wainwright, eds., *Baptism and Eucharist: Ecumenical Convergence in Celebration.* Faith and Order Paper 117. Geneva, Switzerland/Grand Rapids, Michigan: World Council of Churches/Eerdmans, 1983.

Welles, Bradford, ed. *The Excavations at Dura-Europos: The Final Report VIII, Part I: The Christian Building.* New Haven: Dura-Europos Publications (distr. J. J. Augustin, Locust Valley, N.Y.) 1967.

Whitaker, Edward C. *The Baptismal Liturgy,* 2nd ed. London: SPCK, 1981.

_____. *Documents of the Baptismal Liturgy,* 2nd. ed. London: SPCK, 1970.

Ysebaert, J. *Greek Baptismal Terminology.* Nijmegen: Dekker-van de Vegt, 1962.

Synoptic Table: The Fathers on Baptism and the Catechumenate		
Century	West Syria	East Syria
Second	*Didache* Melito of Sardis	*Odes of Solomon* *Gospel of Philip* *Acts of Judas* *Thomas*
Third	*Didascalia* *Apostolorum*	
Fourth	Cyril *Apostolic* *Constitutions* Gregory of Nyssa Chrysostom (Theodore of Mopsuestia)	Aphrahat Ephrem
Fifth	Theodore of Mopsuestia *Ordo of* *Constantinople* Dionysius the Pseudo- Areopagite	Narsai Jacob of Serugh *The Teaching* *of St. Gregory*
Sixth		

Note: A work or an author in parentheses means that work or author reflects the customs of the century even though the work or author is dated later.

Italy	North Africa	Egypt
Shepherd of Hermas Justin Martyr Abercius *(Apostolic Tradition)*		*Excerpts of Theodotus* Clement
Apostolic Tradition Novatian	Tertullian Cyprian	Origen
Zeno Ambrose	Optatus	Serapion Didymus the Blind *Canons of Hippolytus*
Innocent I Leo the Great John the Deacon *Leonine Sacramentary*	Augustine	Cyril The Coptic Rite
(Gelasian Sacramentary)		

Index

Abraham, 139, 162, 189
Acts of Judas Thomas, 111,
    127–129
Adam (First Adam), 6, 26–27,
    70, 73, 87, 95, 139, 152–156,
    165, 168, 170–174, 182–183,
    192
Adam (Second Adam), 26 (*see*
    Christ as)
Adherence to Christ (*see* Al-
    legiance)
Adoption, 79–80, 86–87, 93, 95,
    105, 201
Agathangelos, 198
Alexandria, 30, 31, 42
    School (*see* Typology, Types
    of Baptism)
Allegiance to Christ (Rite of,
    Submission to, *see* Contract)
    7, 46, 51, 71 77–78, 99–100,
    105
Ambrose of Milan, 11, 20–21
Anastasis (Church of), 52, 53,
    54
Anointing
    of Jesus, 181–182
    Messiah/Christos, 18
    postbaptismal (Chrismation),
    18–22, 40, 49–52, 59, 82,

87, 102, 105, 109, 115, 189
    prebaptismal, 18–22, 39–40,
    47–48, 56–57, 58, 78–79, 83,
    84, 105, 114–115, 121, 126,
    130
    Syrian, 20–21, 39, 114–115,
    202
Two Traditions (Syriac-
    speaking, Greek-speaking),
    19–21, 114–115
Antioch, Antiochene, 29, 31, 39,
    56, 71, 81, 98, 116, 170
    School of, 31, 81, 115, 170
Antitype, 42, 48, 50
Aphrahat *(Demonstrations),* 19,
    37, 111–113, 134–136, 151
Apocryphal Acts, 127–128
Apostolic Constitutions, 55–60
Apostolic Tradition of Hippoly-
    tus, 10, 15, 20, 55
Apotaxis (*see* Renunciation), 98
April (Easter Mystery), 153–154
Aquarii, 112
Arians, 152
    Arianism, 152, 153, 160
    Baptism, 13
Armenia, 31, 36, 115, 197–199
    Catechism, 115, 197–199
Asceticism, 112, 113, 136–138

Asia Minor (Turkey), 36
Augustine, 12–13, 25

Baptism
  and faith, 14–15, 74–75, 152
  as burial (death), 48, 50,
    65–66, 75, 85–86, 89–108,
    116–117, 148, 153–154, 180,
    186
  efficiency of (*see* Symbolic
    participation), 10–11, 83,
    90–91, 113–114, 200
  form, 36, 39 48, 66, 79,
    90–92, 131, 134, 154, 185
  infant, 14–15, 115
  sacrament of faith, 14
Baptismal
  font (*see* Womb [baptismal]),
    7, 79–80, 87–88, 167
  register, 104, 168
  water; consecration (*see* Bap-
    tismal font), 56, 59, 61,
    87–88, 102, 125, 136, 157,
    166, 167
Baptizands, 4, 99
Barsai (Bishop), 151
Barsauma (Bishop), 170
Basil the Great, 60, 199
Bible
  and baptismal liturgy (*see*
    Typology), 22–27
  Greek, 111
  Syriac (*see* Peshitta)
Bishop and baptism, 15, 40–41,
  56, 77, 90–97, 98, 103–105,
  108, 151, 152
Bridal
  Chamber *(Nymphon),*
    121–125, 127, 190, 195
  Feast, 120
Bride (*see* Marriage), 119,
  190–191, 195–197, 204, 205

Bridegroom, 119, 190–192,
  195–197

Caesarea
  (Cappadocian), 60–61, 197
  (Palestinian), 42
Candle (baptismal), 72, 125, 130
Cappadocia, 36, 60, 197
Catechesis (*see* Instruction), 5,
  97–98, 132
Catecheses, mystagogical, 42–55
Catechist, 25, 205
Catechumen(s), 3–7, 199
Catechumenate, 3–7, 98, 128,
  152
Catholicos, 197
Celebacy, continence, 128
Chalcedonians, 182, 187
Chorepiscopus, 188
Chrein, 18
Chrism, 50, 51, 57, 59, 123–125
Chrismation, 21–22, 49–52,
  96–97
Christ
  Baptism of (*see* John the Bap-
    tist), 19, 63, 94–96, 114,
    151, 156, 157, 164, 177–182,
    184, 192–194, 198–205
  Incarnation of, 119, 160, 161,
    162, 189–190
  Nativity of, 151, 158–159
  pierced side of, 17–18, 146, 152
  Second Adam (*see* Adam,
    First), 26–27, 171–175, 183
  "Christs" (newly baptized as),
    158
Church-order (*see* Didache,
  Didascalia), 2
Church of the East, 170
Circumcision (Baptism as), 39,
  116, 117, 137–141, 148
Confirmation, 21

Consecration, priestly (Ordination), 101
Consignation, 21
Constantinople, 29, 97
  The Golden Church, 71
Contemplation, 101-102, 105-109
Contract (*see* Allegiance), 100
Conversion, 2-3, 5, 128-134
Coptic Rite, 12, 112
Council
  Arles, 13
  Chalecedon, 81, 112, 170, 188
  Ephesus, 81, 112, 171
  Florence, 14
  Orange, 14
Covenanters, 112-113, 134-136, 150-151
Creation and baptism, 113-114
Creed, 53, 57-58
  baptismal, 48, 57-58, 82, 99
  (handing over: *traditio symboli*), 53
Crown, coronation, 17
Cup of Water (baptismal), 116
Cyprian, 15
Cyril of Alexandria, 81, 171, 187
Cyril of Jerusalem, 9, 20, 24, 41-43

Didascalia Apostolorum (The Teaching of the Apostles), 38-41, 55
Deification (assimilation to God), 103, 107, 108
Deodore of Tarsus, 31
Descent of Christ (into Hell), 116, 133
Didache (The Teaching of the Twelve Apostles), 8, 15, 32-36, 38, 55

Dionysius the Pseudo-Areopagite, 101-102
Diophysitism, 171
Dura Europos, 8

Easter
  Baptism, 16, 52
  (Pasha), 37, 39, 52
  mystery, 153
  Week, 16, 54-55
Edessa, 29, 30, 111, 116, 127, 135, 151-152, 169, 189, 199
Egeria, 41, 51-55, 127
Elect, 4
Elijah (*see* types of Baptism), 64, 67-68, 153, 154, 163
Elisha (*see* types of Baptism), 65, 67-68, 165, 168
Enrollment, 4, 71, 82
Ephrem, 20, 111, 150-153, 160-161, 164, 166, 189, 199
Epiclesis, 128
Epiphany, 26, 61-62, 82, 158, 164, 170, 172, 189, 196, 197
Eucharist, 4, 16-17, 45, 50, 79-80, 105, 109, 121, 125, 128, 130-131, 134, 155, 161, 162, 163
Eutyches, 171
Eve, 194
Ex opere operato, 13
Exodus and baptism (*see* types of Baptism), 25, 44, 67, 135, 146
Exorcism, 5-6, 75-76, 81-82, 129
Exorcists, 48
Exsufflation, 99, 104

Faith and baptism, 14-15, 74-75, 152
Family (community as), 16-17
Fasting, 53, 133, 150

Fall (the), 73, 170–173, 183
Fire (*see* Chrism and Holy
 Spirit), 123, 161–162, 163,
 167, 193–194
Flesh: hinge of salvation, 8, 12,
 22–23

Garment
 (Christ as; *see* White gar-
  ment), 117
 (of light), 127
Gentiles
 Church of, 204
 Church of (the Peoples),
  143–144
Gnostic *(gnosis, gnostikos)*,
 120–122
Good Friday, 71, 87, 135–136,
 149
Gospel According to Philip, 112,
 120–122
Greek-speaking Christianity, 112
Gregory the Illuminator,
 197–199
Gregory of Nazianzus, 61
Gregory of Nyssa, 14, 26,
 60–62, 70, 198

Harrowing of Hell, 116
"Hearer," 39
Holy Spirit
 and anointing, 18–22, 50, 79,
  96–97, 181
 baptism (*see* entries under
  Anointing), 50, 63–64, 75,
  85, 86, 87, 88, 89, 90, 91,
  93, 95, 105, 113–119,
  136–138, 155, 161, 162, 165,
  166, 169, 177, 181, 182,
  185–186, 192–196, 200
Holy Week ("Great Week"), 52,
 54

Hymnal, 115–116
Hymns, 115, 152–169

Ignatius (of Antioch), 36
Illumination: Baptism as, 71,
 101, 102, 103, 106, 118,
 126–127, 130, 158–160, 199
Image (of God), 171–173, 183
Immersion (*see* Baptism as burial), 8, 48–49, 65–66, 71, 79,
 84, 91–92, 95, 105, 109, 116,
 122, 155–156, 167, 181, 201
Imposition of hands, 15, 59, 90,
 92
India, 127–128
Initiation, Baptism as, 3,
 104–106
Innocent I, 21
Instruction
 (*see* Catechesis), 4–5, 39, 75,
  82
 creedal, 39, 43
 Prebaptismal, 52–54, 57, 82
 manual, 82, 83
Intercessory prayer, 80
Islam, 31

Jacob (Bishop of Nisibis),
 150–151
Jacob of Serugh, 11, 17, 25,
 188–189
Jerusalem, 41–42
Jews, Jewish community, 36,
 115, 135–136, 146
Jews and Christians, 99, 115,
 135–136
John the Baptist (*see* Christ:
 Baptism of), 23, 94–95, 148,
 152, 164, 165, 166, 175–179,
 183, 188–197, 198–205
John the Deacon, 21
John Chrysostom, 17–18, 31,
 70–72, 81, 98

Jordon (River, Baptism as), 11, 67, 113, 124, 140, 151–152, 157, 158, 163, 164, 166, 175

Joshua/Jesus, 139–141

Judas Thomas (Didymus), 127–128

Kiss (of peace), 15, 72, 79–80, 204

Last Supper: footwashing, 135, 149, 151

Lent, 7, 41–42, 52–54 ("Forty Days"), 7, 52, 53, 54, 71

Leo the Great, 12

Liminality, 3

Linen stole, 84

Lord's Prayer, 16, 17, 60, 71, 80, 132, 189

Macrina, 60

Madrashe, 151

The "Man" Jesus, 31, 81, 171–172, 185–186

Manashar, 132–134

Manicheans (Mani), 112, 135, 151

Manual (textbook for Catechumens), 82

Martyrium (Church of), 52, 53, 54

Marriage, baptism as, 17, 119–122, 123, 184, 192–193

Mary (*see* Bride, Christ, Rebirth, Virgin), 151, 162, 203

Masah, 18

Matter and form, 8

Melito of Sardis, 36–38

Memra/Memre, 115, 189

Mingana, Alphonse, 170–171

Mescha (oil), 153–157

Meschicha (Christ) 153–157

Mesopotamia, 127, 135, 150

Mesrob (Mastoch), 198

Milk, 116, 118, 155, 204

Milk and honey, 116

Minister of Baptism (*see* Bishop), 13–14, 18, 75

Monks, order of, 101

Monophysites (Eutyches), 187–188

Mopsuestia (*see* Theodore of), 81

Moses, 25, 113, 141, 146–147, 159, 202, 203

Mygdonia, 127–131, 133, 134

Mystery *(Mysterion),* 8, 102, 123, 141, 148, 192, 202

Mysteries, 43, 47, 62, 90, 109, 125–127, 142, 144, 147, 180

Mysticism, 101

Nag Hammadi, 120

Namaan the Syrian, 164, 165, 168

Narkia, 127–131

Narsai, 11, 112, 169–171, 188–189

Neoplatonic Philosophy, 101

Nerses (Bishop), 197

Nestorians, 170

Nestorius, 31, 81, 112

Nisebis, 29, 30, 111

Nicaea, 152

Noah, 139

October (this world), 153–154

Odes of Solomon, 26, 112, 115–116

Oil, 153–157 consecration of, 101 olive, 47–48

Ointment, 50

Ordo of Constantinople, 17, 97–98

Orientation, 46, 60, 99
Origen (on baptism) 8–9, 19,
    24–25, 61

Pasch, *Pascha,* Paschal, 37
Paradise and baptism, 9–10,
    25–27, 43–44, 70, 73–74, 83,
    117–118, 152, 158, 170–171
Participation in God, 107
Passover, 24–25, 37, 39, 43,
    135–136, 139, 141–150
Passion of Christ, 43, 135, 149
Pattern of Baptism (*see* Christ:
    baptism of), 11–12, 19, 94–95,
    113–114, 198
Paul of Tarsus and baptism, 24
Persia, 27, 197
Persians, 111, 134
Peshitta, 112, 135, 137
Peter Lombard, 21
Philoxennus of Mabbug, 22, 189
Photizands, *photizomenos,* 4, 71
Poetry
    (didactic), 151
    symbolic (and bible), 113–114,
        150
Postbaptismal Rites, 15–18
Prayer, postbaptismal (*see*
    Lord's Prayer), 60, 71, 80
Proclus of Constantinople, 98
Promised Land, 17, 113, 139,
    146–147
Proselyte baptism, 24, 33
Psalms, 150

Quartodeciman (Easter), 37,
    135–136, 141, 145–146

Redditio Symboli, 5, 53
Redemption (Rite of: Ransom),
    121–123, 156
Red Sea (*see* Exodus)

Regeneration (baptismal, see Re-
    birth), 65
Renewal and baptism, 75,
    89–90, 173–175, 182–185
Remission of sins and baptism,
    48, 49, 62, 63, 88–90, 131
    152, 153–156, 168, 169
Renunciation (of Satan), 7,
    43–46, 57, 77–83, 98–101, 104,
    136
Repentance, Baptism of,
    192–194
Resurrection and baptism, 75,
    85–86, 89, 93, 95, 96, 114,
    123–125, 134, 138, 160
Rites of passage/of initiation, 3
Ruha (Spirit), 114
Rushma (*see* "seal"), 114

Sacraments (*sacramentum,*
    sacramenta), 8, 12, 123–125
Sacrament
    and baptism, 64, 68, 123–125
    as sign, 12–13
Saint Thomas (School of),
    127–128
Sardis, 36–38
Satan (Devil, Evil One), 7, 44,
    45, 74, 75, 76–78, 99 166,
    169, 196
Scapegoat, 146
Scrutiny, 6–7
Seal (*Sphragis),* 19, 21, 39, 41,
    84, 104, 150, 167, 187, 199
Semitic (Christianity), 111, 114
Serapion of Thmuis, 12
Severus of Antioch, 22, 188
Shanak (Bishop), 197
Shapur II (King), 135
Sifur, 131
Spirit (*see* Holy Spirit and
    baptism)

Sponsors (God parents), 39,
53–54, 76–77, 83, 104
Staging post, 190
Stripping, ritual of, 43, 47, 75,
78–79, 83, 87, 104, 107, 117,
128, 168
Symbolic participation, 8–10,
42–43, 48, 82–84, 103, 107,
113–114
Synagogue, 111, 115, 135–136
Syntaxis (*see* Allegiance), 98
Syria
East, 21, 22, 29, 30, 111–203
Hellenized, 39, 55, 111–112
West, 21, 22, 29–109
Syriac/Syrian (*see* Syria, East,
West), 1, 19–21, 25, 111–115
Syriac-speaking Christianity, 10,
20, 29, 42, 111–112
Syrians, 29–30

Teaching of St. Gregory (*see*
Armenia), 151, 197–199
Tertia, 132–134
Tertullian, 8, 11, 12, 13, 15, 19,
23
Theodore of Mopsuestia, 9–10,
11, 21–22, 30–33, 81–83, 170
Torah (oral), 114
Traditio Symboli, 5
Translators, 55
Trinity and baptism, 22, 39, 59,
79, 90–93, 131, 134, 154, 185,
202
Two Ages, 83

"Two Ways" (of life, of death),
32–36, 82–83
Type, 121, 203
Type and Antitype, 24, 43
Types of Baptism, 61, 66–68,
113, 135, 165, 202–203
Typology (*see* Bible and Baptismal liturgy), 22–27, 42–43
Antiochene, 31, 42–43
East Syrian/Syriac, 113, 114,
135, 139, 146–147, 156, 202,
203
figure, image, shadow, 24, 43
reality, substance and truth,
24, 43

Unleavened Bread, 136

Valentinus, 121
Vigil, 136, 141
Virgin, Virginity, 153–157,
158–159, 189
Visan, 132–134

Washing of the feet and baptism, 148–149
Way, the, 119
White Garment (baptismal
robe), 16–17, 71–72, 77, 96,
109, 116 126–127, 128,
168–169
Womb (baptismal), (*see* Rebirth
and baptism), 12, 151, 155,
163, 185, 191–195, 200, 205